The Journalist's Legal Guide

Second Edition

Michael G. Crawford, B.B.A., LL.B.

CARSWELL
Toronto • Calgary • Vancouver
1990

Canadian Cataloguing in Publication Data

Crawford, Michael G., 1959-
  The journalist's legal guide

2nd ed.
ISBN 0-459-33867-6 (bound) ISBN 0-459-33877-3 (pbk.)

1. Press law — Canada. 2. Mass media — Law and
legislation — Canada. 3. Broadcasting — Law and
legislation — Canada. I. Title.

KE2550.C73 1990   343.7109'98   C90-093495-6
KF2750.C73 1990

© 1990 Carswell — A Division of Thomson Canada Limited.

Dedicated to the Bear,
Casey May and S. Sue Hanna

Preface

As with the first edition, *The Journalist's Legal Guide* aims to provide a comprehensive, yet basic outline of the rights and obligations of Canadian journalists.

As before, care was taken to create a reference book that is useful to journalists at all levels of experience. For example, in many topic areas, explanatory footnotes — complete with case law citations — have been provided for those with an intrepid desire to know more about a point of law that's cited.

Several new features have been added to this second edition. First, I've placed checklists at the end of most chapters to provide journalists with a concise reminder of key points in each area of law. Second, almost every chapter has been completely re-written to anticipate readers' frequently asked questions and to make it easier to find important points. Third, there's an improved index and some new sections dealing with emerging issues, such as the handling of confidential information.

As near as possible, this edition is current to the beginning of 1990.

At this point, I'd also like to pass on a note of appreciation to Toronto media law counsel Brian MacLeod Rogers of Blake Cassels & Graydon. In recent years, Brian has always had time to lend me an ear or an opinion on the latest wrinkle in the law affecting journalists. I thank him for his patience and thoughtfulness.

Finally, a thought on why it's important for every journalist to strive to understand the law affecting the news media.

This book isn't just about avoiding expensive lawsuits. The true benefits of knowing the legal rights and limits of a journalist are confidence and improved quality. Without an understanding of the legal rights and limits, the journalist's work suffers and the public, in turn, suffers.

Sometimes, the fear that comes from a lack of knowledge about the law can kill a story the public should know. On the flip side, ignorance or recklessness in publishing or broadcasting news can end up distorting the truth.

By knowing how the law affects the news media, a journalist can produce a far more valuable story.

Contents

1

Freedom of the Press:
Revisited and Updated

In the first edition of this book in 1986, it was optimistically noted that the proclamation of the Canadian Charter of Rights and Freedoms[1] and its guarantee of "freedom of the press" promised the dawning of a new era in defining the legal rights and responsibilities of Canadian journalists.

That has proved to be correct, although not always to the journalist's advantage. Indeed, the more liberal and progressive expansion of media rights predicted by some has failed to materialize. In some areas of law, attempts to challenge restrictions on the news media have been shot down in flames as courts have asserted that the press have no special status.

But there have also been many victories and there's no escaping the fact that the Charter's promise of freedom of the press has forced both courts and legislators to now regularly grapple with the questions of news media rights and, consequently, the public's "right to know."

There's reason to remain optimistic that there will be other victories and that the Charter's guarantee of freedom of the press will expand the media's rights. As the Charter nears the end of its first decade, only a handful of cases involving freedom of the press issues have made it up to the level of the Supreme Court of Canada. A greater number of cases have been heard by provincial courts of appeal and even more issues have been tackled by trial courts, but there is not yet a solid body of case law setting out the full meaning and limits of freedom of the press. For example, the Charter's impact on defamation statutes is only now being explored

---

1 Part 1 of the Constitution Act, 1982, being Schedule B of the Canada Act 1982 (U.K.), 1982, c. 11 (hereinafter, Charter).

by legislators and courts.[2] As more court challenges are launched in the future, journalists can hope to see other changes, such as greater television access to court hearings or a broader privilege to criticize public figures.

FREEDOM OF THE PRESS BEFORE THE CHARTER

The entrenchment of "freedom of the press" in the Charter in 1982 formally acknowledged the special role of the news media in society. Section 2(b) of the Charter states that everyone has the fundamental freedom:

> ... of thought, belief, opinion and expression, including freedom of the press and other media of communication.

Courts and legislators have always recognized that the media are an integral part of society, but freedom of the press had never before been formally noted in a Canadian constitutional document. The Charter's classification of "freedom of the press" as a fundamental freedom gives courts more authority to closely define the limits of media rights. In fact, soon after it came into force, the constitutional guarantee was having an effect on media-related law, invalidating some long-standing statutory provisions which limited the media's news gathering opportunities.

To understand why entrenching freedom of the press in the Constitution is important, it helps to know from whence we came.

Historically, the news media in Canada, as in most democracies, has always fought for the right to express opinion and report news freely. In one of the most famous court cases in Canada's early history, Nova Scotia newspaper editor Joseph Howe was tried in 1835 on a charge of criminal libel after he criticized local government officials in his publication. Although he was technically guilty of the offence, the jury acquitted him after his emotional plea for a free press.

In the United States, the Fathers of the American Revolution had already seen the need for a constitutional recognition of press freedoms after suffering under the oppressive and restrictive rule of the English monarchy. The First Amendment of the U.S. Constitution promised in 1791 that no law of Congress shall abridge the freedom of speech or the press. The early presence of this constitutionally-entrenched guarantee helped shape an approach to defining the role of the news media in American society which is somewhat more liberal in many areas of the law than the rights accorded to the press in Canada. For example, the First Amendment has helped American reporters win the right to televise court

---

2 See "The Law of Defamation, An Issues Paper," March, 1989, Ontario Ministry of the Attorney General.

proceedings in most states and allowed for broader criticism of public figures.

A "Freedom of the Press" Myth

The danger in the term "freedom of the press" is that it implies a special right has been imparted upon the news media which is above the rights of the general public. That is not the case. The issue of whether the press enjoy some sort of special privilege has been dealt with by the courts on many occasions over the years, as can be seen in the 1914 British case of *Arnold v. The King-Emperor*, which dealt with a charge of criminal libel brought against a journalist who had accused a magistrate of improper conduct:[3]

> Their lordships regret to find that there appeared on the one side in this case the time-worn fallacy that some kind of privilege attaches to the profession of the Press as distinguished from the members of the public . . . but, apart from statute law, his privilege is no other and no higher.

While the news media are not considered to have any greater privileges than the average citizen, an important corollary is that the courts have recognized that the news media are members and representatives of the public.

This is not to say that Parliament has not recognized the role of the news media. In 1961, Parliament enacted the Canadian Bill of Rights which listed, among other rights, freedom of the press.[4] Unfortunately, the Bill of Rights is not a part of our Constitution, it applies only to Federal statutes and has been narrowly interpreted by the courts as simply being an instrument for statutory interpretation. But on occasion, the principle behind the Bill has not been ignored by the courts.

In 1977, a British Columbia court quashed a search warrant which gave the federal Department of Consumer and Corporate Affairs permission to search the offices of a newspaper for information about picketers who had interfered with an inquiry.[5] The newspaper's only involvement in the picketing was in covering it as a news event. As it turned out, the only reason why the search warrant was directed at the newspaper was because its reporters had been seen speaking with the demonstrators and the investigators wanted the reporters' notes to find who the demonstrators were and what they said.

The court, noting the Bill of Rights' promise of freedom of the press,

---

3 (1914), 30 T.L.R. 462 at 468 (P.C.).

4 R.S.C. 1985, App. III, s. 1 (f).

5 *Pacific Press Ltd. v. R.*, [1977] 5 W.W.R. 507 (B.C. S.C.).

nullified the warrant after determining that the government investigators had failed to prove that all other reasonable channels to get the information had been exhausted. In other words, the court was saying that freedom of the press should only be infringed upon as a last resort.

How Courts Have Viewed Press Rights

Over the years preceding the Charter, the onus to protect and develop the legal rights of the news media in Canada largely fell on the courts. The courts have used many diverse sources to develop media rights, with sometimes cumbersome and conflicting results. Our media law is actually a mish-mash of law imported from Britain and the United States, with some of our own creations thrown in. In addition, the peculiarities of our own history have resulted in some rights of the press evolving differently in various parts of the country. For example, the law of defamation in Québec, which is largely drawn from its European-based Civil Code, can be substantially different in some respects from the law of defamation in the English-based common law provinces. The socialist background of Alberta had early ramifications for the press in that province and most provinces to this day place their own peculiar restrictions on the news media in certain areas.

The result is that equal treatment of the media throughout Canada in many areas of the law has been sporadic, depending on the political and social characteristics of each province. Fortunately though, Canadian courts have held a generally consistent view of the basic right and value of "freedom of the press."

One of the first major assaults on freedom of the press was attempted by the Social Credit government of Alberta in 1938. The provincial legislature enacted a law which sought to control any statement in newspapers relating to any policy or activity of the government. Bill No. 9 was entitled "An Act to ensure the Publication of Accurate News and Information."[6] The preamble of the law stated that it was

> . . . expedient and in the public interest that the newspapers published in the Province should furnish to the people of the Province statements made by the authority of the Government of the Province as to the true and exact objects of the policy of the Government and as to the hinderances to or difficulties in achieving such objects to the end that the people may be informed with respect thereto.

The so-called "Press Bill" gave a designated official of the provincial government the right to demand that newspapers publish official rebuttals

---

6 See *Ref. re Alberta Legislation*, [1938] 2 D.L.R. 81 (S.C.C.).

to any criticisms or misleading statements in the news media about the government's social credit system. The Act also gave the official the authority to demand to know the identity of the author and sources of a story. The official could also levy penalties prohibiting the publication of the newspaper and gag specific reporters by prohibiting any further publication of their stories.

The nation's press vehemently opposed the law. As a result of the adverse press reaction, the "gag law," as it was called by journalists, and two other related bills were referred to the Supreme Court of Canada for an opinion as to whether they were within the provincial government's constitutional powers.[7] Not surprisingly, the court found the proposed Press Bill to be beyond the legislature's powers.

In its landmark decision, the high court reiterated the public's right of expression, particularly in the news media:[8]

> Freedom of discussion is essential to enlighten public opinion in a democratic State; it cannot be curtailed without affecting the right of the people to be informed through sources independent of the Government concerning matters of public interest. There must be an untrammelled publication of the news and political opinions of the political parties contending for ascendancy.

The Supreme Court has since spoken on many occasions on the question of freedom of expression and, consequently, freedom of the press. For example, the court indirectly dealt with the limits of freedom of expression in the 1979 case of *Gay Alliance Toward Equality v. Vancouver Sun*, which involved the right of a newspaper to refuse advertising.[9] In this case, a homosexual group wanted to run an advertisement for its newspaper, "Gay Tide," in the Vancouver Sun. But the ad was refused. The gay organization then alleged the newspaper had infringed the Human Rights Code of British Columbia by denying a class of persons, without reasonable cause, "a service customarily available to the public," as guaranteed by the Code.

A majority of the Supreme Court justices felt the Sun had not violated the Code. They found that, while newspaper advertising is a service available to each member of the public, the nature and scope of that service is determined by the newspaper itself:[10]

> The law has recognized the freedom of the press to propagate its views and ideas on any issue and to select the material which it publishes. As a corollary to that, a newspaper also has the right to refuse to publish material which runs contrary to the views which it expresses.

---

7 *Reference re Alberta Legislation*, [1938] 2 D.L.R. 81 (S.C.C.).
8 *Ibid.*, p. 119.
9 (1979), 97 D.L.R. (3d) 577 (S.C.C.).
10 *Ibid.*, p. 591.

Although the decision wasn't directly on point in dealing with journalists' rights, it once again reiterated the view that the news media are an important instrument for disseminating public opinion — even opinions others do not agree with.

The Limits of a Free Press

While the courts recognized the value of freedom of expression and freedom of the press, they did not allow the news media complete freedom to report news where other equally important interests are at stake. For example, the courts and legislators have been very careful to balance the freedom of the press against the rights of individuals to a fair trial (for example, the Criminal Code[11] allows the court to ban publication of evidence given at a preliminary hearing).

Fortunately, attempts to make the news media's rights less than those enjoyed by the general public have failed. In *Re F.P. Publications (Western) Ltd. and R.*, a trial judge barred a reporter, but not the rest of the public, from attending a trial where charges of keeping a common bawdy house were being heard. The reporter had earlier refused to agree not to publish the names of witnesses. The exclusion order was clearly directed at preventing publication of the names. The Manitoba Court of Appeal held that the presiding judge cannot use section 486(1) of the Criminal Code to exclude members of the public and to create a select audience or censor the news. The appeal court said the reporter was only doing his job and his presence in the courtroom was not causing any disturbance in the proceedings. The court held that the lower court order was an unjust infringement on the freedom of the press and ran against the principle of an open court.[12]

THE CHARTER AND FREEDOM OF THE PRESS

While it may seem that judges were doing a fairly good job of defending the rights of the press before the Charter came along, freedom of the press was not an easy issue for them. The rights of parties to a court action and the existence of express statutory provisions restricting the news media's reports, all served to act as an imposing barrier to the rights of the press in the eyes of many judges. The main problem was that there were few grounds beyond the common law to justify the courts making radical changes to media-related laws.

However, that changed with the Charter which carries the full authority

---

11 R.S.C. 1985, c. C-46.
12 (1979), 51 C.C.C. (2d) 110 at 125-126 (Man. C.A.).

of being part of the Constitution, the Supreme Law of the Land. When it came into effect many people accurately predicted that the Charter would give judges new powers and authority to strike down inconsistent laws and practices. The Charter had special significance for those who followed media law since it appeared that it would finally deliver the necessary authority for judges to quash restrictive legislation and outmoded case precedents.

For the most part, the constitutional entrenchment of freedom of the press has proved to be a valuable tool for the news media in expanding their rights. But, as numerous unsuccessful court cases have illustrated since 1982, freedom of the press is not an absolute right and it must still compete with other rights and freedoms, such as the right to a fair trial.

The "great equalizer" in determining the extent and limits of freedom of the press is section 1 of the Charter, which says that constitutional rights and freedoms are

> subject only to such reasonable limits prescribed by law as can be demonstrably justified in a free and democratic society.

This is the test against which all laws and practices that infringe upon rights and freedoms are subjected to. If a law restricts a fundamental right, such as freedom of the press, and it cannot be "demonstrably justified" by the individual seeking to uphold the restrictive law, then it will be declared unconstitutional. This provides the authority courts have needed to help extend the boundaries of freedom of the press. But it's also a two-edged sword which can work against the press.

How Courts Apply the Test

One of the first laws to be successfully challenged by the news media under the Charter was a section of the now-repealed Juvenile Delinquents Act[13] which barred the public from attending any juvenile trial. The Ontario Court of Appeal held the absolute ban on the new media's right to attend trials (and conversely, the juvenile accused's right to a public trial) without any use of judicial discretion, was a violation of the Charter's guarantee of freedom of the press.[14]

The court said that an absolute ban on public access is rarely a reasonable limit in all circumstances. The judges felt the absolute ban cast too wide a net for its intended purposes and society lost more than it gained because of it. While the court struck down this provision, it also noted that the guarantee of freedom of the press is not absolute. The judges

---

13 S. 12.
14 *Re Southam Inc. and R. (No. 1)* (1983), 41 O.R. (2d) 113 (C.A.).

said the invalid section would have withstood the Charter's scrutiny if it had provided for a discretionary use of judicial power.

That rationale has been carried on to other cases. The Ontario Court of Appeal again dealt with the meaning of freedom of the press in *Canadian Newspapers Co. Ltd. v. A.G. Canada*.[15] This 1985 case involved a challenge of a Criminal Code provision which allows a complainant (that is, victim) in a sexual assault case to ask for a court order banning publication of the complainant's identity. According to the Code, once the request is made, the judge has no choice in issuing the ban. At the time, section 442(3) (now section 486(2)) stated:

> Where an accused is charged with an offence mentioned in section 246.4, the presiding judge, magistrate, or justice may, or if the application is made by the complainant or prosecutor, shall, make an order directing that the identity of the complainant and any information that could disclose the identity of the complainant shall not be published in any newspaper or broadcast.

The newspaper challenged the section not because it wanted to reveal the identity of sexual assault victims, but because of an unusual problem the story presented for journalists. The victim had brought the assault charge against her own husband. If the newspapers followed the letter of the law and did not report the victim's name but did report the accused's identity, it would not be able to report the unusual nature of the case because it would reveal the victim's identity. In court, the newspaper objected to the fact that the Code imposed an absolute ban on the publication of the victim's identity if the complainant or prosecutor requested it.

The provincial appeal court used the section 1 test to determine whether the infringement on freedom of the press was in violation of the Charter. As in any Charter case, the onus was on the party upholding the present law to prove it's a reasonable limit that can be justified in a free and democratic society. The Crown, in this case, had to prove it was reasonable to allow an absolute publication ban in all sexual assault trials. The Crown called a witness who testified that many victims worry that their identity will come out at trial and one concern was that women might not bring charges against sexual offenders if names could possibly be released.

The Ontario court noted that the concern of a sexual assault victim is a social value which should be protected and that a publication ban is a reasonable limit. But the court then went on to question whether it is a limit which must be applied in all cases. The judges suggested there may be occasions when it may be necessary to publish a victim's name — perhaps to bring forward more witnesses or where someone has

---

15 (1985), 49 O.R. (2d) 557 (C.A.).

previously accused other people of sexual assault without justification.

In the end, the provincial appeal court held that an absolute ban is not reasonable because it does not allow a judge to exercise any discretion once the complainant has asked for the ban.

While this was a significant victory for advocates of a free press, the case went on to the Supreme Court of Canada. There, the lower court decision was overturned.[16] The Supreme Court justices agreed that the mandatory publication ban was a *prima facie* infringement of freedom of the press. However, applying the same section 1 test, they held that the mandatory ban was required to achieve Parliament's objective of facilitating complaints by victims of sexual assaults. Thus, the two-edged sword of section 1 swung back against the press, in favour of a greater public end.

But this decision hasn't spelled the end of the news media's court challenges of absolute bans or limits on the press. There have been many other successful challenges since that decision.

Indeed, it's important to note that "freedom of the press" is such an all-encompassing concept covering so many different aspects of the public's interests that no single case can be expected to set the tone for interpreting the Charter's free press guarantee.

As almost every chapter in this book illustrates, the courts have had to consider the effect of the guarantee in a multitude of different areas of the law. In each case, varying degrees of importance are placed on factors such as society or the public's interests, the right to a fair trial and the value of having a free press. In some areas, such as in challenging publication bans and gaining access to documents and hearings, the news media have won many more victories than they've lost. In other areas, such as contempt and protection of news sources, courts have generally ruled against giving the news media any special status.

Still, the Charter has done much to further the position of the news media in challenging restrictions and barriers on their activities.

CHALLENGING INFRINGEMENTS ON THE PRESS

What many journalists may not know is that the Charter has given them more authority than ever before to challenge infringements on their "right" to gather and disseminate news. Commonly, the most imposing restrictions or barriers are set out by courts or statutes. What is important to note these days is that judges are now more open than ever to hearing legal arguments as to why a court order or statute is unjust.

In almost every case, the challenge of a court order or law will involve

---

16 (1988), 43 C.C.C. (3d) 24 (S.C.C.).

legal counsel. But if a journalist is at a proceeding where an application is made to exclude the public or ban the publication of information, and he or she feels the order is unjust, the reporter should respectfully request that the proceeding be adjourned to allow the reporter to contact his or her lawyer. The judge may refuse the request, but it is worth trying.

The Ontario Court of Appeal in the *Canadian Newspapers* case, mentioned above, spoke extensively on the right of journalists to challenge a court-imposed restraint.[17] While this particular case dealt with an order barring the publication of a sexual assault victim's name, it has relevance to the challenge of any court order or law.

First, the court said the news media has no express right to intervene in a criminal proceeding.[18] That doesn't mean a judge won't listen to a request from a journalist or anyone else at a criminal proceeding. Just the same, a judge can ignore a request to be heard. The court said the news media would most certainly have no right to appeal a judge's decision not to allow an intervention in a criminal matter. The rationale is that the time involved in an appeal of a decision on any court order would unjustly delay the fair trial of an accused.

Still, the court did hold that it is important for the news media to have their rights determined before the courts. The appeal judges then went on to say that the news media did have an express right to apply through a civil proceeding for a "declaration" that the court order or legislative provision in question is unconstitutional. If the application is heard through a civil process, the court said the news media then would be entitled to appeal the decision without fear of interfering with the criminal trial. If a province's court rules allow it, the civil application may even be heard by the same judge conducting the criminal trial. But the court noted that the presiding criminal court judge or any other judge can still choose not to hear the civil application.

---

17 Note 16, above.

18 The Court noted the Ontario decision in *R. v. Thomson Newspapers Ltd.* (1984), 4 C.R.D. 525.40-01 (Ont. S.C.), where it was held the news media did not have a right to intervene in a trial involving criminal charges brought under the Combines Investigation Act.

However, courts in other provinces may disagree. In *Re Edmonton Journal and A.G. Alberta* (1983), 4 C.C.C. (3d) 59 (Alta. Q.B.), the court considered whether a reporter had "standing" or a justifiable interest in criminal proceedings. The Alberta court concluded a reporter did have standing as a "concerned citizen" and could challenge the exclusion order. In the recent case of *R. v. Harrison* (1984), 14 C.C.C. (3d) 549 (C.S.P.), a Québec court held that the media had "standing" to challenge a publication ban issued during a preliminary hearing because the media's role as the public's agent was hampered by the ban.

SOME FINAL THOUGHTS

While the rights of the news media will continue to expand, as stated in this book's first edition, the Charter is unlikely to change the principle that the news media have no greater rights than the average citizen. For example, in *R. v. Thompson Newspapers Ltd.*, the court said the Charter does not give the media or even the public a general constitutional right to require a judge to allow public access to any court document during a trial.[19]

However, the opportunity is now here to assert a Canadian version of what Americans refer to as "the public's right to know," using the Charter's guarantee of freedom of the press.[20] The Charter holds a great potential to expand the rights of the news media and, at the same time, the public's rights, and it can be safely predicted that the constitutional entrenchment of the fundamental freedom of the press will play an ever increasing role in activities of the news media.

---

19 *R. v. Thomson Newspapers Ltd.*, *ibid.*

20 In fact, in the case of *R. v. Harrison*, note 18, above, at 552, the court said in light of the Charter "the media are now the custodians of the public's right to know." The phrase was first used by American journalist Kent Cooper in the 1940's.

In Eugenia Zerbinos, "The Right to Know: Whose Right and Whose Duty?," v. 4, No. 1, Winter, 1982 edition of Communications and the Law, at page 33, the author discusses the lack of an all-encompassing definition of the "right to know" in the United States. There is no "right to know" mentioned in the U.S. Constitution, but it is argued that the public's right to know is inherent in a democratic system of government. The author suggests the right to know is actually an umbrella term for several specific rights accorded to the public (of which, the press is the self-declared agent).

2

Defamation

Generally, defamation is the publication of a statement which harms another individual's reputation. For most journalists, defamation is one of the primary areas of concern. And rightly so. In the past two decades, the news media have increasingly found themselves under attack in the courts, embroiled in lengthy and expensive defamation actions.

Aside from the high cost of defending a defamation lawsuit, court awards to plaintiffs have also been increasing. Some of the highest recently have been well over $100,000, and awards between $10,000 and $25,000 are not uncommon.

And it's not just the controversial or spectacular stories that attract lawsuits. Sometimes, stories of the most innocent appearance or intention can prompt someone to call their lawyer. So, it's vital these days for journalists to keep watch for the danger of defamation when preparing a story for publication. As they say, the best offence is a defence.

WHAT IS DEFAMATORY?

Over the years, the courts have developed several definitions of what is defamatory. A defamatory statement tends to discredit or lower an individual "in the estimation of right-thinking members of society generally."[1] It may also expose an individual to other's hatred, contempt, ridicule or injure his or her reputation in an office, trade or profession.[2]

A report presented at the 65th Annual Meeting of the Uniform Law Conference of Canada in August 1983, suggested this all-encompassing definition of what is defamatory:

"Defamatory matter" is published matter concerning a person that tends to:

(a) affect adversely the reputation of that person in the estimation of ordinary persons; or

(b) deter ordinary persons from associating or dealing with that person; or

(c) injure that person in his occupation, trade, office or financial credit.

A defamatory statement can harm the reputation not only of a person, but also corporations,[3] unions[4] or any legal entity.[5]

The courts in Canada have been reluctant to allow defamation actions by groups which do not enjoy a legal status (for example, *ad hoc* citizen's

---

1 *Sim v. Stretch* (1936), 52 T.L.R. 669 at 669-670 (H.L.). It is important that society generally, and not just a few select individuals, find the statement defamatory. For instance, in *Burnett v. C.B.C. (No.1)* (1981), 48 N.S.R. (2d) 1 (T.D.), the court said it could not find a statement defamatory if a person's reputation is only lowered within a particular class or section of the community which has a "standard of opinion" the courts cannot identify or approve.

2 For example, see *Thomas v. C.B.C.*, [1981] 4 W.W.R. 289 at 302 (N.W.T. S.C.), where an engineer was defamed by allegations that he had acted negligently in his job.

3 The defamatory matter must injure the company in the way in which it does business or functions. In *Price v. Chicoutimi Pulp Co.* (1915), 51 S.C.R. 179 at 188-189, the Supreme Court of Canada said the defamatory words must be directed at the corporation as apart from its employees or owners and attack the corporation in the method of conducting its affairs (for example, accusing it of fraud or mismanagement). The case of *Georgian Bay Ship Canal Co. v. World Newspaper Co.* (1894), 16 P.R. 320 at 322, states a company could also be defamed if a defamatory statement wrongly alleges that officers or employees, while acting in the best interests of the company or in the regular conduct of business, have committed a criminal act.

The defamation action may fail if the corporation is not capable of the alleged act. Corporations cannot themselves commit murder, rape or actually perform an act. For example, the court in *Church of Scientology of Toronto v. Globe & Mail* (1978), 84 D.L.R. (3d) 239 at 242 (Ont. H.C.), held that while a non-profit corporation could be defamed, the one in this case could not sue for a statement alleging that its members were practising medicine without a licence. The court said the statements were in reference to the members only and a corporate entity itself could not practise medicine.

4 *P.P.F., Loc. 488 v. CBC* (1979), 97 D.L.R. (3d) 56 (Alta. T.D.). Also see, *Pulp and Paper Workers of Canada v. International Brotherhood of Pulp, etc.* (1973), 37 D.L.R. (3d) 687 (B.C. S.C.), where one union sued another for libel.

5 In *Prince George v. B.C. Television System Ltd.*, [1979] 2 W.W.R. 404 (B.C. C.A.), a municipal corporation was found to have the legal capacity or standing to sue for defamation.

committees).[6] But, a member of an identifiable class or group may be able to successfully sue if a defamatory statement directed at the class or group can be proven to be reasonably understood to refer to that person as a member.[7]

The responsibility for publication of a defamatory statement does not stop with the journalist — it continues throughout the chain of command, so that editors, news directors, producers, owners, publishers, announcers and even those delivering the publication can be held responsible. Anyone who has knowledge, or should have knowledge, of the defamatory statement and subsequent control over its publication, is potentially responsible.[8]

THE PECULIARITIES OF DEFAMATION

One aspect of a defamation lawsuit that makes it different from any other civil action is that the plaintiff (the offended individual) does not have to prove the defamatory matter is false. Under the common law, the courts immediately presume that any statement which adversely affects someone's reputation is false.[9]

Indeed, even a true statement can, technically speaking, be defamatory in accordance with the definition that it subjects someone to ridicule or contempt. As the saying goes, the truth hurts. But, in all provinces except one, proving the truth of a statement acts as a complete defence to a defamation action.

This leads to an important point to remember. A statement may be defamatory, but may not be actionable (in other words, successful) in court.

---

6 Manitoba is the only province that protects against libel of a race or creed in its defamation statute. The Uniform Law Conference's report mentioned at the beginning of this chapter suggests "group defamation" is a difficult issue because the group and its membership often cannot be defined. The report says supplying a civil remedy for defaming such a group might also stifle public debate on important issues.

7 *Knupffer v. London Express Newspapers Ltd.*, [1944] A.C. 116 (H.L.). The defamation must clearly point to the plaintiff as a member of the group. For example, in *Booth v. BCTV Broadcasting System* (1982), 139 D.L.R. (3d) 88 (B.C. C.A.), a news report quoted a hooker saying two members of the narcotics squad "that are high up — right up on top — take payoffs." The court held that only the two senior officers in the squad could sue and dismissed lawsuits brought by nine other members of the squad who felt they were implicated.

8 *Popovich v. Lobay*, [1937] 3 D.L.R. 715 (Man. C.A.). In the English case of *Emmens v. Pottle* (1885), 16 Q.B.D. 354 (C.A.), the court stated that, to be found not liable or responsible, there must be no knowledge of the libel, no negligence in not knowing of it and that the defendant did not know, or should have known, the publication was of a bad character.

9 *Belt v. Lawes* (1882), 51 L.J.Q.B. 359 at 361 (D.C.). The Uniform Law Conference report argued against including a requirement for "falsity" in any definition of defamation because it would mean that the plaintiff would first have to prove an offending statement is false before claiming it was defamatory. The report reasoned that because a person's reputation is at stake, the onus should always be on the defendant to prove the truth of defamatory statements or call some other defence.

As will be discussed later, a statement may be proven true, or there may be a special defence available which can permit even a completely false statement to be published (for example, qualified privilege). It is for this reason that journalists can still write controversial or critical stories.

A word of warning, though. There are certain circumstances in which a true, yet defamatory, statement may still be successfully pursued in the courts. As mentioned above, the truth is a complete defence in all provinces, but one. The exception is Québec, where the true defamatory statement must also be in the public interest and made without malice. Also, the rare charge of defamatory libel under the Criminal Code[10] has a "truth" defence which requires that the defamatory statement must have an element of public benefit at the time of publication. A final warning about publishing true defamatory statements is that in some provinces, a civil action may be successfully pursued under provincial Privacy Acts if the offending statement is not made in the public interest.[11]

WHAT'S THE DIFFERENCE BETWEEN LIBEL AND SLANDER?

Historically, defamation has fallen into two categories. *Libel* is defamation through a permanent form, such as writing.[12] *Slander* is defamation by the spoken word or gesture.[13] There is a reason for the distinction. In a case of libel, the plaintiff does not have to offer proof that the defamation caused any actual damage to his or her reputation.[14] In a case of slander, the plaintiff must show that actual damage (for example, loss of credit) resulted from the defamatory words.[15] The distinctions are less important today.

For instance, a court action against a broadcast journalist will be in libel because alleged defamations in broadcasting are usually preserved in a permanent form, such as audio or video tape[16] and most provinces have legislation which states that a defamation in broadcasting is libel.[17]

---

10 R.S.C. 1985, c. C-46.

11 See the chapter on "Invasion of Privacy."

12 *Osborn's Concise Law Dictionary*, 6th ed. (London: Sweet & Maxwell, 1976), p. 203.

13 *Ibid.*, p. 307. But, in *Stopforth v. Goyer* (1978), 87 D.L.R. (3d) 373 at 375 (Ont. C.A.), the court said it is settled law that when a person speaks defamatory words to the press with the intention or knowledge that they will be republished, the speaker is responsible in libel instead of slander.

14 This was recognized in *Thorley v. Lord Kerry* (1812), 128 E.R. 367 at 371.

15 There are occasions when the common law will allow a slander action without proof of damage. *Gatley on Libel and Slander*, 8th ed. (London: Sweet & Maxwell, 1981), p. 73, states that slander is actionable without proof of actual harm where a crime has been imputed, an infectious or contagious disease has been suggested, a business reputation has been hurt or the chastity of a woman or girl is questioned.

16 A 1981 report by the Law Reform Commission of British Columbia, L.R.C. 50, "Report on Cable Television and Defamation," suggests a broadcast delivered from a script or played back from a recording is libel. But it suggests a "live" broadcast remark is slander.

17 British Columbia, Ontario, and Nova Scotia expressly state that defamations in broad-

DEFAMATION CAN EVEN BE A CRIMINAL OFFENCE

Defamation can be the subject of either civil or criminal proceedings. The law applying to criminal defamation is, for the most part, substantially different from civil defamation laws. The standard of proof called for in a criminal case is much more demanding than that found in civil cases. Also, because of different historical backgrounds, criminal and civil offences and defences in defamation actions are sometimes a world apart.

Most court actions against the news media are civil, with the plaintiff seeking compensation for his damaged reputation. Criminal actions are rare and involve serious and malicious defamations likely to incite public hatred, contempt or ridicule against the individual.[18] The criminal charge of defamatory libel punishes the offence against society, not just the offence against the individual. While a criminal charge of defamatory libel is rare, a journalist should realize that a seriously defamatory statement could be the subject of criminal proceedings.[19]

THE CIVIL LAW OF DEFAMATION

Assessing the Risk of Defamation

Journalists can best avoid losing a defamation lawsuit by understanding how the law examines a story. There are essentially three key questions:

Is There Defamatory Matter?

Based on plain meaning of the words.   To succeed in court, one of the first things the plaintiff must prove is that the words are defamatory. But it is not good enough that the plaintiff feels the words are objectionable. The court (the jury or judge sitting alone) must also be convinced. If there is a dispute about whether the words are defamatory, the judge will use the clear and obvious meanings of the words, such as set out in a dictionary, to decide what they could mean.

---

casting are libel. Alberta, Manitoba, New Brunswick, Newfoundland, Prince Edward Island, the Northwest Territories and the Yukon have eliminated the distinction between libel and slander altogether, making all defamations actionable without proof of damage. Saskatchewan's legislation provides only for "newspaper libel," leaving broadcasters to the common law distinctions between slander and libel. Québec's Civil Code does not recognize a distinction between slander and libel. Québec's Press Act allows anyone who "deems himself injured" to initiate an action against a newspaper.

18 *R. v. Cameron* (1898), 7 Que. Q.B. 162 at 163.

19 The Canadian Centre for Justice Statistics recorded 36 people charged with criminal libel offences between 1963 and, the last year recorded, 1973.

 The Law Reform Commission of Canada has recommended that criminal defamatory libel be repealed and it is likely to be taken off the books.

If not clearly defamatory, is there an innuendo? Sometimes, a plaintiff may allege that the words, while not defamatory by definition, may carry a defamatory innuendo to people with knowledge of special facts.[20] The essence of defamation is the transmission of ideas which adversely affect a person's reputation despite whether it is express or by implication. While the plaintiff can always allege that a statement carries an innuendo, he has the burden of proving that there is an innuendo.[21]

Unfortunately for well-meaning journalists, innuendos can happen quite innocently. For instance, the use of file footage or stock photographs which single out an identifiable person can be dangerous when coupled with a controversial story. In one case, stock footage of a hospital worker preparing an operating room was used in connection with a story on abortion. The hospital worker was a devout Roman Catholic and felt that people who knew him would think he condoned abortion. Another example would be pictures showing two people talking on a street in the context of a story on illegal drug trafficking, insinuating that either person deals in narcotics. If either person proves he could be identified, he could sue, putting the onus on the journalist to prove the truth of the innuendo.

Is it defamatory in the context of the entire story? Since words can be defamatory on their own, but perhaps not when considered in the context they were used, a judge may also consider the tenor of the whole story or, at least, relevant segments. For example, in a case involving Soviet defector Ivan Gouzenko in 1976, the court stated that although isolated words in a story may be defamatory, the entire article must be considered. Although the journalist used some strong language to describe Gouzenko, the judge said words like "traitor" and "defector" were accurate descriptions of the plaintiff.[22]

Once it is decided that the words are capable of being defamatory, the jury or judge sitting alone must decide if the statements are truly defamatory in this case. As mentioned, the statement must be defamatory in the estimation of "right-thinking members of society" as represented by the jury or the judge in non-jury trials.

---

20 In *Mark v. Deustch* (1973), 39 D.L.R. (3d) 568 at 571 (Alta. T.D.), the court stated the plaintiff does not have to prove that everyone derived a defamatory innuendo from a statement, only that it could be understood that way and that such people exist.

21 In the case of *Pherrill v. Sewell* (1908), 12 O.W.R. 63 (Div. Ct.) the court said the innuendo must be clear to the "reasonable man." The appeal court judge borrowed (at p. 65) this clever quote from a Scottish judge: "I am unwilling to torture innuendoes out of words that do not in a reasonable manner bear the interpretation sought to be put upon them."

22 *Gouzenko v. Harris* (1976), 13 O.R. (2d) 730 (H.C.).

Does The Defamatory Matter Refer to the Plaintiff?

Is it a direct or indirect reference? It is important to the plaintiff's case to prove that the offending statement refers to him or her, even if he or she is not expressly identified.[23] As an example, if a story made defamatory references to an unnamed "senior city hall official," a highly placed city official might successfully sue if he could prove that society in general would understand the defamatory statement to be referring to him.

What if there was no intention to defame the plaintiff? It is irrelevant that there was no intention to defame someone.[24] For example, a fictitious story that unintentionally uses the name of a real person can be the subject of a successful defamation action.[25] The test is whether a reasonable person receiving the defamatory statement would be likely to think it refers to the individual.[26]

Was The Defamatory Matter Published?

Why it's important to know about publication. Journalism being what it is, this is somewhat of a moot question. Still, there can be no defamation unless the words are published.[27] Publication happens when the defamatory statement is received by someone other than the allegedly defamed victim.[28] A person can even be held responsible for an unintentional publication if it was foreseeable or likely in the circumstance.[29]

---

23 In the English case of *Le Fanu v. Malcolmson* (1848), 9 E.R. 910 (H.L.), the House of Lords said in cases of alleged innuendo, the plaintiff must prove that at least one person would think it refers to the plaintiff.

24 *Planned Parenthood Nfld./Labrador v. Fedorik* (1982), 135 D.L.R. (3d) 714 at 719 (Nfld. T.D.). In *Loos v. The Leader Post Ltd. and Williams*, [1982] 2 W.W.R. 459 at 468 (Sask. C.A.), this appeal court held it does not matter what the defendant intended his words to mean or even what they were understood to mean by the audience. They need only have the potential to be understood in a defamatory manner.

25 *Jones v. E. Hulton & Co.*, [1909] 2 K.B. 444 (C.A.).

26 *Bulletin Co. v. Sheppard* (1917), 55 S.C.R. 454 at 461.

27 In *Jenner v. Sun Oil Co.*, [1952] O.R. 240 at 251 (H.C.), the court held the essential element of the defamation was not the statement itself, but its publication.

28 In *Gallant v. Calder* (1883), 23 N.B.R. 73 (C.A.), referring to the Supreme Court of Canada decision in *Dewe v. Waterbury* (1881) 6, S.C.R. 143, the New Brunswick court held that the defamatory words were spoken only to the plaintiff and the judge properly dismissed the case. But in the Québec cases of *Peters v. Tardivel* (1899), 15 C.S. 401 and *Beaudoin v. Vaillancourt* (1926), 42 K.B. 42, the offending words were published only to the plaintiffs and they won nominal damages under Québec's Civil Code. None of the common law provinces have followed this line of thought.

29 *McNichol v. Grandy*, [1931] S.C.R. 696. In *Hills v. O'Bryan*, [1949] 1 W.W.R. 985 (B.C. S.C.), the plaintiff showed a defamatory letter, written by the defendant and addressed only to the plaintiff, to others. The court said the defendant could not foresee that this would happen.

What if someone else published it too? Unless there is a special privilege or defence, it is irrelevant that a journalist is only repeating what was said or published by another person.[30] In addition, there is no protection offered to a journalist who uses defamatory material, even though another news agency, such as a wire service, originally published it.[31]

WHAT ARE THE DEFENCES?

Co-existing with hundreds of years of case law on defamation, is legislation in each province and territory which sometimes modifies the common law and, in other instances, codifies it. In general, the legislation supersedes any areas of direct conflict with the common law. But, for the most part, the common law rules have been adopted. In qualified privilege, for instance, defamation statutes specifically allow the use of the common law to supplement the legislative provisions.

While all jurisdictions have defamation legislation, individual provincial statutes vary widely in some respects. The most prominent differences are between the common law provinces and Québec. Even the common law provinces have developed their own particular defamation statutes.[32] For instance, Saskatchewan's legislation only addresses defamation actions against newspapers while all others include both print and broadcasting. Some provinces have incorporated more of the common law into their legislation than others. The cumulative effect of all these variations is confusion for journalists and plaintiffs alike. There has been an attempt to get provinces to adopt a Uniform Defamation Act, but differences still exist even in the provinces which have the uniform Acts. The following section will outline the common law and statutory defences in Canada. Variations among provinces will be highlighted and the civil law in Québec will be discussed separately.

---

30 *MacDonald v. Mail Printing Co.* (1900), 32 O.R. 163 at 170 (H.C.). Also see, *Thomas v. CBC*, [1981] 4 W.W.R. 289 at 298 (N.W.T. S.C.), where the court said a reporter is responsible for proving the truth of any hearsay statement or quote he uses in his story. A hearsay statement is one in which the person speaking does not have direct knowledge of the truth and is only repeating what he heard from someone else, who is not available to testify.

31 See *Allan v. Bushnell T.V. Co.* (1968), [1969] 1 O.R. 107 (H.C.) and *Chinese Cultural Centre of Vancouver v. Holt* (1978), 7 B.C.L.R. 81 (S.C.), for cases where defamatory news reports in one publication were repeated in another news medium.

32 Defamation Acts, R.S.A. 1980, c. D-6; R.S.M. 1987, c. D-20; R.S.N.B. 1973, c. D-5; R.S.N.S. 1967, c. 72; R.S.P.E.I. 1974, c. D-3; R.S.Y. 1986, c. 41; Libel and Slander Acts, R.S.B.C. 1979, c. 234, as amended; R.S.O. 1980, c. 237, as amended; Press Act, R.S.Q., c. P-19, as amended; Libel and Slander Act, R.S.S. 1978, c. L-14, as amended.

The Defence of Truth or Justification

Most responsible journalists believe that everything they write is true and based on facts. Justification is the defence of truth and it is the one defence which most journalists think they can rely on. But, it can be a problematic and difficult defence.

As mentioned at the beginning of this chapter, the law places a heavy onus on the publisher of a defamatory statement to "justify" it or call some other defence.

Proving It

Proving the truth of a statement is not as easy as it sounds. For example, the defence of truth does not simply involve proving that a quoted source did really say the defamatory statement that was published. A journalist and his lawyers will have to present actual proof to the judge and jury of the truth of any source's statements, as well as the journalist's own statements. The evidence, as in any other trial, will have to be admissible and relevant. The court is unlikely to accept hearsay evidence, which is any proof based on the word of a person who is not at the hearing to testify to the truth of the statement. In other words, it is second-hand information. It also does not help to be partly correct. In one extreme case, a publication said the plaintiff owed $59.35 (a large amount of money in 1892). In reality, the plaintiff only owed $24.33 and the court held the plea of justification was not established through partial proof.[33]

To succeed with the defence of justification, a journalist must be able to prove that the alleged facts are true in both fact and substance.[34] That means the plain meaning of the published words must be true, including any alleged innuendo. In the common law, it is unnecessary to prove the truth of every single word, but there must be justification for the gist of the statement.[35] Ontario and Nova Scotia have adopted a statutory equivalent of the common law requirements for the "truth" defence. The provision in both provinces states that[36]

> a defence of justification shall not fail by reason only that the truth of every charge is not proved if the words not proved to be true do not materially in-jure the plaintiff's reputation having regard to the truth of the remaining charges.

---

33 *Green v. Minnes* (1892), 22 O.R. 177 (C.A.).

34 In the English case of *Walker & Son, Ltd. v. Hodgson*, [1909] 1 K.B. 239 at 253 (C.A.), the court said: ". . . . the defendant must prove not only that the facts were truly stated, but also that the innuendo is true. He must justify every injurious imputation."

35 First stated in *Edwards v. Bell* (1824), 1 Bing 403 at 408.

36 Libel and Slander Act, R.S.O. 1980, c. 237, s. 23; Defamation Act, R.S.N.S. 1967, c. 72, s. 8.

The Standard of Proof Required

With one exception, the standard of proof needed to prove the truth of a statement is the same as in any other civil trial. The statement must be proven to be true "on a balance of probabilities based on the preponderance of evidence." This means that the jury or judge will have to be convinced that the statements of fact are in all probability true, based on the evidence.

The exception to the standard of proof is when a criminal or corrupt act is alleged. The standard of proof required of the defendant in such instances is automatically raised to a higher level. While the criminal act does not have to be proven "beyond a reasonable doubt" as in criminal law, the courts have determined that a higher degree of probability than normal is necessary.[37]

Proving the commission of a criminal offence may be extremely difficult. Someone charged with murder and awaiting trial cannot be called a murderer. Even evidence of a conviction itself may not be enough, sometimes, to support an allegation that a crime has been committed. For example, if a person has been convicted of possession of stolen property, a journalist could not say that the plaintiff is a thief. If the plaintiff had been convicted of theft, the record of conviction would strengthen the defendant's case, but evidence might still have to be offered to prove that an offence had been committed by the plaintiff.

Therefore, to rely on the defence of truth, a journalist must keep in mind who can be called as a witness to offer direct evidence as to the veracity of a statement. As well, it is important to retain all notes, documents and recordings used while gathering the information for the story.

The Defence of Consent

It is rare that anyone would consent to be defamed, but it can happen. The defence of consent is rooted in the legal principle of *volenti non fit injuria* (that to which a person consents cannot be considered an injury). The principle is that anyone who knowingly and voluntarily exposes himself to a danger, should be thought to have assumed the potential consequences.

For this defence to succeed, the defendant must be able to prove that the plaintiff caused the defamatory statements himself or that the plaintiff knew what defamatory statements were to be published and gave a full

---

37 This was stated in *York v. Okanagan Broadcasters Ltd.*, [1976] 6 W.W.R. 40 (B.C. S.C.). The court went on to say that even though there was no direct evidence of the alleged criminal acts in this case, the judge could find that it was "reasonably probable" that the plaintiff had committed the acts based on indirect evidence.

and knowledgeable consent to the defamation.[38] For example, in one Western case, a person agreed to appear on a radio program to refute a defamatory rumor in the community. However, the person made it clear that he only wanted to make a statement that the rumour was not true and did not want to be challenged or subjected to questioning by listeners resulting in further spreading of the rumor. Unfortunately, a caller did just that and the plaintiff successfully sued the radio station for allowing the caller's defamatory remarks to go out over the airwaves.[39]

The Defence of Absolute Privilege

While the law seeks to protect the reputation of individuals, it also must consider the right of society as a whole to public debate in certain forums, such as Parliament or the courts. If the laws of defamation applied to comments in these forums, no one would be willing to bring up controversial issues. Therefore, the law has developed an exception for defamatory statements arising from certain public forums. The special defence of absolute privilege allows the publication of a defamatory statement even if it is made with malicious intent. This defence is usually only available to certain public representatives in government or judicial proceedings. But the privilege is extended to journalists in two situations which will be discussed.

Government Proceedings

Traditionally, elected members of legislative forums enjoy an absolute privilege while performing their legislative duties. However, an absolute privilege does not exist in everything an elected official says or does. Members of Parliament, the Senate or a provincial legislature enjoy this privilege only during votes, in reports and papers presented during proceedings and during the actual proceedings of the House, a provincial

---

38 In *Jones v. Brooks* (1974), 45 D.L.R. (3d) 413 (Sask. Q.B.), the plaintiff secretly hired two investigators to ask the defendant about the plaintiff's reputation. The court found the resulting defamatory statements were caused by the plaintiff's own actions and he was thus consenting to their publication.

In *Burnett v. CBC (No. 2)* (1981), 48 N.S.R. (2d) 181 (T.D.), the defendant argued unsuccessfully that since the plaintiff did not object to a story being done about him (he had refused to participate but, of course, could not stop the reporter from doing the story), the plaintiff had thereby consented to any defamatory comments made by other people in interviews. The court said there was no consent here and the plaintiff had a right to expect subsequent comments to be within the confines of the law of defamation.

39 *Syms v. Warren* (1976), 71 D.L.R. (3d) 558 (Man. Q.B.).

legislative assembly or committee meetings.[40] Their absolute privilege exists only in connection with the formal transaction of business in the House, assembly or committee.[41] For example, comments made outside of the proceedings (even on the steps of a legislature) would not enjoy absolute privilege even though the words may be a repetition of statements made in the proceedings.[42]

Judicial Proceedings

Judges, lawyers and witnesses also enjoy absolute privilege during judicial proceedings, except in Québec.[43] In Québec, all words spoken in a judicial proceeding are not absolutely privileged. The absolute privilege only extends to words which are relevant and reasonably necessary to the purpose of the case and spoken without malice.[44]

An absolute privilege can also be extended to bodies which are not formal courts, but do exhibit judicial or quasi-judicial qualities.[45] This can include coroners' inquests, public inquiries and compensation board hearings. But there is a restriction as to how far the absolute privileges of these bodies go. Most of these public bodies, such as coroners' inquests, are not considered "courts of record" (that is, with a formal record of their proceedings and the ability to fine or imprison). Bodies which are

---

40 Parliament of Canada Act, R.S.C. 1985, c. P-1, ss. 7-8. The common law offers similar protection as seen in the case of *Vezina v. Lacroix* (1936), 40 Que. P.R. 1.

41 See Maingot, *Law of Parliamentary Privilege In Canada*, (Toronto: Butterworth & Co., 1982), pp. 69-72.

42 *Stopforth v. Goyer* (1978), 20 O.R. (2d) 262 (H.C.). But, there may be a qualified privilege available.

43 First stated in the English case of *Munster v. Lamb* (1883), 11 Q.B.D. 588 (C.A.). In *Henderson v. Scott* (1892), 24 N.S.R. 232 at 238 (C.A.), the court said the privilege applies even when the defamatory words have nothing to do with the issues in the case. The case of *Hall v. Baxter* (1922), 22 O.W.N. 207 at 209 (S.C.), states the absolute privilege for participants extends to statements made in their writs, pleadings and affidavits. But, the Supreme Court of Canada in *The Gazette Printing Co. v. Shallow* (1909), 41 S.C.R. 339, said the publication of pleadings by the news media, before being admitted as evidence or read into open court, would not be protected by any privilege whatsoever.

44 *Langlois v. Drapeau*, [1962] B.R. 277 at 280-281.

45 *Stark v. Auerbach*, [1979] 3 W.W.R. 563 at 567 (B.C. S.C.), dealt with whether absolute privilege could be extended to bodies other than courts. The court said it can be extended if the public body exercises a judicial function (i.e., weighs evidence, gives reasons for its decision and acts judicially). In the English case of *Royal Aquarium and Summer and Winter Garden Society, Ltd. v. Parkinson*, [1892] 1 Q.B. 431 (C.A.) the court also agreed that the absolute privilege at common law extends only to inquiries of a judicial or quasi-judicial nature. For example, see the Canadian case of *Halls v. Mitchell*, [1926] 4 D.L.R. 202 (Ont. S.C.), where a worker's compensation board was found to have absolute privilege.

not courts of record lose their absolute privilege if the defamatory statements are made outside the authority or purpose of the hearing.[46] As long as the statements are within the purpose of the proceedings defamatory statements can be made, even with malicious intent.

A Limited Privilege for Journalists

Journalists enjoy absolute privilege in two cases. The first occasion involves reports of government proceedings. If tabled reports, papers, votes or proceedings of Parliament or a legislature are published by the news media in their entirety they will enjoy absolute privilege.[47] However, it is rare that such matters would be published in their entirety and the more common journalistic practice of publishing extracts of reports, papers, votes or proceedings only enjoys a qualified privilege.[48]

Most provinces also extend a limited form of absolute privilege in their legislation to fair and accurate reports of public judicial proceedings. It is actually an absolute privilege in name only because of its restrictions. British Columbia and Nova Scotia simply extend a "privilege" to court reports, with no mention of an absolute privilege. In addition, Saskatchewan's Act only applies to newspapers, leaving broadcasters to the common law principles. This is representative of many of the enacted provisions:

> A fair and accurate report published in a newspaper or by broadcasting, of proceedings publicly heard before any court is absolutely privileged if,
>
> (a) the report contains no comment;
> (b) the report is published contemporaneously with the proceedings that are the subject-matter of the report, or within thirty days thereafter; and
> (c) the report contains nothing of a seditious, blasphemous or indecent nature.

As the provision states, protection from a defamatory statement will only be offered to reports of judicial proceedings held in public. Therefore, a report of details of *in camera* or closed door proceedings will not be

---

46 For example, in *MacKenzie v. McArthur*, [1981] 4 W.W.R. 692 (B.C. S.C.), a coroner was held liable for directing a jury to find that a doctor had carelessly treated someone and caused their death. That type of verdict was outside the authority of the coroner in that province.

47 Parliament of Canada Act, R.S.C. 1985, c. P-1, ss. 7-8. The common law principle was first set out in the English case of *Wason v. Walter* (1868), L.R. 4 Q.B. 73, where the court said the advantage to the public far outweighs the private injury that results. In *Lake v. King* (1670), 1 Saund. 131 (K.B.), the court recognized the need to protect the publication of Parliamentary petitions and papers.

48 Parliament of Canada Act, note 47 above, s. 9. See also Maingot, *Parliamentary Privilege In Canada*, note 41, above, at p. 46.

privileged. There is also a requirement for a "fair and accurate" report. That means it must be properly balanced and not one-sided. But, it does not have to be word-for-word. The report must be substantially correct and carry the same meaning as a word-for-word account.[49]

The report must also contain no comment on the proceedings. This provision is intended to prevent journalists from speculating on such things as the quality of the evidence or the possible outcome of the proceedings. This does not mean that a journalist cannot report what he sees in court. But, it is fair to say there are limits to what is observation and what is comment. For instance, a journalist should not make a subjective comment, such as "The accused looked worried about his case."

According to the statutes, the report must also be published contemporaneously or within a reasonable period after the proceedings, usually no more than 30 days. In the common law, fair and accurate reports of any judicial proceedings, regardless of the time frame, are entitled to a qualified privilege.

The law also adds these two qualifications. First, there must be an opportunity for the right of reply:

> No privilege will apply where the newspaper or broadcasting outlet refuses to publish a reasonable statement of explanation or contradiction.

And, second, headlines and captions are considered a part of the story. Only British Columbia's legislation makes no reference to the right of reply. As well, British Columbia and Ontario statutes do not make reference to headlines or captions. But the common law clearly states that the headline is part of the story.[50]

---

49 *Nowlan v. Moncton Publishing Co.*, [1952] 4 D.L.R. 808 at 812 (N.B. C.A.). In *Geary v. Alger*, [1925] 4 D.L.R. 1005 (Ont. C.A.), the defence was lost because the journalist added to his report the name of a person who the Crown had not expressly identified in open court. In *Mitchell v. Times Printing and Publishing Co. (No. 2)*, [1944] 1 W.W.R. 400 (B.C. S.C.), the court stated that adding extra comment which imputes guilt will destroy the defence of absolute privilege. The report in question said that a "long-sought killer" had "finally been caught." The accused was later found not guilty. But the court in *Wesolowski v. Armadale Publishers Ltd.* (1980), 3 Sask. R. 330 (Q.B.), said if a journalist correctly describes the situation in court without malice, despite an error in describing the charge, the report is still fair and accurate. In this case, a person was named in the indictment with the accused, but was not charged. The court said the newspaper's reference to the person as "an unindicted co-conspirator" was fair and accurate because it adequately described that part of the judicial proceedings.

50 *Bennett v. Sun Publishing Co.* (1972), 29 D.L.R. (3d) 423 at 436 (B.C. S.C.). Also see *Tedlie v. Southam Co.*, [1950] 4 D.L.R. 415 (Man. Q.B.), where a headline wrongly suggested that negligence in the operation of a train had caused deaths.

The Defence of Qualified Privilege

As noted, the defence of absolute privilege is necessary to allow certain public representatives to speak freely on important matters in the public interest even if there is an underlying malicious motive. The courts have also recognized there may be important occasions in which general members of the public will have a duty to publish statements which could turn out to be defamatory.

Thus evolved the defence of qualified privilege, which can be used to defend statements published in the public interest while carrying out a recognized duty, protecting an important interest or reporting on public proceedings.[51] One of the major differences between this defence and absolute privilege is that there must be an absence of malice in the publication of the defamatory statements.

The Statutory Defence

Journalists regularly take advantage of this privilege when publishing extracts of government proceedings and accounts of public meetings, public hearings or other matters of public interest or concern. In some provinces, the legislation also includes private societies, clubs and agencies in the list of bodies offering opportunities of qualified privilege.

As will be seen, this is a complex defence and the statutes do not try to spell out all occasions of qualified privilege. In fact, all the statutes expressly state that any privilege existing by law is not limited or abridged by the legislation, thereby allowing the common law cases to supplement the statutes. But because of the complexities of this defence and the nature of journalism, journalists may find few opportunities outside the statutory occasions to claim a qualified privilege.

All provinces and territories offer a qualified privilege in their defamation legislation for reports of government and other public proceedings. This is representative of the provision in most Acts:

> A fair and accurate report, published in a newspaper or by broadcasting of a public meeting or, except where neither the public nor any reporter is admitted, of proceedings in
>
> (a) the Senate or House of Commons of Canada;
> (b) the Legislative Assembly of any province;

---

51 The principle of qualified privilege was first stated in the English case of *Toogood v. Spyring* (1834), 1 Cr. M. & R. 181, where the court said, "If fairly warranted by any reasonable occasion or exigency, and honestly made, such communications are protected for the common convenience and welfare of society; and the law has not restricted the right to make them within any narrow limits."

(c) a committee of any of such bodies;

(d) a meeting of commissioners authorized to act by or pursuant to statute or under lawful warrant or authority; or

(e) any meeting of

     (i) a municipal council;

     (ii) a school board;

     (iii) a board of education;

     (iv) a board of health; or

     (v) any other board or local authority formed or

constituted under any public Act of the Parliament of Canada or the Legislature of any province, or a committee appointed by any such board or local authority;

is privileged, unless it is proven that the publication was made maliciously.

Notice that the report must be "fair and accurate." This means it must be balanced, but it does not have to be verbatim. The report must be substantially correct and carry the same meaning as a word-for-word account.

The legislation also provides for claims of qualified privilege for reports of public meetings. But, not all public gatherings or meetings will be occasions to claim a qualified privilege. A "public meeting" is defined elsewhere in the legislation as "a meeting bona fide and lawfully held for a lawful purpose and for the furtherance or discussion of any matter of public concern, whether admission is general or restricted." A closed door meeting is not a public meeting according to the statutory defence which states that it will not apply where "neither the public nor any reporter is admitted." A public meeting has been further defined by the courts as one which has some element of public control[52] — it does not include a lecture, a church sermon or a partisan political rally.

The defence will be lost if there is any evidence of malice underlying the publication of the defamatory statements. This will be discussed more fully below, but an example of such malice would be any sensationalized statements. For instance, a plaintiff may prove malice if a journalist published defamatory remarks made in a public meeting which the reporter knew were untrue.

The legislation also provides for a qualified privilege for some public documents:

The publication in a newspaper or by broadcasting, at the request of any government department, bureau, office or public officer, of any report, bulletin,

---

52 *Hefferman v. Regina Daily Star*, [1930] 3 W.W.R. 656 (Sask. K.B.). The court also stated that the statutory privilege extends only to reports of matters relevant to the discussion at the public meeting. Therefore, a journalist should not publish a defamatory statement merely because it was made at a public meeting.

or other document issued for the information of the public is privileged, unless it is proved that the publication was made maliciously.

Ontario extends a qualified privilege to reports of publicity releases arising out of public meetings.

The statutory privilege in most provinces is accompanied by three requirements. The first stresses that some matters should never be published under the guise of a privilege:

> No privilege will apply in any of the above situations if there is publication of seditious, blasphemous or indecent matter.

Another important requirement is that the defamed party must be allowed to present his or her side of the story in order for a journalist or news organization to rely on the statutory defence:

> No privilege will apply where the plaintiff shows that the newspaper or broadcasting outlet refused to publish a reasonable statement of explanation or contradiction.

Also, for the statutory defence to succeed, the defamatory statement must involve the element of public interest:

> No privilege will apply where the publication is not of public concern or for public benefit.

At least two provinces have added further explanation to what kinds of occasions offer a qualified privilege. The legislation in Ontario and Nova Scotia expressly extends a qualified privilege to reports of the findings or decisions relating to a person who is a member of, or subject to the control of, certain associations. The legislation includes the following associations:

   (i) Those formed for the purpose of promoting or encouraging interest in art, science, religion or learning, or

  (ii) formed for the purpose of promoting or safeguarding the interests of trade, business, industry or professions, or

 (iii) formed for the purpose of safeguarding the interests of any game, sport or pastime to the playing or exercising of which members of the public are invited or admitted.

The Common Law Defence

The common law has identified several other occasions in which a qualified privilege can be claimed. Essentially, the courts look to see if the defamatory communication between the maker of the statement and those receiving it is important and necessary. For this reason and others outlined below, the news media, which publish statements to the world at large will rarely have occasions, other than those listed in the legislation, to claim a qualified privilege.

There are several requirements to the common law defence:

1. the defamatory statement must be fair and accurate;
2. the defamatory statement must involve an important matter of public interest;
3. there must be a legal, social or moral duty to publish the defamatory information and any person receiving the information must have a valid interest in receiving it; and
4. there must be no actual malice in publishing the statement or knowledge that the statement is untrue.[53]

The defamatory statement must involve an important matter of public interest. The fact that a statement would be "interesting" to other members of the public is not good enough to prove that the matter is one of "public interest." There must be "valid, social reasons" to report the statement.[54] It is irrelevant that the journalist thinks it is a matter of public interest.[55] The "reasonable person," represented by the jury or the judge, must feel it is of important general or public interest.[56] Some examples of matters of public interest are: State matters, the public conduct of those involved in public affairs, legal matters, church matters and literary and artistic works. And even if you do prove that the statement did concern a matter of public interest, it will not be enough to sustain this defence.[57]

The crucial element to the common law defence of qualified privilege is this next requirement, which can be the most complex and

---

53 There are rare instances in which someone may be protected by qualified privilege even though the statement is known to be false. *Gatley on Libel and Slander*, 8th ed. (London: Sweet & Maxwell, 1981), p. 333, states the privilege will exist when someone has a legal, moral or social duty to report another person's statement even if he does not believe it. The English case of *Horrocks v. Lowe* (1974), [1975] A.C. 135 at 150 (H.L.), stated that sometimes, there may be a duty to pass on a defamatory statement without endorsement. An example is given by *Gatley*, p. 242, where an accountant may be bound to report that evidence surrounding a suspected theft leads to one employee, even though the accountant does not believe the employee did it.

54 As stated in *Littleton v. Hamilton* (1974), 4 O.R. (2d) 283 at 285 (C.A.).

55 *Hare v. Better Business Bureau of Vancouver*, [1946] 2 W.W.R. 630 at 633 (B.C. S.C.).

56 *Halls v. Mitchell*, [1928] S.C.R. 125 at 133.

57 In *Brown v. Elder* (1888), 27 N.B.R. 465 (C.A.), the court said the mere fact a matter is of public interest is not enough. There must be an "exceptional" duty imposed upon someone to publish the statement. Also see *Parks v. C.A.I.M.A.W.* (1981), 122 D.L.R. (3d) 366 (B.C. S.C.), where the court found defamatory remarks broadcast over the radio about a lawyer were not of interest to the public generally and not protected by a qualified privilege. The remarks stemmed from a dispute between the lawyer and a union leader who made the comment.

difficult element to prove. The person making or publishing the defamatory statement must have a legal, social or moral duty to convey the information and any other person hearing or reading it must have a reciprocal duty or interest to receive the information.[58] The duty must be clear and it is irrelevant that a person simply believes there is a duty to convey or receive defamatory information.[59]

Why the Media Rarely Can Use the Common Law Defence

Since the cornerstone of qualified privilege is that the maker of the statement has a duty to publish it and the receiver of the statement has a legitimate interest in hearing it, the privilege will be lost if the information is published to anyone who does not have an interest in receiving it.[60]

It is this element of the common law defence which most often defeats the use of it by the news media. The Supreme Court of Canada has said the news media will rarely be in a position of qualified privilege when publishing to the general public.[61] The Supreme Court has said the *duty* to report on a matter of public concern must not be confused with the *right* to comment fairly on issues. In other words, the defence of qualified privilege must not be confused with the defence of fair comment. The duty must be one which would be recognized by the "reasonable man."[62]

There have been rare occasions in which the law has recognized a right of the press to report defamatory matter and claim the defence of qualified privilege. It appears that this usually only happens when someone

---

58 See, for example, *Planned Parenthood Nfld./Labrador v. Fedorik* (1982), 135 D.L.R. (3d) 714 at 721 (Nfld. T.D.), where the court found there was no social or moral duty for the defendant to allege through a radio interview that the plaintiff's sex education program was responsible for an increase in teenage abortions and illegitimate births.

59 As stated in *Wing Lee v. Jones*, [1954] 1 D.L.R. 520 at 528 (Man. Q.B.). In *Arnott v. College of Physicians and Surgeons of Sask.*, [1954] S.C.R. 538 at 541, the Supreme Court of Canada said the duty must be recognized by "people of ordinary intelligence and moral principles." In *Bennett v. Stupich* (1981), 30 B.C.L.R. 57 (S.C.), the court found there was no public duty on the part of a columnist to suggest that the Premier of the province was drunk in the Legislature.

60 In *Jones v. Bennett* (1968), [1969] S.C.R. 277, a politician was defending himself at a party meeting and issued some defamatory remarks. The Supreme Court of Canada said at p. 284 that the occasion of qualified privilege was lost by the politician because he knew the news media was present and whatever he said would be published to the general public.

61 As stated in *Globe and Mail Ltd. v. Boland*, [1960] S.C.R. 203.

62 *Ibid.*, p. 207. In *Littleton v. Hamilton* (1974), 4 O.R. (2d) 283 (C.A.), the court dealt with a book that made defamatory statements in connection with the history of an organization which was established with public funds and had received substantial publicity. Though the topic was one of public interest, the court found there was no "special duty" of the author to tell all Canadians the defamatory statements.

has a duty to make the comment through the news media and the subject-matter is of important public interest. One of the most prominent examples of this involved defamatory statements made by a federal minister outside Parliament. The minister claimed in the House that a particular senior civil servant was grossly negligent and had misled him and then when the minister was outside the proceedings, he repeated the same allegations to the waiting press. The Ontario Court of Appeal held that this was an occasion of qualified privilege because the public has a real and *bona fide* interest in the issue and the person making the statement has a corresponding public duty or interest to make the statement. The court said the public had an interest in knowing whether the comments in the House were justified and the minister had a duty to "satisfy that interest" as long as the comment was made without malice.[63] Other than in reporting remarks of other people, this exception to the general rule does not seem to apply to comments by journalists themselves.

The Dangers of Malice

The issue of malice is important in this defence and laced with potential pitfalls for reporters. The fact that a qualified privilege exists does not allow a reporter to knowingly publish false and defamatory statements.[64] If the publication is out of spite, ill will, to sensationalize or gain audience ratings at the risk of injuring someone, the court will find there was malice. The courts have even found malice where the reporter used stronger language than the circumstances warranted.[65] The

---

63 See *Stopforth v. Goyer* (1978), 20 O.R. (2d) 262 at 271 (H.C.). In *Mallett v. Clarke* (1968), 70 D.L.R. (2d) 67 at 72 (B.C. S.C.), the principal of a hairdressing school made some defamatory remarks about the plaintiff in the media after the plaintiff made some serious allegations about the school. The court found the principal was under a "duty" to respond in the media to the allegations because the school's reputation had been called into question. In the case of *McGugan v. Davidson* (1984), 58 N.B.R. (2d) 103 (T.D.), a trial court held that a qualified privilege applied to defamatory remarks made by a union leader on television. The court accepted the argument that during a strike, as was the case here, the union could only communicate with its province-wide membership through the media and the remarks were thus made to a group which had a rightful "interest" in receiving the comment. The remarks were in response to an unjustified attack on the union.

64 In *Hefferman v. Regina Daily Star*, [1930] 3 W.W.R. 656 at 665 (Sask. K.B.), the court held that simply because a false and defamatory statement was made at a public meeting it was not automatically privileged. In *Vogel v. CBC*, [1982] 3 W.W.R. 97 (B.C. S.C.), the court said a lack of belief in a defamatory statement can be proof of malice.

65 *Burnett v. CBC (No. 2)* (1981), 48 N.S.R. (2d) 101 at 223 (T.D.). Other examples of proof of malice are failing to check the accuracy of information (*Robinson v. Dun* (1897), 24 O.A.R. 287) and careless exaggeration of information (*Brown v. McCurdy* (1888), 21 N.S.R. 201 (S.C.)).

plaintiff must be able to prove there was malice and offer actual proof of it.[66]

As stated before, this is sometimes a confusing and complicated defence. There has been some suggestion that the guarantee of freedom of the press in the Canadian Charter of Rights and Freedoms[67] may loosen the restrictions in this defence and allow journalists to claim qualified privilege on more occasions, particularly where public officials are concerned.[68]

The Defence of Fair Comment

Journalism not only involves the reporting of the news, but also the interpretation and analysis of the news. Journalists also express their own opinions in stories or repeat someone else's opinion. On occasion, these opinions and interpretations may be severely critical of other individuals and, in keeping with the definition of defamation, can be defamatory. The defence of fair comment is specifically designed to allow people to express their own opinions on important public matters even if the opinion is technically defamatory.

The Common Law Defence

In the common law, there are several elements to the defence:

1. the comment must be on a matter of public interest;
2. the comment must be a fair and honest expression of the author's opinion;

---

66 In *Silbernagel v. Empire Stevedoring Co.* (1979), 18 B.C.L.R. 384 (S.C.), the court said there must be more than a "mere possibility" of malice and if there is not enough proof of malice the benefit of the doubt must go to the defendant.

67 Part 1 of the Constitution Act, 1982, being Schedule B of the Canada Act 1982 (U.K.), 1982, c. 11 (hereinafter, Charter).

68 In Doody, "Freedom of the Press, The Canadian Charter of Rights and Freedoms and a New Category of Qualified Privilege," (1983), 61 Can. Bar Rev., pp. 124-150, the author argues that the guarantee of freedom of the press now creates the opportunity to broaden the defence of qualified privilege to allow more criticism of public officials, as in the United States. The landmark American case of *New York Times Co. v. Sullivan*, 376 U.S. 254 (1964) allowed unlimited criticism of a public official except where there is proof of malice, such as a reckless disregard for the truth.

The author notes that subsequent American decisions have toned down the effect of this case by narrowly defining what is a "public official." As it now stands, a public official in the U.S. is someone who has the opportunity to counter the views expressed in the press and is in a legitimate public controversy, not just someone who is a topic of public interest. American law has also created the "limited purpose" public official who represents a particular cause or issue, but is not constantly in the public eye.

3. the comment must be based on known and provable facts; and
4. there must be no actual malice underlying the comment.

The first important factor is that the subject-matter of the comment be of public interest. It should be a genuine interest and not just mere gossip.[69] It does not appear though, that the courts call for as stringent a test for the public interest requirement in fair comment, as they do in the defence of qualified privilege. It is irrelevant that the author of the statement felt it was a matter of public interest. It will be up to the judge or jury as representatives of the "reasonable person" to determine whether it was an important matter of public interest.[70]

It is essential that the defamatory comment must be seen to be an honest opinion of the author based on fact and the opinion itself must not appear to be an assertion of fact.[71] For example, in one case it was reported that an expert witness testifying at a trial was being paid $1000 a day plus expenses. The journalist then commented that the witness is an example of an expert hired to give favourable testimony for his client. That was an "opinion" which was not based on any of the stated facts in the story. Moreover, to the average person, it would have been considered a statement of fact instead of opinion.[72]

It must be obvious to the reader, viewer or listener that the defamatory statement is simply an opinion. It is not even necessary for the opinion to be one which everyone would hold. Although the defence is called "fair comment," the courts have held that the opinion does not really have to be "fair" as most people understand the word (for example, reasonable or moderate). It does not even have to be a reasonable perspective on the facts.[73]

---

69 *Cook v. Alexander*, [1973] 3 All. E.R. 1037 (C.A.).

70 *England v. CBC*, [1979] 3 W.W.R. 193 at 214 (N.W.T. S.C.).

71 *Bulletin Co. v. Sheppard* (1917), 55 S.C.R. 454 at 466.

72 *Barltrop v. CBC* (1978), 86 D.L.R. (3d) 61 (N.S. C.A.).

73 In *Vander Zalm v. Times Publishers*, [1980] 4 W.W.R. 259 (B.C. C.A.), a political cartoon showed the plaintiff pulling the wings off a fly in apparent glee. The court said at p. 265 it was fair comment so long as the author has an honest belief in what he says and it is unnecessary for the comment to be a reasonable perspective on the facts. The court said the opinion may even be exaggerated or prejudiced, as long as it is an honest view that could be held by someone. In *Pearlman v. CBC* (1981), 13 Man. R. (2d) 1 (Q.B.), the plaintiff was referred to as a "slum landlord" with "no morals, principles or conscience." Based on the facts as stated in the story, the court said at p. 8, it was a fair comment made without malice. And in *Gouzenko v. Harris*, note 22, above, the court held that the words "traitor" and "defector," used to describe a Soviet turncoat, were fair and true descriptions of the plaintiff.

The Test

The "cardinal test" for succeeding in this defence is whether the author himself honestly believed the opinion and whether it is one which could be drawn from known facts.[74]

Though an opinion does not have to be "fair" or a reasonable perspective on the facts, it should be noted that there are limits. The courts have held that a comment which accuses an individual of illegal, corrupt, criminal or morally reprehensible conduct is beyond the limits of fair comment.[75] For instance, it would not be a fair comment to say a politician is using his public office for private gain without specific evidence supporting the accusation and it would not matter that the commentator believed what he was saying.

This brings up an important point. The facts stated in the story must be true and provable. It is not enough to say that it is reasonable to believe the facts to be true or that everyone knows it is true.[76] In court, a journalist using the defence of fair comment will have to prove that each of the facts which formed the basis of the opinion are true. There is a special allowance made for comments based on information originating in a public forum which carries absolute privilege (such as Parliament). For example, if a Member of Parliament alleges that an industrial plant is polluting the atmosphere, it is only fair that journalists and other members of the public should be able to comment on the remark as well as report it. As a rule of public policy, comments on "facts" raised in such public forums are deemed to be true for the purposes of comment.[77]

The Statutory Defence

Six provinces and both territories have enacted statutory versions of the fair comment defence. Ontario and Nova Scotia have legislated a general provision which saves a defendant from having to prove all the facts stated in a defamatory comment:[78]

> In an action for libel or slander in respect of words consisting partly of allegations of fact and partly of expression of opinion, a defence of fair comment shall not fail by reason only that the truth of every allegation of

---

74 *Chernesky v. Armadale Publishers and King*, [1978] 6 W.W.R. 618 (S.C.C.). In England, see *Slim v. Daily Telegraph Ltd.*, [1968] 1 All E.R. 497 at 503 (C.A.).

75 The English case most commonly referred to is *Campbell v. Spottiswoode* (1863), 3 B & S 769.

76 *Man. Free Press Co. v. Martin* (1892), 21 S.C.R. 518 at 529.

77 *Mangena v. Wright*, [1909] 2 K.B. 958 at 976-977.

78 Libel and Slander Act, R.S.O. 1980, c. 237, s. 24; Defamation Act, R.S.N.S. 1967, c. 72, s. 9.

fact is not proved if the expression of opinion is fair comment having regard to such of the facts alleged or referred to in the words complained of as are proved.

Ontario, Alberta, Manitoba, New Brunswick, Newfoundland and the two territories also have a special form of a fair comment defence, which was designed to protect newspapers publishing letters to the editor. However, the provision could be used to support fair comments by a journalist sometimes. For example, Manitoba has enacted this provision:[79]

> Where the defendant published alleged defamatory matter that is an opinion expressed by another person, a defence of fair comment shall not fail for the reason only that the defendant did not hold the opinion if
>
> > (a) the defendant did not know that the person expressing the opinion did not hold the opinion; and
> > (b) a person could honestly hold the opinion.

Alberta, Newfoundland and both territories have a provision similar to Manitoba's. In Alberta, the defence is only available to defendants (such as journalists) if the opinion published is one of non-employees and non-agents of the publishing outlet.

There are some other distinctions in the other jurisdictions. In the territories, there is no obligation on the part of the defendant to inquire whether the person expressing the opinion holds that opinion. In New Brunswick, there is an additional requirement that the person expressing the opinion must be identified in the publication. In Ontario, the statutory defence is very broad. In that province, the defence will not fail even if neither the publisher nor the author of the comment holds the opinion, as long as someone honestly could hold the opinion.

The latter statutory fair comment provision was in reaction to the Supreme Court of Canada's decision in *Chernesky v. Armadale Publications Ltd.*, which involved the publication of defamatory opinions in a letter to the editor in a newspaper.[80] The remaining provinces must rely on this Supreme Court of Canada decision. The court ruled the defence of fair comment was not available to the newspaper or its editors because they did not hold the same opinion as the authors of the published letter nor did the newspaper know if the authors themselves honestly held the opinion expressed (the authors had left the province). The basis of the fair comment defence in common law is that it is an opinion that is honestly held by the author and the newspaper could not prove that this was so. The court said its decision does not mean that a newspaper cannot publish views it disagrees with. The court said that what its decision means is that a

---

79 Defamation Act, S.M. 1987, c. D30, s. 9(1).
80 [1978] 6 W.W.R. 618 (S.C.C.).

newspaper cannot publish a defamatory letter or comment and then automatically claim the defence of fair comment without knowing if it is an honest opinion. The legislation enacted in the provinces mentioned above now either requires the publisher to identify the author of an opinion or absolves the publisher of having to ask about the beliefs of the author.

How to Avoid Losing this Defence

When writing a story which expresses an opinion, it is important to include all of the necessary facts. Every known background fact does not have to be stated, but enough facts must be published to support the opinion.[81] In addition, the way in which the facts are stated must be fair and they cannot be twisted or taken out of context. There must not be any large difference between the facts as stated and the known truth.[82]

The Special Case of Québec

The Civil Law

A civil defamation lawsuit in Québec is subject to a substantially different system of law than that in the rest of Canada. Québec relies on its Civil Code. The particular provision which is applicable to defamation is Article 1053:

> Every person capable of discerning right from wrong is responsible for the damage caused by his fault to another, whether by positive act, imprudence, neglect or want of skill.

Québec law requires that the plaintiff prove three elements. Each element must be proven on the balance of probabilities.[83] The plaintiff must first prove there is *fault* on the part of the defendant.[84] The plaintiff

---

81 *Holt v. Sun Publishing Co.* (1979), 100 D.L.R. (3d) 447 at 450 (B.C. C.A.).

82 *Ibid.*

83 *Thibeault v. Porlier Transport* [1971], Que. C.A. 518.

84 The courts presume fault once the plaintiff proves the circumstances existed for it. It is unnecessary to prove the defendant intended his act or omission. Fault is defined as a mode of behaviour of a person, who is capable of realizing the nature and consequences of an act or omission, and does something contrary to law or fails to meet a standard of care set out by the courts. It can be proven with evidence of malice, imprudence, neglect or want of skill. See Nicholls, *Offences and Quasi-Offences in Québec* (Toronto: Carswell, 1938), pp. 22, 38-39.

must also prove that he has suffered damage[85] and there is a causal relationship between the fault of the defendant and the damage.[86]

The standard of care expected is that of the reasonable journalist (the generically-applied Civil Code standard of *bon pere de famille*) acting in the same circumstances.[87] This is determined from an objective point of view and it does not matter that the journalist thought he was acting with the proper standard of care (if other journalists in the same circumstance would act differently).

Québec is the only province where publication of the defamation is unnecessary. Sometimes, the objectionable statements were made only to the plaintiff and no third parties.[88] Québec also allows living descendants to sue for defamations of their ancestors, where the defamation injures the descendant's reputation.[89]

In Québec, one of the most important issues in a defamation action is whether the publication of the words was in the public interest. The presence of public interest can serve as a complete defence in this province provided there is no proof of malice.[90]

Even truth is not a complete defence. A failure to prove that the defamation was in the public interest, or that the publication's only purpose was to injure the person, can destroy the defence of justification.[91] The defences of absolute and qualified privilege are not recognized

---

85 *Ibid.*, p. 39, where the author points out "damage" can even include hurt feelings or sensibilities. Also, in *Cass, April 26, 1810; Pandictes Francaises, vo. Diffamation; Injure No. 25*: "Anything which, with intention or malice, gives offence or affronts another is injurious."

86 Nicholls, note 84, above, at p. 21. Even if fault is proven, the plaintiff will not succeed unless he can prove the causal link between the fault and damage.

87 *Ibid.*

88 *Ibid.*, p. 39.

89 In *Chiniquy v. Begin* (1915), 24 D.L.R. 687 (Que. C.A.), a publication questioned the marriage of the plaintiff's parents. The court allowed an action by the daughter because the publication suggested she was illegitimate. The court said, at p. 693, the action allowed her to "vindicate" her parents memory.

90 Nicholls, note 84, above, at p. 40, where the author suggests even a private affair of a public official can be published if it is indicative of public performance (citing *Belleau v. Mercier* (1882), 8 Q.L.R. 312 (S.C.) and other cases).

91 *Ibid.*, p. 41. The defence of truth may be established if the defendant can prove there was reasonable and probable cause to believe in the truth and public interest of his statements. If a statement is not in the public's interest, but is true, it may help reduce the damages. The courts have also adopted this rule stated in *Cass, April 26, 1810; Pandictes Francaises, vo. Diffamation; Injure No. 39*: "Any truth causing injury, made other than in the course of justice, is punishable even if it brings a crime to light which it would have been well to punish in the public interest."

in Québec[92] (except for statutory privileges set out below). While the privilege defences are somewhat different, the defence of fair comment is relatively unchanged in comparison.[93]

The Legislation

The Press Act,[94] the only Québec legislation dealing with defamation, refers only to newspapers. Broadcasters must rely largely on the case law in Québec. This Act provides limited protection for journalists.

Privilege, similar to that offered in the common law provinces, is granted for accurate reports, published in good faith, of:

1. proceedings of the Senate, House of Commons, the Assemblée nationale du Québec, and committees from which the public are not excluded;
2. reports of the Public Protector laid before the Assemblée nationale;
3. any notices, bulletins or recommendations from a government or municipal health service;[95]
4. public notices given by the Government or a person authorized by it respecting the solvency of corporations and the value of security issues; and
5. judicial proceedings held in public.

As in the common law provinces, the privilege will not apply to reports of *in camera* proceedings of courts. As well, the Act states that it does not "affect or diminish the rights of the press under common law."

However, the Act does expressly state no newspaper may avail itself of the provisions of this legislation in either of the following cases:

1. when the offended party is accused by the newspaper of a criminal offence; or

---

92 Nicholls, note 84, above, at p. 38. For example, defamatory comments made during a judicial proceeding are actionable if the words are beyond the subject-matter of the proceedings. See note 43.

93 In *SRJ Consultants Inc. v. Fortin* (1982), 20 C.C.L.T. 221 (C.S. Qué.), the court said the defendant municipal councillor had a right to question and comment on the viability of a proposed skihill development. The court said a statement is untrue when it is based on a lie and a lie is an assertion which is *knowingly* against the truth. This is similar to the common law requirements of honest opinion based on facts.

94 R.S.Q. c. P-19.

95 In *La Tribune Ltee. v. Restaurant Chez Toni Sherbrooke Inc.*, Qué. C.A., July 11, 1983, a newspaper published false information from a health officer regarding the seizure of meat from a restaurant. It was found not to be privileged within section 10 of the Press Act because the health officer was not warning the public. The information was false, not issued in good faith or in the public interest. The health officer did not confirm the information and was not acting as the "bon père de famille."

2. when the offending article refers to a candidate in a parliamentary or municipal election and was published within the three days prior to nomination day and up to the polling day.

FACTORS THAT CAN MITIGATE A LOSS

The defences outlined above are all that journalists have to call on. In the unfortunate event that none of the defences can be established and the plaintiff wins, it is worth mentioning there are several factors which can help to mitigate the damages or lessen the blow. Some of these mitigating factors must be present before the case goes to trial and so it is wise to keep them in mind.

Apology or Retraction

Many defamed individuals will be quite happy to simply get a written apology or a formal retraction of the defamatory story. Unfortunately, such apologies are not a complete defence. The damage to a person's reputation can still exist despite an apology — even an apology immediately after the defamation.

But an apology can go a long way in reducing the damage award to a plaintiff. The important factor is that the publisher of the derogatory statement must show regret for his mistake and the apology must be full and fair.

Statutes in all the provinces and territories state that a formal "retraction" can completely preclude the awarding of any "general" or non-specific damages. If the proper circumstances are met, the courts will confine the award to what are called "special damages." These are damages which are a foreseeable result of the defamation, such as the loss of financial credit. These special damages must be specifically pleaded and proven. The circumstances for mitigation of special damages are quite particular:[96]

The plaintiff shall recover only special damage if it appears on the trial,

    (a) that the alleged defamatory matter was published in good faith; and
    (b) that there was reasonable ground to believe that the publication thereof was for the public benefit; and
    (c) that it did not impute to the plaintiff the commission of a criminal offence; and

---

96 See, for example, s. 17(1) of the Defamation Act, R.S.N.B. 1973, c. D-5; *LeBlanc v. L'Imprimierie Acadienne Ltee.*, [1955] 5 D.L.R. 91 (N.B. Q.B.) invoked a similar predecessor provision. The wrong person was named in a story as being charged with theft. An apology was made within three weeks. The court restricted an award to special damages in accordance with the legislation, for the public benefit and because there was an apology.

(d) that the publication took place in mistake or misapprehension of the facts; and

(e) [that there was] a full and fair retraction . . . and . . . apology [as required by the legislation] . . . before the commencement of the action.

The time limit for the publication of the retraction varies from province to province and depending on whether a newspaper or broadcasting outlet makes the apology. Usually the retraction has to be made after the notice of the defamation action is received or soon after. The retraction must also be complete. To say, "I apologize for calling you a thief," is not good enough. The apology must clearly establish the truth of the matter.[97]

The legislation also attaches special importance to defamations which happen during election campaigns because of the potential for far-reaching damage. Retractions involving candidates for public office must be made within the time period set out in the legislation, which is usually at least five days before the election.

In Québec, under the Press Act, which as stated, governs only newspapers, a newspaper may escape "prosecution" by publishing a full retraction in good faith in the next issue published after the notice of the defamation lawsuit was received and allowing the plaintiff to publish in the newspaper a reasonable reply to the defamatory statements. If the retraction and reply are published without comment, the plaintiff will not be able to sue at all. If a newspaper only publishes the retraction and the plaintiff does not exercise his right to reply, the court will only award actual (special) damages. The Press Act does not offer any protection to newspapers where an article defaming a candidate in an election is published within three days before nomination day and up to polling day.

Offer of Settlement

Another way to mitigate damages is to settle out of court. In one province, an offer to settle before the matter reaches trial can also have an effect on damages awarded if the plaintiff still wants to go to court.

Nova Scotia's law has a provision allowing an "innocent defamer" to make an offer to amends. The "innocent defamer" is a someone who did not intend to defame the plaintiff and did not know of any circumstances which might allow the defamatory words to be understood to refer to the plaintiff.

An innocent defamer can also be someone who publishes words which

---

97 In *Thompson v. NL Broadcasting Ltd.* (1976), 1 C.C.L.T. 278 (B.C. S.C.), the court said the news outlet's apology should have said the editorial was unfounded, published without knowledge of the facts and that the incident was regretted.

are not defamatory on their face and is not aware of the circumstances by which they might be taken in a defamatory manner. The latter requirement is not available to a publisher who is not the author, unless he or she can prove the author wrote without malice. If the offer to settle is refused, the Nova Scotia court will consider the refusal a valid defence to the innocent defamation.

Distribution

The distribution area of the newspaper or broadcasting signal can also affect the size of the award. For example, in a case against a network such as the Canadian Broadcasting Corporation, an award may reflect the fact that the defamation was national in scope. A small town newspaper is unlikely to be saddled with as large an award.[98]

Reputation of the Plaintiff

Since the law of defamation aims to compensate someone for lost reputation, it only stands to reason that a person with a bad reputation will have little to preserve. Although it should never be a consideration in deciding whether to use a defamatory comment, the courts have kept damages to a nominal level when the plaintiff has a bad reputation. In one case, a newspaper published a story which said the plaintiff was involved in drug trafficking. In the defamation trial, evidence showed the plaintiff associated with known criminals, that he did indeed have a criminal record and that earlier news reports had also connected him with drug trafficking and he did not sue them. The court held the plaintiff had been defamed and awarded him one dollar while saying the plaintiff had no reputation capable of being injured.[99]

THE CRIMINAL LAW OF DEFAMATION

The Criminal Code creates offences for the publication of defamatory statements and certain other objectionable remarks. The potential punishment is harsh. For example, a defamatory libel under the Criminal Code carries a maximum sentence of two years or a maximum of five years if the statement is known to be false when it is published. Unlike the mixed bag of legislation in civil defamation actions, the criminal law is the same

---

98 For example, see *Stieb v. Vernon News*, [1947] 4 D.L.R. 397 (B.C. S.C.), where the court considered that the small newspaper had apologized and that most of its readers were paid subscribers.

99 *Leonhard v. Sun Publishing Co.* (1956), 4 D.L.R. (2d) 514 (B.C. S.C.).

in all provinces without exception. But it is generally recognized that the Criminal Code provisions dealing with defamation are obsolete and some may be struck down eventually under the Charter or simply wiped off the books by Parliament.

Defamatory Libel

As mentioned at the beginning of the chapter, prosecutions for criminal libel are rare and it has been suggested that the offence should be repealed.[100] Criminal prosecutions are reserved for serious and malicious defamations likely to incite hatred, contempt or ridicule against the individual.[101] But, the definition of defamation in the Code is very similar to the definition in civil law and therefore the potential is there for a criminal charge to be laid for almost any defamation. Section 298(1) states:

> A defamatory libel is matter published, without lawful justification or excuse, that is likely to injure the reputation of any person by exposing him to hatred, contempt or ridicule, or that is designed to insult the person of or concerning whom it is published.

Section 298 then goes on to state defamatory libels can be expressed through express words "legibly marked upon any substance" or "by any object" and by innuendo:

> A defamatory libel may be expressed directly or by insinuation or irony
>
> (a) in words legibly marked upon any substance, or
> (b) by any object signifying a defamatory libel otherwise than by words.

The wording in this part of section 298 is cumbersome and vague. It seems to expressly rule out defamations by slander and it may be difficult to prove that broadcasters who speak without a script have expressed a defamatory libel because the words are not "legibly marked upon any substance." There may be some argument that a video or audio tape of the defamatory broadcast could be considered "any object." But, the answer is unclear.

Section 299 defines what is the "publication" of a defamatory libel. With the usual definitions of publication, the section also states that a criminal libel will be published even if it is only seen by the person whom it defames. This is a departure from the common law.

---

100 The Law Reform Commission of Canada in *Defamatory Libel* (Working Paper 35, 1984) proposed that the Criminal Code offence of defamatory libel be struck from the books because there are enough civil remedies available. The L.R.C. said (at pp. 33-44) that the defamatory libel section infringes on the guarantees of freedom of expression, it is poorly worded, confusing and inconsistent with the civil law tort of defamation.

101 *R. v. Cameron* (1898), 7 Que. Q.B. 162.

It appears that, contrary to most other criminal offences, there does not have to be an intention to injure the reputation of the victim. Certainly, in one British Columbia case the lack of an intention in the publisher to defame his subject did not matter. The newspaper published an article awarding a local judge a satirical "honour" which was quite derogatory (a Pontius Pilate Award). The court said it did not matter that the libel was intended as a joke and found the newspaper guilty.[102]

Seditious Libel

One of the grander aims of the Criminal Code is to protect the government from acts of sedition. Sedition is anything which incites people to commit treason or anything which advocates the use of violence in overthrowing or reforming the government. Section 59 says a "seditious libel" is one which expresses a seditious intention and a "seditious intention" is as follows:

Without limiting the generality of the meaning of the expression "seditious intention," every one shall be presumed to have a seditious intention who

(a) teaches or advocates, or
(b) publishes or circulates any writing that advocates, the use, without authority of law, of force as a means of accomplishing a governmental change within Canada.

Section 60 provides this defence:

No person shall be deemed to have a seditious intention by reason only, that he intends, in good faith,

(a) to show that Her Majesty has been misled or mistaken in her measures;
(b) to point out errors or defects in
     (i) the government or constitution of Canada or a province,
     (ii) Parliament or the legislature of a province, or
     (iii) the administration of justice in Canada;
(c) to procure, by lawful means, the alteration of any matter of government in Canada; or
(d) to point out, for the purpose of removal, matters that produce or tend to produce feelings of hostility and ill-will between different classes of persons in Canada.

Section 59 was the focus of a 1951 Supreme Court of Canada case.[103] It involved a Jehovah's Witness who was convicted at trial of seditious libel after he published pamphlets which severely criticized the Québec government and the Québec courts. A majority of the court ordered a

---

102 *R. v. Georgia Straight Publishing Ltd.* (1969), [1970] 1 C.C.C. 94 (B.C. Co. Ct.).
103 *Boucher v. R.* (1950), 99 C.C.C. 1 (S.C.C.).

new trial on the basis that the trial judge did not properly explain to the jury the defence in section 60. The court took the opportunity to discuss the scope of the crime of seditious libel. The court said a seditious intention is one which intends to incite violence or create a public disorder or disturbance against the Crown or any institution of government. They said it can also include any act with a view to inciting the public such that it defeats the functioning of the courts.

Blasphemous Libel

This is a rather outdated offence which involves the publication of inflammatory or outrageous statements about a religion. The penalty for the offence is set out in section 296, but it offers no express definition of what is blasphemous libel. It does say that it is a question of fact whether any matter that is published is a blasphemous libel. In other words, a judge or a jury will decide in each particular case if a statement is blasphemous. The offence carries a maximum sentence of two years in prison, but no convictions or charges have resulted from this section in recent years.

The courts have been left to properly define blasphemy. The case law says a blasphemous libel is an attack on the Deity or expressions grossly repugnant to religious sentiments, exceeding the limits of decent controversy and having as their sole object the outraging of the feelings of every believer in religion.[104] An attack on the clergy or a doctrine of the church is not a blasphemous libel.[105]

Section 296(3) does offer this defence which allows fair discussion and comment on religious matters:

> No person shall be convicted of an offence under this section for expressing in good faith and in decent language, or attempting to establish by argument used in good faith and conveyed in decent language, an opinion upon a religious subject.

The Criminal Code Defences

The Criminal Code lists many defences to the offence of defamatory libel. Generally, the defences fall into the same categories as the common law defences (such as, absolute privilege, fair comment). But the list is not exhaustive. Section 8(3) preserves any defence that exists in the common law, except where it is inconsistent with the provisions of the

---

104 *R. v. St. Martin* (1933), 40 R. de Jur. 411 (Que.). In *Bowman v. Secular Society Ltd.*, [1917] A.C. 406 (H.L.), the court said a corporation promoting anti-Christian beliefs could not be charged with a criminal offence simply because it denied Christianity.
105 *R. v. Kinler* (1925), 63 Qué. S.C. 483.

Code. For example, the common law defence of absolute privilege enjoyed by Members of Parliament, which is not listed in the Code, can be used to defeat a criminal charge.

In many respects, the specific Code defences vary greatly from the common law. Some Code defences are broader in scope than civil defamation law defences, others are narrower and at least one is non-existent in the civil law of common law provinces (the defence of public benefit). As with the libel offences listed in the Code, many defences are obsolete and could be challenged in the future or wiped off the books.

Judicial Proceedings and Inquiries

Section 305 states that no person shall be deemed to have published a defamatory libel for publishing defamatory matter:

(a) in a proceeding held before or under the authority of a court exercising judicial authority; or

(b) in an inquiry made under the authority of an Act or by order of Her Majesty, or under the authority of a public department or a department of the government of a province.

This section protects individuals (such as witnesses, lawyers, judges) participating in judicial proceedings or inquiries from prosecution for defamatory libels.[106] A strict reading of this section suggests that this does not apply to journalists, who publish reports of judicial proceedings or inquiries and do not make defamatory statements "in" these proceedings. This is strengthened by the fact that the defence of qualified privilege for reports or extracts is in a later section.

Parliamentary Papers

Section 306 states that no person shall be deemed to have published a defamatory libel for publishing defamatory matter contained in petitions presented to the House of Commons, the Senate or a legislature and in papers published by order or under the authority of one of those bodies. Journalists may publish extracts of these petitions and papers without prosecution providing the publication is in good faith and without ill-will to the person defamed.

---

106 The Law Reform Commission of Canada suggests at p. 22 that this is a wider defence than that offered in the common law because it includes all inquiries, including those which are not judicial or quasi-judicial.

Fair Reports of Government or Judicial Proceedings

Section 307(1) states that no person shall be deemed to have published a defamatory libel by reason that he:

> publishes in good faith, for the information of the public, a fair report of the proceedings of the Senate or House of Commons or the legislature of a province, or a committee thereof, or of the public proceedings before a court exercising judicial authority, or publishes, in good faith, any fair comment on any such proceedings.

This is very similar to the common law defence.[107] Note that it includes the common law principle that fair comments on matters brought up in absolute privilege forums are privileged when published in good faith.

Fair Reports of Public Meetings

Section 308 protects anyone who publishes in good faith a fair report of the proceedings of any public meeting, if the meeting is lawfully convened for a lawful purpose and is open to the public. This only applies to newspapers and the report must be fair and accurate. There also must be no refusal to publish a reasonable explanation or contradiction offered by the person defamed.

Public Benefit

Section 309 is a defence which is unavailable in the common law.[108] It makes a publication for the public benefit a complete defence. It says no person shall be deemed to have published a defamatory libel who:

> publishes defamatory matter that, on reasonable grounds, he believes is true, and that is relevant to any subject of public interest, the public discussion of which is for the public benefit.

Fair Comment on a Public Person or Art

Section 310 protects anyone who publishes a fair comment on:

> the public conduct of a person who takes part in public affairs

---

107 The defence failed in *R. v. Buller* (1954), 108 C.C.C. 352 at 344-355 (Que. Sup. Ct.), because the newspaper article suggested in extra comment that the accused's guilt was known or established.

108 For instance, in *Banks v. Globe and Mail Ltd.* (1961), 28 D.L.R. (2d) 343 at 350-351 (S.C.C.), a defamatory editorial supposedly published for the public's benefit was held not to be protected by any privilege in civil law.

or fair comment on a book, artwork, performance

or on any other communication made to the public on any subject, if the comments are confined to criticism thereof.

Truth

Section 311 is the defence of justification and it protects anyone who prove that the publication of defamatory matter was

for the public benefit at the time when it was published and that the matter itself was true.

This is a narrower version of the "truth" defence than that found in civil defamation law which only requires the allegation to be true. The Code defence requires that a statement not only be true, but also published for the public benefit at the time of publication.

Publication Invited or Necessary

Sections 312 says no person shall be deemed to have published a defamatory libel if the defamatory matter arises on the invitation or challenge of the defamed person. It also protects a person who finds it necessary to answer to defamatory matter published by another person.

The accused person seeking to rely on this defence must believe that his statement is true and the statements must be relevant to the invitation, challenge or necessary refutation without exceeding what is reasonably sufficient to say in the circumstances.

Answer to Inquiries

Section 313 says no person shall be deemed to have published a defamatory libel if the defamatory matter is in answer to an inquiry made by a person who the publisher believes, on reasonable grounds, has an interest in knowing the truth.

The person seeking to rely on this defence must publish the information in good faith for the sole purpose of answering the inquiry, he must believe the defamatory material is true, it must be relevant to the inquiry and cannot exceed what is reasonably sufficient to say in the circumstances.

Giving Information to an Interested Person

Section 314 says no person shall be deemed to have published a defamatory libel if the defamatory information is given to someone who, he believes on reasonable grounds, has an interest in hearing the truth about a certain subject.

This is different from section 313 since no one has made an inquiry which has prompted the defamatory libel. The accused is making the defamatory statement of his own volition. The conduct of the person giving the information must be reasonable in the circumstances, the defamatory information must be relevant to the subject-matter and it must be true, or if not, it must be given out with no malice to the person defamed and with the belief it is true.

To Redress a Wrong

Section 315 says no person shall be deemed to have published a defamatory libel if the defamatory information is published in good faith:

> for the purpose of seeking remedy or redress for a private or public wrong or grievance from a person who has, or who on reasonable grounds he believes has, the right or is under the obligation to remedy of redress the wrong or grievance.

The accused must believe the defamatory matter in question is true and that the defamatory matter is relevant to the remedy in question and the statements do not exceed what is reasonably sufficient in the circumstances.

GENERAL PROBLEMS IN DEFAMATION

Many questions reporters commonly ask have been addressed by case law and legislation. While any specific problems should always be referred to legal counsel, the following list highlights the danger zones plus a brief discussion of the related law.

Consumer Reports

Although most consumer organizations are reliable, journalists must be on guard for possible untruths in consumer reports which could unjustly damage the reputation of a product or a company. In situations where the public's health or safety is in immediate danger, a qualified privilege may be claimed in theory by a consumer report, consumer organization or consumer journalist if the defamatory statement is honestly believed. In one case, the defendant was told by a seemingly reliable source that a certain product was dangerous. Motivated by a concern for the public welfare, the consumer journalist published a story identifying the dangerous product. While the information from the source was wrong, the court held there was a qualified privilege because the report was honestly believed (that is, no malice), it was an important matter of public interest, it was done out of a sense of public duty and the general public had a valid interest to hear the information.[109]

But, there is a danger that a court may not always feel that a consumer report was made on an occasion of qualified privilege. For example, the "danger" may not be such that there is a pressing public duty to reveal it or a court may feel that a journalist could have found out the truth about the product or company through further investigation.

Contagious Diseases

Many provinces have legislation which prohibits the publication of any information identifying a person who has a venereal disease. Caution should be exercised whenever it is suggested that a person has a contagious disease. The common law does not require any proof of actual damage for a defamation action to succeed if a contagious disease has been imputed. The damage to a person's reputation can be significant and it may be difficult to prove at trial (for example, a doctor may refuse to reveal test results).

Corporations

It is possible to defame a corporation. The defamatory matter must attack the corporation in its method of conducting its affairs, accuse it of fraud or mismanagement or harm its financial position. To be successfully pursued in court, the defamatory matter must damage the reputation of the corporation as distinct from defaming the individuals who run it.[110] The defamation of a corporate official, such as the chief executive officer, is usually not enough to sustain an additional action by the company. But it may be defamatory of the corporation to accuse its employees, officers or agents of criminal or corrupt conduct while doing their regular duties or while acting in the best interests of the corporation such that it appears to be an action of the company.[111]

While a corporation is considered a legal entity on its own, it can only sue for defamation if it is capable of doing the act which is alleged.

109 *Camporese v. Parton* (1983), 150 D.L.R. (3d) 208 (B.C. S.C.). Also, see *Upton v. Better Business Bureau of the Mainland of B.C. Ltd.* (1980), 114 D.L.R. (3d) 750 (B.C. S.C.), where defamatory credit information about the plaintiff was found to have a qualified privilege because the information was distributed only to B.B.B. members and not the general public.

110 *Price v. Chicoutimi Pulp Co.* (1915), 51 S.C.R. 179.

111 *Georgian Bay Ship Canal Co. v. World Newspaper Co.* (1897), 16 P.R. 320.

For instance, a corporation cannot commit murder or bribe a city official. Its officers can, but the corporation itself cannot. In one case, a journalist accused the members of a non-profit corporation of practising medicine without a licence. The court said it may be defamatory of the members of the corporation, but not the corporation itself, since it is not capable of practising medicine.[112]

Criminal Charges

When criminal charges have been laid and the accused is awaiting trial, a journalist must be careful not to suggest that a person or business is guilty of the crime.[113] This could happen if you speak of the charge as being a fact. For example, saying the accused "stole the money last month and is now awaiting trial" is both defamatory and a contempt of court.

The exact wording of the charge should be used as much as possible in the story. It is dangerous to paraphrase some criminal charges or state them incorrectly. For example, there is a great difference in penalty between theft and possession of stolen goods.[114]

As will sometimes happen, an accused can have the same name as another person in a community. Whenever possible, street addresses and full names should be used to identify people accused of a crime in order to avoid confusion.

Criminal Records

A criminal record is public information and not in itself defamatory. Therefore, you can publish the fact that someone has a criminal record if it is important to the story except, of course, when criminal charges are pending. If someone is charged with a new offence, it is highly likely to be a contempt of court to report his or her criminal record before a matter is adjudicated or the record is brought out in court.

---

112 *Church of Scientology of Toronto v. Globe and Mail Ltd.* (1978), 84 D.L.R. (3d) 239 (Ont. H.C.).

113 *Lumsden v. Spectator Printing Co.* (1913), 14 D.L.R. 470 (C.A.).

114 In *Desmarais v. La Presse Ltee.*, [1977] Que. C.A. 224, the "accused" was charged with possession of stolen goods, not theft, as was reported (a more serious charge), and was served with a summons, not arrested, as was reported. The court felt this story gave an impression of a much more serious crime having been committed. The plaintiff offered proof that his business as a notary had suffered since the news report.

Deceased Persons

It is not possible to defame the dead because they can no longer enjoy a reputation or suffer any sort of further injury.[115] It may be possible though to defame a family name such that a defamatory image is cast on certain members of the deceased's living family.[116]

Editing

Reports and quotes of speeches or other people's comments or statements must reflect the material meaning of their message. Any paraphrasing or editing cannot expand on the meaning of the actual statement. In one case, a story reported that a politician had imputed that a nearby village was guilty of gross immorality. He said nothing of the kind and the error was due to paraphrasing by the journalist.[117]

Journalists must also be careful in editing material received on newswires or from other sources. The meaning of the words or the effect of the actual story should not be changed or generalized to the point of defaming someone. In one instance, a criminal charge was generalized to the point where it was a different and more onerous one.[118]

Evidence and Exhibits

Any document or evidence which is entered into evidence in open court can be included as a part of a privileged report on judicial proceedings.[119] There is some disagreement about whether all documents filed in a court proceeding can be published under a privilege if they are not referred to or read out in open court. One case has taken the view that all documents filed become a part of the judicial proceedings.[120]

---

115 This ruling can be found in *Small v. Globe Printing Co.*, [1940] 2 D.L.R. 670 (Ont. H.C.). In England, see *R. v. Labouchere*, 12 Q.B.D. 320 at 324, where a defamation action by a representative of the deceased's estate was rejected.

116 In *R. v. Ensor* (1887), 3 T.L.R. 366, an English court said defamation of the dead was not actionable unless it caused injury or annoyance to the living. It has been suggested that it is possible to defame the dead in Québec. The decision in *Chiniquy v. Begin* (1915), 24 D.L.R. 687 (Que. K.B.) ambiguously suggested the memory of the dead could be defamed, but dealt more with the fact that living family members had been defamed. In this case, the gist of the defamatory statement was that the deceased man had never formally married the mother of the plaintiff thereby suggesting the daughter was illegitimate.

117 *Pottle v. The Evening Telegram Ltd.* (1954), 34 M.P.R. 101 at 102 (Nfld. S.C.).

118 See, *Allan*, note 31 above, where sloppy editing and use of sources distorted the facts.

119 *Hansen v. Nugget Publishers Ltd.*, [1927] 4 D.L.R. 791 (Ont. C.A.).

120 *Butler v. Saskatoon Star-Pheonix Ltd.* (1929), [1930] 1 D.L.R. 1009 (Sask. K.B.).

Headlines and Captions

A headline or caption is part of a fair and accurate report. Most provinces have stated expressly in defamation legislation that headlines are considered a part of reports of judicial proceedings and the common law applies the same principle to any news stories. The headline cannot make a comment on the story which is unsupported by fair and accurately presented facts.[121]

Inquests

Inquests are not courts. Reports of defamatory statements made in coroners' proceedings are privileged, but an inquest is not a trial and blame or fault (that is, criminal guilt or civil negligence) is not within the jurisdiction of a coroner or a coroner's jury. An inquest delivers a finding as to how a person died or was injured, without attributing blame to anyone in particular.

Members of a Class or Group

Members of a class or a group can be defamed if the objectionable statement points directly at identifiable individuals. The plaintiff has to be able to prove that the defamatory words clearly identify him in the minds of the reasonable person.[122] For example, to say that "the lawyers in this country are crooks" encompasses such a large group, that no one lawyer could reasonably claim to be identified. But, to say that "the lawyers in this village are crooks" points to a smaller or more identifiable group. It does not matter that there was no intention to defame the plaintiff.

It should be noted that Manitoba's Defamation Act protects against libel of a race or creed which causes unrest or disorder and exposes members of the race or religious creed to hatred, contempt or ridicule. The only remedy though, is an injunction against further publication of the libel.

---

121 *Tedlie v. Southam Co.* [1950] 4 D.L.R. 415 (Man. K.B.).

122 In *Booth v. BCTV Broadcasting System* (1982), 139 D.L.R. (3d) 88 (B.C. C.A.), two police officers successfully sued for a story saying two highly placed members of the narcotics squad were taking bribes. Even though names were not mentioned, the court held it would have been clear to the average citizen that the two officers in charge of the unit were the ones being accused of taking the bribes. It should be noted that actions brought by nine other members of the narcotics squad were rejected by the court because they could not be considered as highly placed as the two senior officers.

Open-Line Talk Shows

A broadcaster is responsible for the statements made by participants in a live program. In one case, the radio host did not take advantage of his ability to censor, stop or delay calls on his phone-in show. As a result, the radio station was held responsible for a defamatory telephone call which was broadcast.[123]

Pleadings, Affidavits and Other Pre-Trial Documents

Unlike accounts of open court proceedings, reports of documents such as pleadings, affidavits and transcripts of examinations for discovery are not privileged until entered into evidence or read out into open court.[124] Pleadings are merely summations of the arguments which may be presented in open court and can be very one-sided and defamatory. An affidavit may be untrue even though it is given under oath and transcripts of discoveries, while also under oath, can be inadmissible or incorrect.

Alberta's Judicature Act partly-restricts the publication of any civil pleadings, affidavits, discovery transcripts or other documents before the beginning of a trial in the province or, if no trial, the proper determination of any other type of action started in Alberta. According to the Act, a journalist in this province can only publish the names and addresses of the parties and their solicitors, and the general nature of the claim.[125]

Police Information and Investigations

A reporter enjoys no privilege in publishing police comments or police information. The police are no different from any other person and their comments can be defamatory.[126] All provinces have legislation which extends a qualified privilege to publications of official reports, bulletins, notices or other documents issued by a public officer for the information of the public.[127] For example, this would include a police bulletin issued for the safety of the public. But other than reporting details of official

---

123 In *Syms v. Warren* (1976), 71 D.L.R. (3d) 558 (Man. Q.B.), a public official who had been the subject of local rumours agreed to speak on a radio show to explain the truth. But, he made it clear that he did not want to further debate the allegations on the air. Unfortunately, a caller took the opportunity to accuse the official of lying and further defamed him. The court criticized the radio station for not making use of its ability to censor calls.

124 *Gazette Printing Co v. Shallow* (1909), 41 S.C.R. 339.

125 R.S.A. 1980, c. J-1, s. 30(2).

126 *Farrell v. St. John's Publishing Co.* (1982), 35 Nfld. & P.E.I. R. 181 (Nfld. T.D.).

127 See above, "The Civil Law Defences," particularly the section on "Qualified Privilege."

documents released to the public, stories containing general police comments to the press are not privileged.

Journalists should also be cautious when publishing reports of an ongoing police investigation. It could be defamatory to accuse a person or a business of a crime simply because there is a police investigation involving them.[128] For example, a person may be suspected of a crime but the investigation may turn up nothing and charges may not be laid.

Public Figures

A journalist can comment on the public acts of people, but the private life or moral character of a public figure is regarded in the same manner as a private individual.[129] In fact, the courts have awarded higher damages to defamed public officials because they are more "sensitive to attack than the ordinary man."[130] It has been suggested that the Charter may change this rule and allow Canadian journalists, like their American counterparts, to comment more freely on the public and private activities of public figures.[131]

Public Performances

Similar rules apply to reviews of public performances. A person who enters the public arena invites public comment. But the comment must

---

128 An analogy may be found in *McDonald v. Sydney Post Publishing Co.* (1906), 39 N.S.R. 81 (C.A.), where a liquor inspector successfully sued a newspaper for reporting that he was accused of attempted bribery by a local citizen. No criminal charges had been laid at the time of the report and the citizen's accusation was only made with the aim of getting the inspector fired by the city council. Because the accusation was not actually made at a public council meeting nor in any judicial proceeding, the court held that the newspaper was confined to comment on, or criticism of, the accusation and could not print unsubtantiated "facts" unless it was willing to prove them.

129 *Sheppard v. Bulletin Co. Ltd.* (1917), 55 S.C.R. 454.

130 *Farrell*, note 126, above.

131 See Doody, note 68 above, where the author argues the Charter now creates the opportunity to broaden the defence of qualified privilege to allow more criticism of public officials, as in the United States. The landmark American case of *New York Times Co. v. Sullivan* 376 U.S. 254 (1964) allowed unlimited criticism of a public official except where there is evidence of malice, such as a reckless disregard for the truth. The author notes that subsequent American decisions have toned down the effect of this case by narrowly defining what is a "public official." As it now stands, a public official in the U.S. is someone who has the opportunity to counter the views expressed in the press and is in a legitimate public controversy, not just someone who is a topic of public interest. American law has also created the "limited purpose" public official who represents a particular cause or issue, but is not constantly in the public eye.

be fair. The public acts of a person can be criticized, but the comment cannot extend to the private life of any individual.[132]

Quotation Marks, "Alleged," Attributions

Generally, the use of quotation marks or words like "alleged," "it is claimed" or "reportedly" offer no protection in a defamation action.[133] Similarly, attributing a defamatory statement to another person won't protect you from being sued. A journalist is as responsible for the comments of those he quotes as he or she is for his own comments (unless the statements are made on an occasion of absolute or qualified privileged).

An exception is in the reporting of a criminal charge. In that case, a journalist should avoid any suggestion of guilt before the verdict is rendered and should note the accused is "alleged" to have committed the crime.

Satire and Humour

Any story attempting to take a humorous or satirical bent should be examined closely before publication. The courts have generally allowed the defence of fair comment to be used by journalists for satirical or humourous stories or illustrations. The courts have held that a fair comment does not even have to be "fair" in that the comment does not have to have any sort of reasonable perspective on the facts, so long as the author of the comment honestly believed in it and it was a comment which could reasonably be held by anyone.[134]

But, there are limits to humour and the defence of fair comment. The courts have taken the stand, and rightly so, that any comment or opinion which accuses someone of criminal, illegal or morally reprehensible conduct is beyond the limits of fair comment.[135] For example, in 1985, a popular magazine columnist wrote a satirical article in which it was noted that two lawyers were rising quickly through their Vancouver law firm. The columnist then said the lawyers had been "cementing their connections through the lawn tennis circuits and wife-swapping brigades." Despite a printed apology later, the trial judge found that the comment went too far in insinuating that the lawyers and their wives "were capable of such immorality" and ordered damages of $10,000 to each lawyer.[136]

---

132 *Sheppard*, note 129, above.
133 *Steiner v. Toronto Star Ltd.* (1955), 1 D.L.R. (2d) 297 at 300 (Ont. H.C.).
134 *Vander Zalm v. Times Publishers*, [1980] 4 W.W.R. 259 (B.C. C.A.).
135 See the English case of *Campbell v. Spottiswoode* (1863), 3 B & S 769.
136 *Hunter and Swift v. Fotheringham*, summarized (1986), 35 A.C.W.S. (2d) 360 (B.C. S.C.).

Another occasion to note is the after-dinner speech where a person jokes about himself or tells a personally embarrassing story; the journalist must keep the remark within the context in which it was made. The reader or listener must not be lead to believe the remark was made as a serious comment or admission.

Sensationalism

Facts which are innocent and undefamatory on their own can carry a defamatory meaning when presented in a sensationalized manner. For example, one story reported that police had seized documents from a lawyer's office, that he was unavailable for comment and went on to suggest that the police investigation was the reason he had resigned from his public office several weeks earlier. In reality, the police were searching the lawyer's office to find documents belonging to a company which he happened to represent, the lawyer was not involved in any crime, he truly was unavailable for comment and he had resigned from his public position for unrelated reasons.[137]

A journalist should also carefully weigh his or her choice of words. For example, to say that someone was "ousted" from an office, when in fact the person resigned or was not reappointed for other reasons, is defamatory because it implies that the person was removed for wrongdoing.[138]

Sloppy Journalism

Failure to corroborate facts or to check the accuracy of documents or sources can contribute to the amount of damages awarded to the plaintiff. When serious accusations are being levelled, at least one court has punished journalists who did not confront the plaintiff before publication.[139] Gross negligence, such as running a story based on an unconfirmed "tip," will only add to the size of court awards.[140]

Defamation of Title or Property

A journalist must be careful of defaming the marketability of property or the title to tangible or intangible property. The plaintiff must prove

---

137 See *Wells v. Daily News Ltd.* (1976), 13 Nfld. & P.E.I.R. 80 (Nfld. T.D.).

138 *Roberge v. Tribune Publishers Ltd.* (1977), 20 N.B.R. (2d) 381 (N.B. Q.B.).

139 *Munro v. Toronto Sun Publishing Co.* (1982), 39 O.R. (2d) 100 (H.C.).

140 *Tait v. New Westminster Radio Ltd.* (1984), 58 B.C.L.R. 194 (C.A.). Despite a prompt apology, which was taken into account by the court, damages were set at $17,500.

that there was malice, that actual damage has been suffered and that the statements were untrue.[141]

For example, falsely stating that a product infringes on a patent is a slander of title.[142] To say that a house is haunted and uninhabitable is an example of defaming a property.[143]

Visuals

The careless use of visuals (that is, video, graphics or photographs) can be hazardous. There are a number of different areas to beware of. Television journalists must be careful when matching script with pictures. Watch for references to improper or illegal acts when showing identifiable individuals (for example, protestors or crowd shots).

It is defamatory, for instance, to comment on how some business people use bankruptcy proceedings to escape debts, while at the same time showing an identifiable person or place of business on the screen.[144] The innuendo is that the person or business being shown practices these techniques. It is irrelevant that the comment was not directed at the person or business and the plaintiff would only have to prove that the defamatory comment could be understood to be referring to him.

Visuals are considered a part of a story and must reflect the facts as reported. This is important when considering the use of stock footage or photographs. A picture is a "freeze-frame" in a person's lifetime and what was true once may not be true now. For example, to use a photo of a child who once received social assistance, but is no longer in need, in connection with a story about poor children, could be defamatory of the child and her family if they are no longer on welfare and the present situation has not been made clear to the audience.[145]

Another problem can arise when stock footage or photos are used which show identifiable individuals in situations different from what is being portrayed. In one instance, a story about abortion showed stock footage of a young hospital worker setting up an operating table. When the visuals were shot the worker was setting up the table for a different type of operation. It turned out that he was a devout Roman Catholic and took offence to being shown setting up the table for an abortion.

Even if you have obtained a formal release or consent from someone to use their picture, you must be careful. A person's consent must be

---

141 *Cross v. Bain, Pooler & Co.*, [1937] O.W.N. 220 (H.C.).
142 *Cousins v. Merrill* (1865), 16 U.C.C.P. 114 (C.A.).
143 *Manitoba Free Press Co. v. Nagy* (1907), 39 S.C.R. 340.
144 *Burnett v. CBC (No. 1)* (1981), 48 N.S.R. (2d) 1 (T.D.).
145 *Dennis v. Southam Inc.* (1954), 12 W.W.R. (N.S.) 379.

informed and if you use their picture in a context which they could not have been expected to foresee, they could sue. For example, a model who signed a general release form may not expect to see her picture accompanying a story about prostitution.

Journalists must also be careful in choosing graphics or illustrations which may suggest a defamatory message. The graphics and pictures used in connection with a story must reflect true and provable facts. For example, it was held in one defamation case that it added to the defamatory effect of the story to use a graphic of tipped "scales of justice" in a story alleging that a public official interfered with the justice system.[146]

CONCLUSION

There is pressure on several fronts to alter the law of defamation in Canada. As noted above, the Law Reform Commission of Canada has recommended that sweeping changes be made to the criminal libel legislation. The Uniform Law Conference has recommended that the provinces adopt uniform statutes to do away with the inconsistencies between jurisdictions. And there may be even more significant changes coming based on challenges under the Charter.

The concluding point comes from the ombudsman for a major Toronto newspaper. That newspaper's editors have found that many of the legal and ethical problems in news stories could be avoided by including comments from both sides in a contentious issue in the same story:[147]

> "If the target of an attack cannot be reached for comment, the reporter should consider the possibility of withholding the story until he can get the needed comment, rather than slap on an 'unavailable-for-comment' ending."

This fundamental principle of fairness could go a long way in defusing a possible defamation court action.

A DEFAMATION CHECKLIST

The following areas should be considered before a story is published or broadcast:

1. Is there "defamatory matter"? Expressly or by implication, does this story contain any of the following (in a written or visual form):

---

146 *Vogel v. CBC*, [1982] 3 W.W.R. 97 (B.C. S.C.).

147 Rod Goodman, The *Toronto Star's* Ombudsman, in a letter to the author, dated August 17, 1984.

- statements or suggestions of criminal, illegal, immoral or improper behaviour or practices?
- statements about someone's financial status?
- insults or slurs?
- statements about someone's health?
- critical statements relating to a person's profession, business, product or trade?
- statements that might adversely affect the reputation of a person or entity in the eyes of ordinary people?
- statements that would deter ordinary people from associating or dealing with that individual or entity?

If so, chances are there is defamatory material in the story. But this doesn't mean it can't be published. Please continue through the checklist.

2. Does the defamatory matter refer to someone directly or indirectly? Regardless as to whether an individual or entity (group, association or corporation) is named, is it possible that even one person might think the defamatory matter refers to a specific person, entity or its members? If so, this story probably has the basic elements to attract a defamation action (that is, defamatory matter referring to a prospective plaintiff). This doesn't mean the story must be dropped or changed. Chances are there's either a defence or a way to re-write the story to avoid defaming an individual. A lawyer should be called.

3. Is a defence available?

   (a) Is there proof of the defamatory statements, such as:

      - documents?
      - a witness with first-hand knowledge who is willing to appear in court on your behalf?
      - one or two extra sources of corroboration?
      - detailed notes from key interviews?
      - tape recordings of key statements?

The more of the above you have, the better your chances of relying on the "truth" defence (justification). Please re-read that section.

   (b) Was the defamatory matter derived from:

      (i) open proceedings of Parliament, a Legislature, a government committee, a municipal council meeting, a public meeting or a judicial or quasi-judicial hearing?
      (ii) an official report or news release of a government or judicial/quasi-judicial body?

If so, a defence of qualified or absolute privilege may exist. Please re-read that section.

> (c) Is the defamatory matter an honest, non-malicious expression of someone's "opinion" and is it based on provable facts concerning a matter of public interest?

If so, there may be a defence of fair comment. Please re-read that section.

4. Common areas of legal concern include:

- pre-trial court documents or exhibits not dealt with in open court
- wording of criminal charges
- sensationalism distorting the true situation
- headlines, cut lines and captions
- visuals juxtaposed with other stories, casting a defamatory light on an individual
- innuendos in visuals
- generic visuals using recognizable people or businesses in connection with a defamatory subject matter
- satire or humour that goes too far, perhaps suggesting immoral or illegal behaviour
- presence of malice (for example, reckless or careless reporting)
- subjective comments in court reports
- refusing to allow the subject of defamatory matter the opportunity to reply to the statements

3

Confidentiality of News Sources

It's a fact of life these days that many news stories, particularly controversial ones, involve confidential sources of information. While it's always best to have information attributed and on the record, it's not always possible. Indeed, many worthwhile stories would go unreported if journalists had to insist that sources be identified.

The offer of confidentiality is a powerful weapon in a journalist's arsenal and it shouldn't be used indiscriminately. Certainly, there are circumstances when it's obvious that a source will suffer if named. A source may fear for his or her job or even personal safety. And then there are the more difficult judgment calls where the source is seeking confidentiality merely for convenience's sake or to avoid minor social embarrassment or perhaps the source isn't confident of the truth of his or her comments.

Whatever the circumstances, there is no law governing when a news source should be offered a cloak of secrecy. That's up to the individual journalist. However, the law does have something to say about when and if a confidential source must be revealed.

WHEN MUST A SOURCE BE REVEALED?

The general rule is that courts will be unlikely to offer a journalist absolute protection against disclosing the identity of a source if it is considered relevant and necessary to the proper adjudication of a matter.

Disclosure in Criminal Proceedings

In a criminal proceeding, courts can turn to the Criminal Code[1] to

---

1 R.S.C. 1985, c. C-46.

compel a journalist to reveal a source. For example, section 545 allows a justice conducting a preliminary hearing to send a witness who refuses to testify to jail for periods of up to eight days. If, at the end of the eight days, the witness still refuses to testify, the judge can continue to issue eight day internments.

If a witness refuses to testify when a criminal matter reaches the trial stage, the judge can cite the offender for contempt of court and order a jail term and/or a fine.

Disclosure in Civil Actions

Journalists more commonly are asked to reveal their sources in civil matters, particularly defamation actions. Unlike a criminal proceeding, a civil action permits the parties to examine each other under oath before the trial begins (known as an examination for discovery). The courts are split in this country on whether a source must be revealed at this stage.

In some provinces, such as Ontario and Québec, the courts recognize the special role of the news media and follow what is called the "newspaper rule." Under this common law rule, a court will avoid ordering a journalist to disclose a source until the matter reaches trial.[2]

The newspaper rule is imported from England, where disclosure is also generally delayed until trial. The United States has taken a statutory approach and some states have passed "shield" laws that limit the situations in which journalists can be ordered to disclose their sources. But even in the U.S., the common law and federal laws recognize no special privilege for news media sources. A few Canadian provinces have toyed with the

---

2 In *Hatfield v. Globe & Mail Div. of Can. Newspapers* (1983), 41 O.R. (2d) 218 (Ont. M.C.), it was held that a newspaper may refuse to disclose its sources of information prior to the trial. In the Ontario High Court decision of *Reid v. Telegram Publishing Co. Ltd.* (1961), 28 D.L.R. (2d) 6 (Ont. H.C.), the court said that in a libel action invoking truth and fair comment defences, unless exceptional circumstances exist, the judge should refuse a request to order source disclosure because witnesses would have to be called anyway. In *Drabinsky v. MacLean-Hunter Ltd.* (1980), 108 D.L.R. (3d) 391 (Ont. H.C.), where *Reid* and the English case of *Lyle-Samuel v. Odhams Ltd.*, [1920] 1 K.B. 135 (C.A.), were followed, the court said it is not necessary to disclose sources even if malice is claimed by a plaintiff because the source would likely have to be called by the defendant to prove his defence.

In the recent case of *McInnis v. University Students' Council of University of Western Ontario* (1984), 14 D.L.R. (4th) 126 (Ont. H.C.), the decision in *Reid* was reaffirmed with the court only allowing the reporter's notes to be produced at discovery with the source's name blacked-out. The court said the protection of sources at the discovery stage is a matter of public policy. Also see *Hays v. Weiland* (1918), 42 O.L.R. 637 at 642-643 (C.A.), where the court suggested news gathering can only serve its proper service to the public by keeping its sources secret where possible.

idea of enacting their own shield laws (for example, Québec), but no such law has been proposed to date.

A few provinces, notably British Columbia and Saskatchewan, have largely rejected the idea that news media enjoy any special privileges and believe the examination for discovery should be full and revealing.[3]

Sometimes it may not be necessary to reveal the name of a source. In the New Brunswick case of *Baxter v. CBC*, the court refused to order the network to disclose the name of a person who gave a journalist a confidential document.[4] Although the court noted it wasn't recognizing any special privilege for journalist's sources, it decided the document itself was more relevant to the trial. If the information in the document had been relayed to the journalist orally, the court said only then would it have ordered the disclosure of the source's identity.

It also may not be necessary to reveal all the confidential sources involved in a news story. The Nova Scotia appeal court illustrated this in the defamation action involving the *Ottawa Citizen* and Robert Coates, the one-time Conservative defence minister who resigned after the newspaper alleged he had compromised security by visiting a West German nightclub.[5] In the discovery stage, a demand was made for the names of

---

3 The B.C. courts have ordered disclosure of sources in the discovery process in several cases whenever it is relevant. In *McConachy v. Times Publishers Ltd.* (1964), 49 D.L.R. (2d) 349 (B.C. C.A.), the court said discovery, by its nature, demands broad and searching questions. In this case, the court held that the questions concerning the source of the story's information were proper. In *Wismer v. MacLean-Hunter Publishing Co. and Fraser (No. 2)*, [1954] 1 D.L.R. 501 (B.C. C.A.), the court made a political commentator disclose his source because the defences of fair comment and qualified privilege were being relied upon and the plaintiff was trying to prove that there was malice on the part of the source.

In *Price v. Richmond Review* (1965), 54 W.W.R. 378 (B.C. S.C.), the court held the source had to be revealed at discovery even though the defence was one of justification (that is, truth) and did not involve the issue of malice. The court said the rightful purpose of the demand for the source's name was to ascertain whether the article was pure invention, mere gossip or rumour.

In the New Brunswick case of *Culligan v. Graphic Ltd.* (1917), 44 N.B.R. 481 (C.A.), the defendants were forced to disclose their source of information because the defence of fair comment was being pleaded. The court said the sources would reveal whether the comments were made on "obviously insufficient information."

In the Saskatchewan case of *Wasylyshen v. CBC* (1989), 14 A.C.W.S. (3d) 235 (Sask. C.A.), the court pointed out that the newspaper rule has not been elevated to a category of special privilege for journalists and is merely an exercise in judicial discretion (in other words, it's up to each judge). While the court said the newspaper rule was still valid in Saskatchewan, it affirmed the trial judge's decision not to follow the "rule." The court also noted that, in this case, there was no evidence of the sources requesting or even needing confidentiality. It suggested the journalist simply preferred not to mention the names of sources in such stories.

4 (1978), 22 N.B.R. (2d) 307 at 315 (Q.B.).

5 *The Citizen v. Coates* (1986), 29 D.L.R. (4th) 523 (N.S. C.A.).

five people alleged to be sources for the story.

A chambers judge ruled there was no special privilege for the press and ordered all the names to be revealed. But on appeal, two of the three judges held that while there was no general privilege immunizing the press, the Canadian Charter of Rights and Freedoms' guarantee of freedom of the press[6] must be weighed against the plaintiff's right to disclosure. While the public has an interest in seeing justice done, the judges felt the public also has an interest in seeing that special confidential relationships are respected.

The court then looked at the relevancy of each confidential source in light of what they contributed to the story. There was no evidence of a special confidential relationship for two of the sources and their role was relevant. But the other three sources did not have to be named. One had not given any information used in the story and the other two had merely passed on "gossip and rumours" that had nothing to do with the alleged defamatory statements.

Disclosure in Inquiries or Tribunal Hearings

For public inquiries or bodies like coroners' inquests, the legislation creating and governing the particular body may give it the power to subpoena witnesses. If so, the tribunal may have an inherent common law power to fine or jail tight-lipped witnesses for contempt or the right to ask a Superior Court to order the witness to comply with requests for information.

HOW COURTS LOOK AT THE ISSUE OF CONFIDENTIALITY

Until recently, the issue of source disclosure by journalists had not been specifically and fully dealt with other than in motions at the trial level. However, in 1989, just such a case was considered by the Supreme Court of Canada. While the court's decision was somewhat disappointing and circuitous on constitutional questions of freedom of the press, it did give some indication of the court's thinking on source confidentiality.

In *Moysa v. Alberta (Labour Relations Board)*, a reporter for the *Edmonton Journal* wrote a story about a union's organizing activities.[7] One of the companies targeted for the union's efforts was Hudson Bay Company and one week after the story was published several employees were fired, allegedly for trying to organize a union.

---

6 Canadian Charter of Rights and Freedoms, Part 1 of the Constitution Act, 1982, being Schedule B of the Canada Act 1982 (U.K.), 1982, c. 11 (hereinafter, Charter).

7 *Moysa v. Alberta (Labour Relations Board)* (1986), 45 Alta. L.R. (2d) 37 (Q.B.).

Moysa, the reporter, was called before a labour relations board as a witness and the union indicated it wanted to ask her whether she had spoken with anyone at the company before writing her story and what the details of the conversation were. Moysa refused to testify and disclose her sources of information, claiming that communications between a reporter and sources are protected under common law and the Charter. The board disagreed and ordered her to testify under oath.

The newspaper went to court to get the order quashed. The trial court dealt with the issue in two parts: i) whether there is a common law privilege; and ii) whether the Charter offers any protection to journalists as a special class in society.

The newspaper argued that while there was no special category of privilege for journalists under the common law, a general principle of privilege could be applied since freedom of the press is essential to society. The newspaper's lawyer said sources would dry up if the promise of confidentiality couldn't be protected.

But the trial judge refused to stretch the common law that far, noting that if a question is relevant to an inquiry, it is in the public interest to ask about sources of information. The information may have been concocted or sources may have had ulterior motives. The court also rejected the idea that a journalist should only be called as a witness after all other avenues of seeking the information were pursued.

The argument that the Charter's guarantee of "freedom of the press" protects journalists' sources was also rejected. The judge said this "freedom" refers to a "species of intellectual freedom" extended to everyone, and does not impart a separable right to the press as an entity or class. According to the trial judge, compelling a journalist to testify as to his or her sources does not infringe upon the right to use the press. He refused to quash the labour board's order.

The newspaper appealed, but the provincial appeal court agreed with the trial judge that journalists have no special privilege in common law or in the Charter.[8] One appeal judge added that it's up to the legislators to create a journalist's category of privilege.

The Supreme Court of Canada Decision

Unfortunately, the Supreme Court of Canada agreed with the two lower courts.[9] The judges held that the reporter in this case had no special privilege to refuse to testify before the labour board. While the court declined to answer the constitutional questions, it did express some doubt

8 (1987), 52 Alta. L.R. (2d) 193 (C.A.).
9 [1989] 1 S.C.R. 1572.

that sources would dry up if journalists had to reveal who they spoke with. The judges suggested that clear evidence of that danger would have to be presented to a court in the future to justify the granting of any privilege based on the Charter's guarantee of freedom of the press.

First, though, the court noted that even if a qualified form of testimonial privilege exists in Canada, in this case, it would not apply, since the union was more interested in the information the journalist gave to Hudson Bay officials concerning the organizing campaign than it was in the identities of the people the journalist spoke to. The judges said the claim of privilege couldn't be applied to disclosure of information.

The court also referred to the leading United States Supreme Court case which held that the U.S. Constitution's First Amendment accords a reported no privilege against appearing before a grand jury and answering questions as to either the identity of his or her news sources, or information which he or she has received in confidence.[10]

In that case, one judge said that each claim of privilege should be judged on its particular facts by striking a balance between the freedom of the press and the obligation of all citizens to give relevant testimony. The Supreme Court of Canada appears to agree with that and with the idea that the evidence must be crucial to whomever seeks it and also must be relevant. On the facts presented to the labour board, it was held that the evidence sought from the journalist was crucial to the union's allegation of unfair labour practices, and relevant.

The court also referred to one of its earlier judgments on the general question of when a special privilege against disclosure of confidential communications should be established. This case set out a test that may be applied.

Slavutych v. Baker involved an action for wrongful dismissal and the admissibility in court of confidential appraisals of a university professor's work.[11] The confidential information was intended for use only by a tenure committee, but the University used the report as grounds to fire the professor and wanted to introduce the document into court. In deciding whether the communication should be declared privileged, and thus inadmissible, the court acknowledged the theory of an American author on the subject.

J. Wigmore suggests a privilege should be granted to any communication which fulfills the following conditions:[12]

1. The communications must originate in a confidence that they will not be disclosed.

---

10 *Branzburg v. Hayes*, 408 U.S. 665 (1972).

11 (1975), 55 D.L.R. (3d) 224 at 228 (S.C.C.).

12 *Wigmore: On Evidence*, 3rd ed. (McNaughton Revision, 1961), para. 2285.

2. This element of confidentiality must be essential to the full and satisfactory maintenance of the relation between the parties.
3. The relation must be one which in the opinion of the community ought to be sedulously fostered.
4. The injury that would inure to the relation by the disclosure of the communications must be greater than the benefit thereby gained for the correct disposal of litigation.

Each condition must be fully met in order for a communication to enjoy a privilege from disclosure. The first requirement means that it must be apparent the information is being given only on the condition that it will remain confidential. The second requirement is that the court must be able to recognize there are important reasons for confidentiality. For example, the source could lose his or her job. The third requirement is that the public must agree that the confidential nature of the relationship between the source and recipient of the communication should be protected. The final requirement is that the injury to this confidential relationship resulting from the disclosure of the communications must be greater than the benefit of resolving the court action.

As noted, the Supreme Court avoided the constitutional questions in *Moysa*, but it appears that the Wigmore test will play an important role when the right case does go to the high court. Wigmore's test was also applied in an Ontario case that has some interesting analogies to situations faced by journalists.

That case involved a member of the legislature who refused, during a criminal proceeding, to divulge the name of an informant.[13] Elected members of legislatures and Parliament enjoy many privileges which protect them for such things as defamation actions and arrest arising from civil proceedings.

The question which was directed to the Ontario Court of Appeal was whether the member also enjoyed protection from disclosing his sources while performing his duties in government. The member argued that law enforcement officials, who also work for the Crown, are not required to divulge the names of their informants unless the name would help the accused prove his innocence. The member suggested the same rule should apply here to himself as a servant of the Crown.

It was a difficult issue for the courts. Two of the five judges said there is such a privilege based on public policy grounds. But a majority of the court held the opposite view. Using the Wigmore test, they found the legislative member did not meet the third and fourth requirements. Looking at the third requirement, the Court held that the function of the

---

13 *Reference Re Legislative Privilege* (1978), 39 C.C.C. (2d) 226 (Ont. C.A.).

member is in the field of legislation, and not law enforcement. Similarly, journalists report news, they do not enforce the law.

Continuing with a consideration of the third requirement, the court also found that the relationship between the member and the informant is not one which should be "sedulously fostered." The court made the point that informers should go to the police if they have evidence of crimes. The fourth requirement also failed because the injury created by naming the source was felt not to be greater than the benefit of having the case properly determined.

It's difficult to predict how the Supreme Court's decision in *Moysa* will affect the application of the "newspaper rule." But it's reasonable to expect that courts will still offer journalists limited protection until a matter reaches trial.

OTHER ISSUES INVOLVING NEWS SOURCES

Although the practice is frowned upon, sometimes a journalist will strike a deal with a source regarding the use of his or her comments and information. Handling these agreements with sources properly involves more than questions of journalistic ethics.

Breach of Contract

If a journalist expressly agrees to allow a source to "veto" or even review a story before it is published, a court may hold the reporter to his or her word.[14] A court could find that the reporter and the source have made an enforceable contract. If a journalist disregards the promise, a source may be able to get an injunction stopping the publication of the comments or he could theoretically sue for breach of contract and claim damages.

In 1986, an injunction was granted by an Alberta court barring the national broadcast of a CBC interview with a convicted serial killer. The accused was appealing some of his convictions and, while the program may also have been contemptuous, the judge focused on the fact that the CBC journalist who dealt with the inmate had agreed before a series of interviews to allow him to see the finished program before it aired. The

---

14 An analogy can be found in the case of *Paddington Press Ltd. v. Champ* (1979), 43 C.P.R. (2d) 175 (Ont. H.C.). An injunction was successfully brought against a television network that planned to broadcast an interview with a prominent personality and author. The book publisher alleged that there was an agreement with the reporter not to broadcast the interview until a certain date. But the reporter claimed he made no such deal. Due to the conflicting claims of each side, the judge granted the injunction until the matter could be dealt with in a trial.

judge held that the CBC had broken its agreement with the interview subject and could not broadcast the story.

If possible, a journalist should not make any deals with sources about the end use of their information. In most cases, giving a source or interview subject the right to have a say in how a story is told can spell legal trouble or, at the very least, editorial disputes between the journalist and his source.

Breach of Confidence or Trust

Another factor to consider is that there is a common law action called *breach of confidence* which involves the unauthorized publication of confidential information.[15] This action can be invoked whenever a third party (that is, journalist) becomes privy to private information arising from relationships between others that call for confidentiality.

For example, anyone in a master-servant or employer-employee relationship has a common law duty to keep corporate secrets confidential. If a journalist were to be told something confidential by an employee, the employer could claim there was a breach of confidence and ask for an injunction to prevent further publication of the information. In some cases, the employer may also be able to sue for damages up to the value of the information. Other relationships involving a "confidence" are husband-wife, doctor-patient and solicitor-client.

In addition, if an off-the-record comment is used and traced back to the employee, he or she could be fired. That employee could possibly have grounds to sue you for causing his or her dismissal if the information was supposed to be secret.

There may also be statutory provisions which prohibit some government employees from disclosing confidential information. For example, members of the Canadian Security Intelligence Service are prohibited by law from disclosing the names of sources of information or employees involved in covert activities, as well as any information gained during the performance of their duties.[16] Most governments also require civil servants to take an oath of secrecy.

On or Off The Record?

A common problem arises when a source makes a demand after an interview that all or part of the interview not be used. In that case, the source has no right to make such a demand if there was no mention

---

15 For a good discussion of the tort of "breach of confidence" see Williams, *The Law of Defamation in Canada* (Toronto: Butterworths, 1976), pp. 41-48.
16 Canadian Security Intelligence Service Act, R.S.C. 1985, c. C-23, ss. 18(1) and 19.

beforehand that all comments are not for publication. The courts may suggest, in the absence of any agreement, that it should be presumed that all comments to a journalist are on-the-record.[17]

A SOURCES CHECKLIST

1. The general rule is that courts are unlikely to offer absolute protection to a journalist who does not want to disclose the identity of a source, if it is considered relevant or necessary to the proper adjudication of a matter.
2. In a criminal proceeding, courts may use the Criminal Code to compel a journalist to reveal a source. Section 545 allows a justice conducting a preliminary hearing to send a witness who refuses to testify to jail for periods of up to eight days. At trial, a judge can cite a journalist for contempt and order a jail term and/or a fine.
3. In many provinces, civil courts recognize the special role of the news media and follow what is called the "newspaper rule." Under this common law rule, a court will try to avoid ordering a journalist to disclose a source until the matter reaches trial. However, courts in a few provinces don't follow the rule and may order disclosure in the early stages of a court action.
4. Several courts have found that there is no special privilege for journalists in the common law or under the Charter against disclosing a confidential source's name.
5. A journalist should not make promises to sources that he or she doesn't intend to keep (for example, to let the source see the story before it's published). A court may hold the journalist to his or her word and issue an injunction for breach of contract.
6. Some relationships impose an obligation of confidence on the parties (for example, employer-employee, solicitor-client or doctor-patient). If that confidence is breached by one of the parties passing on confidential information to a third-party (such as a journalist), the other party may be able to seek an injunction restraining publication.

---

17 For instance, in defamation actions the courts have held that anyone who knows the press are present must expect that their comments could be published.

4

Avoiding Legal Risks
in Investigative Reporting

It is said that every reporter is an "investigative reporter." However, the news gathering industry does recognize a special breed of journalist. As one broadcasting executive once testified in court, "an investigative reporter is simply a reporter who gets stories that nobody wants you to have."[1]

Investigative reporting calls for extensive research and, sometimes, the use of exotic or clandestine techniques. When published or broadcast, an investigative story often attracts great attention and someone's reputation may even be ruined or sullied by it.

No judge has ever said that journalists shouldn't engage in investigative reporting (as long as it doesn't interfere with a police investigation or a judicial process). In fact, the courts have generally supported and encouraged the news media's endeavours to inquire into alleged wrongs against society and other individuals.

By its very nature, though, an investigative story carries more weight than so-called "spot news." As a result, the courts may look for a higher standard of care and skill from an investigative reporter. The courts most certainly will not tolerate anything less than the reasonable standard of care expected of all journalists.

In the following case, a judge examined step-by-step how one particularly defamatory investigative story was put together and, in the process, set forth some worthwhile opinions on the potential for abuse that exists in all stories.

---

1 *Vogel v. CBC*, [1982] 3 W.W.R. 97 at 122 (B.C. S.C.).

THE CASE OF *VOGEL v. CANADIAN BROADCASTING CORPORATION*

In March of 1980, the CBC broadcast three television news stories about Richard Vogel, the then-Deputy Attorney General of British Columbia. The programs said that Vogel had used his position to influence, or try to influence, the course of justice in three criminal cases for the purpose of protecting his friends. The programs were the culmination of a long investigation by a then-CBC Vancouver journalist. The reporter had had about ten years' experience as a print journalist before joining the CBC in 1979 as an investigative reporter and was considered more than competent.

The first broadcast was a 14-minute special production on the six o'clock news for the British Columbia region. A condensed version ran that night on the late-night news program that followed the national news. The third broadcast was a short story which ran the next night on CBC's The National and was seen across the country.

Richard Vogel and his family immediately suffered the effects of the story. He was suspended without pay immediately after the story was aired and there was a flood of demands for his resignation. Two weeks later, the Attorney General announced that an investigation had cleared Vogel of any wrongdoing. But the CBC refused to retract the story, publicly announcing that it would stand by it and defend any court actions.

In the defamation lawsuit that followed, the British Columbia Supreme Court awarded Vogel a total of $125,000. It is among the highest awards granted to a victim of defamation in Canada. The court assessed joint damages against the CBC and the journalist for $100,000. Another $25,000 was levied against the CBC as punitive damages to show the court's disapproval of the corporation's behaviour.

The Use of Sources

As it turned out, the journalist's only source for his story was a senior Crown prosecutor in the province's criminal justice branch. Although the reporter went to great lengths to confirm the source's allegations of wrongdoing, his efforts were fruitless. Nevertheless, the reporter chose to interpret certain events as proof of improper and scandalous behaviour by the Deputy Attorney General and ignore the dead ends in his investigation.

As good journalistic policy dictates, the story was reviewed by CBC executives and lawyers before airing. But the court noted it was still aired even though the executive producer of the program knew there was some doubt about evidence supporting the allegations.

The court had a great deal to say about the use of sources, particularly ones who give out information on a confidential basis. The idea for the story began with a lunch meeting between the journalist and a senior Crown prosecutor in Vancouver. The journalist was hoping to get an investigative piece out of a court case which, at that time, linked the then-Chief Justice of B.C. to a prostitute. The hooker's story was later found to be a complete falsehood.

The prosecutor hinted that a better story might be found in the actions of Deputy Attorney General Vogel in that case and others. He promised more information. A series of clandestine meetings between the two men were then held over the next several weeks in deserted areas of Stanley Park or while driving in areas of the city where they wouldn't be recognized.

As was his job, the journalist demanded proof of the prosecutor's allegation that Vogel had interfered in the chief judge's case and two others. The prosecutor produced a confidential file which outlined some of the office correspondence on the cases, but there wasn't much to substantiate the allegations. The journalist pressed for more information, particularly a letter which was said to have been sent to the Attorney General outlining in detail the complaints against Vogel.

The Crown prosecutor agreed to supply the document secretly. The judge in this case recounted this event:

> [The Crown prosecutor], by that time, was showing some aptitude for playing his role of "Deep Throat." The operation involved [the prosecutor], on a Saturday morning, leaving a copy of the letter in a plain brown envelope in a locker in the Vancouver Bus Depot, hiding the locker key in the angle of a Y-shaped beam in an unfinished building and then informing [the reporter] that he might find something of interest were he to look in that place. The smooth progress of the operation was interrupted because [the reporter] looked in the wrong beam and found an old furniture store invoice. After puzzling for some time as to the hidden message intended to be conveyed by that piece of paper, he telephoned [the prosecutor], got further directions, and was thus enabled to find the key, find the locker and thus come into possession of the copy of the letter.[2]

The letter, which was produced in court, didn't substantiate the claims of the prosecutor. In fact, the letter actually dispelled the idea that there had been any wrongdoing. But it didn't seem to matter to the reporter at this stage. The judge noted, "[The reporter], by that time, was convinced that he was on the trail of a major scandal, and found it easy to reject any evidence inconsistent with that view."[3]

After getting all the documents he could from his source, the journalist could still find no corroboration for the allegations. Yet, he was urged on

---

2 *Ibid.* at 123-124.
3 *Ibid.* at 124.

by the source. As it later turned out, the prosecutor had a grudge against the Deputy Attorney General. But the journalist chose to accept the word of this single source as the truth, even though his initial investigation found nothing. The judge here felt he knew why:

> [The reporter] prides himself on being a sceptic, but in his dealings with [the prosecutor] he showed himself incapable of scepticism. That inability may result from his romantic view of the investigative reporter as society's bulwark against corruption — fighting a guerrilla war against the "establishment." What he calls "scepticism" is a sourly cynical assumption that corruption is rampant in the establishment and that all attempts by it to maintain privacy or confidentiality are part of a conspiracy to suppress the truth. He is consequently inclined to regard as something of a hero any member of the establishment who is willing to be a "leak." He is not inclined to accept, even as a possibility, that information provided to him in that way may not be reliable.[4]

The reporter's assigning editors were no less guilty. They blindly accepted the reporter's word that the sole source was reliable. Sometimes, the reporter would even get mad if his source's credibility was questioned. Court testimony showed that it got to the point where editors avoided any questioning of the journalist for fear that he would become further agitated by their doubt.

The moral in this is that even high-level sources can have hidden motives. The word of any source, secret or not, must be thoroughly corroborated in the case of serious allegations. Many top journalists adopt a rule that a source's allegations must be corroborated by two or more independent sources of information.

Ambush Interviews and Deceptive Techniques

The court took a dim view of "ambush interviews" which catch an interview subject off-guard and tend to place the person in a bad light. Invariably, little information of value is added to the story. Similar analogies can be drawn to other "stunts" that appear to be more flash than substance. For example, one might suggest that a television clip showing a reporter beating on a door that no one answers, or shouting for a comment, over-dramatizes the point. The question to be asked is whether the investigative technique justifies the information gained.

While an ambush isn't illegal or even defamatory in and of itself, the court considered its use in Vogel's case as further proof of the reporter's careless and malicious attitude. At one point in the story, a Crown Attorney

---

4 *Ibid.* at 128.

was shown being interviewed in the ambush interview style. The transcript of the story read as follows:

> Nils Jensen's boss is this man: Brian Weddell, the chief prosecutor for the Kootenays area — the man who's complained to his colleagues about Vogel's interference in this case. But he didn't seem to want to shed much light on it.
>
> [REPORTER]: There are several people that say Vogel phoned one of your prosecutors directly and told him to lay the dangerous driving charge and that the guy checked with you and you said it was O.K. Is that not true?
>
> [BRIAN WEDDELL]: Not that I can recall. I don't recall having any contact with Mr. Vogel at all about this case.
>
> [REPORTER]: No, you weren't supposed to have had contact directly with him — but one of your prosecutors did, and you knew about it. Is that true?
>
> [BRIAN WEDDELL]: Not that I recall.
>
> [REPORTER]: Well, you wouldn't forget something like that, would you?
>
> [BRIAN WEDDELL]: I don't know.[5]

The judge saw this as the point in the story in which the theme of the "good guys" and "bad guys" develops. He described how the interview that appeared on camera differed from what had actually happened:

> Weddell was subjected to an "ambush." The first view, which was taken with a hidden camera at some distance, shows him walking across a parking lot. His hat is pulled down over his eyes, his shoulders are hunched into his coat, his hands are in his pockets and a cigarette dangles from his lips. The impression given is one of shiftiness. The fact apparently is that he was on his way to his office on a cold morning, unaware that he was being watched. In those circumstances, few would come off better, either in appearance or in reacting to the series of questions put sternly by the reporter while a camera is pointed from over his shoulder.[6]

The judge went on to note that the telephone call in question had happened more than a year earlier. The viewers were not told that and the innuendo was that there was a cover-up. The result was that the person came off looking badly in the interview and in this case the "ambush" technique hardly seemed necessary.

The court also mentioned, without comment, two other techniques of investigative reporters. The first technique involved the use of "bogus scripts." The journalist claimed they were the prime tool of the investigative

---

5 *Ibid.* at 138.
6 *Ibid.* at 147.

reporter. The scripts were supposedly copies of the story that was ready to go to air. The purpose of the bogus scripts was to lead an interview subject to think that the CBC had solid evidence of the allegations outlined. The script would then be used to persuade the subject to "confirm" the allegations.

A second technique involved the use of hidden microphones and "body packs" to record conversations without the interview subject knowing.

In both cases, the techniques did not turn up any new or corroborating evidence. The interview subjects refused to confirm the allegations and the journalist eventually chose to ignore the results of these investigative methods.

What's important to note here is that the court interpreted the reporter's decision to ignore these investigative results as further proof of malice and an intent to distort the facts.

Manipulation of Facts and Interviews

The Vogel story contained other interviews which the court found slanted or taken out of context in order to produce the story the reporter wanted to portray. One such interview involved another Crown prosecutor in Victoria. The story transcript read as follows:

> The story of Vogel's interference — the phone call to the prosecutor — is common knowledge among some B.C. prosecutors, but no one seems to want to talk about it.
>
> [REPORTER]: You say you don't have any direct knowledge about the phone call, but the story is commonly discussed in Crown counsel circles. How widely is it known?
>
> [NILS JENSEN]: I have no idea — I can't comment on that.
>
> [REPORTER]: How long have the stories been circulating?
>
> [NILS JENSEN]: Again — I can't comment on that.
>
> [REPORTER]: But you have heard the story?
>
> [NILS JENSEN]: I prefer not to comment on that.[7]

This may appear to be a typical "no comment" interview. However, the judge explained the unusual manner in which it came about. At the beginning of the interview, Mr. Jensen had initially said "on-camera" that he had heard "something" about alleged interference and about the alleged telephone call. But, in fact, he had no personal knowledge of the call.

---

7 *Ibid.* at 138.

Realizing that he had gone too far, Jensen asked that the interview not be used.

The journalist agreed not to use the interview if Jensen would consent to start the interview again and state simply "no comment." Jensen agreed and the court noted how the interview was eventually used:

> The interview on screen clearly conveys the impression that Jensen was confirming the truth of what was asserted by [the reporter] in the questions — and [the reporter] agreed that that was the intent. . . . [Jensen's] expression is that of a man anxious to tell the truth and troubled that it is not open to him to do so. Each of his refusals to comment comes after a period of cogitation — the pause, punctuated only by "ah's" of indecision, before he finally says that he would prefer not to comment as to whether he heard the story, is about 15 seconds — a long time, on television.[8]

What was actually an interview with a person who knew nothing of the allegations became a suggestion of a cover-up.

A second interview for the Vogel story was actually rehearsed and then staged to produce a desired effect. The interview was with a friend of a young man who had been caught driving while intoxicated and was charged by police. The accused, a Mr. Rigg, was not convicted and the journalist wanted to portray Vogel as a friend of the family who had helped Rigg out. The reporter set out to ask Rigg's friend what he knew of Vogel's involvement. The judge described the interview that appeared in the story:

> The impression is that [the friend], taken by surprise, gave one responsive answer and clammed up, presumably to protect his friend, Rigg, when the questions turned to the delicate subject of "how he got off." The interview ends with [the friend], looking apprehensive and yet knowing, apparently trying to escape from the interviewer.[9]

In fact, Rigg's "friend" had had a falling out with Rigg soon after the arrest and was more than willing to co-operate with the journalist if it could be done in such a manner that he would appear to be an unwilling participant. The night before the interview, two of the reporters working on the story rehearsed him in the performance he gave.

There was one other staged interview. It was with the Crown prosecutor who was the reporter's source. The interview consisted of the prosecutor refusing to comment on the allegations of wrongdoing. Testimony at court indicated that the object of the interview was to ensure that no one would think the Crown prosecutor was the source of the information.

---

8 *Ibid.* at 146.
9 *Ibid.* at 150.

Sensationalized Packaging

The judge noted that seemingly innocent words on paper can become damning when combined with the right pictures. This should be noted by both print and broadcast journalists. Throughout his ruling, the judge commented on the influence the visual package had on the story. For example, the news began with these headlines:

> This is the CBC Evening News, with Bill Good, Junior.
> British Columbia's Deputy Attorney General has interfered with the judicial system. Tonight, a detailed report.[10]

Of that brief beginning, the judge said:

> The backdrop at this point is a photograph of the plaintiff with a worried, harassed look. That was taken from some film footage obtained by [another reporter] several weeks earlier in preparation for the program, but without the plaintiff's knowledge of the purpose.
> This segment, though brief, was of the most attention-getting kind. Its impact, in its context as the lead item, was far greater than can be visualized from reading the words on paper.[11]

Also, the judge noted the graphic used to introduce the item after the headlines was the scales of justice. But the scales were tilted about 30 percent, which a CBC executive said was considered "just right" for the story. It appeared several times in the story as a type of logo.

The judge felt the combination of these dramatic visual effects helped make the allegations appear to be even more serious and controversial.

Balance and the Right of Reply

As every journalist knows, it's important in any story to accurately portray both sides and, if possible, allow the subject of the story to answer comments about the issues. This story gave the impression, on at least two occasions, that key people who could have offered the "other side" refused to speak with the CBC.

One segment of the story involved attempts to contact Vogel himself. The script reads as follows:

> We offered Dick Vogel an opportunity to answer questions about his actions, but an associate of the Attorney General's Department declined the offer on Mr. Vogel's behalf.[12]

The truth of the matter was that a public relations representative was

---

10 *Ibid.* at 136.
11 *Ibid.* at 143.
12 *Ibid.*

contacted by the journalist about a possible interview. The spokesman was told only that the interview would involve allegations about three court cases. Vogel's spokesman wasn't told what the allegations were about and he saw no urgency in arranging an interview. The court said the request was, at best, a deceptive half-truth.

At another point in the script, it was suggested that a lawyer involved in the incidents was faking an illness to avoid comment. "We tried to contact Mickey Moran," the reporter noted, "but were told he was ill and couldn't talk to us."[13]

In fact, the CBC avoided contact with the lawyer until the story was almost finished. Only one attempt was made to speak to the lawyer — at his house. They were told they couldn't see him and there were no further attempts to get a comment.

Sensationalized Writing

The judge was very critical of the writing technique in the Vogel story. The script was riddled with innuendos and the reporter suggested throughout that there was a cover-up. The truth was there were no facts to back up the allegations.

Even the CBC national news was criticized for its writing. The national reporter in Vancouver at the time reported on the story and the judge was critical of the vague, yet defamatory, style of writing and intonation used by the reporter. For instance, the judge zeroed in on one line in The National report that said: "Dick Vogel *had* used his powerful position . . ."[14]

The judge found that the emphasis on the word "had" gave the impression that it had long been suspected that Vogel was acting improperly. The court found a more serious aggravation of the libel in this closing passage:

> While no cabinet ministers have been implicated in the allegations so far, the whole business is obviously embarrassing to the Social Credit government.[15]

The suggestion was that Vogel wasn't alone and that even cabinet ministers might be involved. There was no proof offered at the trial to justify the statement. The court concluded that it was puffery designed to give the story a more serious tone for the national audience.

The judge had this to say about standards of journalism in this case:

> It is an accepted tenet of our democratic society that the press serves the

---

13 *Ibid.* at 144.
14 *Ibid.* at 172 [emphasis added].
15 *Ibid.* at 190.

public interest by exposing corruption and misconduct by those in public life, and that it is essential that it perform that role. It is, however, sometimes hard to see that any public interest is served other than the interest in being entertained. In this case, that was the interest intended to be served. The program was conceived and executed as a form of entertainment presented in the guise of news. . . .

What was considered was, in essence, the question: "Can we get away with it?" That having been answered in the affirmative, the next question was: "How can we produce the greatest effect?"[16]

Some Final Thoughts

There is much to be learned from the mistakes of others. It's sad to note that soon after the Vogel story aired, the reporter burned all his notes, the dummy scripts and other documents related to the story. It appeared to have been done to prevent them from being available in a court action.

While the Vogel case clearly illustrated the pitfalls of shoddy investigative reporting techniques, it also pointed out how lazy and gullible other journalists can be when such a story breaks. The judge in Vogel's case had some sharp criticisms for the reporting done after the CBC's story broke and the reports on the defamation trial itself. The reporting on the trial sometimes seemed to focus on any hints of incriminating information which might confirm the investigative story — some reporters refused to believe the story was wrong.

The judge felt the "pack mentality" of journalists can lead to further aggravation of a defamation:

When one media outlet suggests scandalous conduct on the part of a public figure, it can be expected that its competitors will, if the story is one of widespread interest, assign reporters, commentators and support staff to get their own story and join in the controversy. It can also be expected that there will be a tendency by some to outdo the others by getting a more interesting angle, which is likely to be one which will put the subject in an even worse light.[17]

Perhaps, one final lesson is found in this sentence which the judge quotes from another judgment:

To only give the public a look at the side of the coin supportive of their comments and opinions and not to show the facts to the contrary on the other side of the coin is to deal in half-truths, and comments made in this way are neither fair nor made in good faith.[18]

---

16 *Ibid.* at 180.
17 *Ibid.*
18 *Thomas v. CBC*, [1981] 4 W.W.R. 289 at 337-338, quoted in *Vogel* at 187.

AN INVESTIGATIVE STORY CHECKLIST

As noted at the beginning, investigative reporting often involves more care and effort than the average story. Here are some points to keep in mind when researching such a story.

1. *Keep notes and outs*: It's a mistake to neglect to make or keep notes during interviews or when doing research. This becomes most apparent when a lawsuit has been launched and you're looking back to justify the story. Admittedly, there are both good and bad points in keeping detailed notes. A journalist's notes can be used by either side in a court proceeding to prove/disprove malice, identify sources or validate quotes.

    Chances are notes will be more valuable than dangerous. For instance, defamation actions often take two years to get to trial and a journalist may need notes to refresh his or her memory. Even if a journalist is taping a conversation, notes should be taken in case the recording fails. Still, one should be careful when taking notes since they can indicate a reporter's attitude at the time. For example, malice could be found in a reporter's jottings that the interview subject "looks shifty" or "is a jerk." One final point. Many journalists now write their notes on computer terminals. Whenever possible, keep these notes in a separate computer file rather than write and edit the story directly from the master file.

    The same guidelines apply to broadcast journalists regarding keeping outtakes or unused video, film or audio clips.

2. *Tape conversations*: It's bothersome and not always possible, but a journalist should record all conversations with key people in a story. Tapes are obviously better than notes for proving that someone said what they said. Remember, however, that simply having a tape of someone saying something isn't good enough to prove the truth of a statement.

3. *Corroborate*: It's essential that all key points or "facts" be backed up by at least one other source. Some journalists insist on corroboration from two to three other sources. In another British Columbia case, a radio station wrongly reported that a local lawyer had been fined for fraud. The story was based solely on an unconfirmed telephone tip. The judge in *Tait v. New Westminster Radio Ltd.* found the reporting to be grossly negligent.[19]

4. *Use an internal checking system*: It would seem obvious, but too many news organizations and editors fail to check and question the reporter's work. The case of *Munro v. Toronto Sun Publishing Corp.* points out

---

19 (1984), 58 B.C.L.R. 194 (C.A.).

the perils.[20] In that case, Munro, a prominent federal cabinet minister was accused of making stock market trades using insider information obtained through his cabinet position. The story was based on "evidence" on a microfiche that a reporter frequently held up before his editors, but never showed them. In fact, no one other than the reporter had looked at the microfiche.

When a second reporter was put on the story to help flesh it out, he didn't look at the microfiche either. After the story was published, Munro promptly denied the allegations of wrongdoing and demanded proof. At that point, the newspaper found it had no proof of its accusations. The key reporter claimed the microfiche was lost or possibly stolen.

As it turned out, the court heard testimony to the effect that this journalist was more determined "to get" the minister than actually find evidence to support the story. The court also determined that the second journalist assigned to develop the story was so driven by a desire to destroy and gain notoriety that he didn't even take the time to look at the documentation alleged to have been available.[21] In the end, the court awarded damages of $100,000 to Munro. The judge said that editors are just as responsible as reporters for the accuracy of a story.

5. *Offer an opportunity for reply*: It's not always possible or desirable, but consideration should be given to allowing the subject of an investigative report the opportunity to respond to allegations. In *Munro*, the supervising editors were chastised by the court for not asking the minister for his comments before the story was published. The judge stated that a journalist should always confront a subject before publishing serious allegations.

However, there are times when it would be imprudent to confront the story subject. For example, the subject may seek an injunction or, in cases involving crime, someone may flee or destroy evidence. A lawyer can help decide whether the subject should be given the opportunity to make a comment before a story comes out.

6. *Review documents carefully*: Documents are nice to have, but they aren't infallible. Affidavits and signed statements, for instance, are only as credible as the person giving the information. Hearsay information sworn under oath is often useless because the person doesn't have personal knowledge of events. Also, someone who gives an affidavit may still have to appear in court and be subjected to cross-examination.

Even court documents and "official" government documents aren't without problems. Pleadings, for example, can be exaggerated or wrong.

---

20 (1982), 39 O.R. (2d) 100 (H.C.).
21 *Ibid.* at 123.

Finally, don't rely on books, magazine articles or newspaper clippings to back up claims. They carry no authority (even if they make the same allegations and no one sued) unless a journalist can convince the authors to hand over their evidence.

7. *Watch internal documents*: A news organization's own internal documents (story drafts, memos, letters, etc.) are also likely to be a part of a court proceeding. Journalists and their editors should be careful to avoid embarrassing or incriminating comments in such documents. In one case, a radio station reported on the dismissal of a town administrator and suggested it had something to do with an unrelated criminal investigation in missing municipal money.[22] The "slug" on the top of the news script was "Town Caper," indicating the attitude of the reporter at the time.

---

22 *Crawford v. CFBC* (1987), Saint John (N.B.Q.B.).

5

Journalists and Invasion of Privacy

In Canada, there is no general right to be protected against invasion of privacy.[1] However, it is a grey area in the law and a confusing mix of federal and provincial laws do offer individuals and even corporations

---

1   Canadian courts have been reluctant to create a separate civil tort of invasion of privacy. But in the case of *Motherwell v. Motherwell* (1976), 73 D.L.R. (3d) 62 (Alta. C.A.), the tort of *nuisance* was broadened to remedy a violation of privacy. The court issued an injunction to stop a woman from making frequent and abusive telephone calls to her father, brother and sister-in-law, that amounted to undue interference with the enjoyment of their premises. Courts in some other provinces have expressly disagreed with this decision. But courts in New Brunswick and British Columbia have gone even further and said there is a common law tort of invasion of privacy. See *Re K.C. Irving Ltd. and R.* (1971), 4 C.P.R. (2d) 120 (N.B. Q.B.) and *Re MacIsaac and Beretanos* (1971), 25 D.L.R. (3d) 610 (B.C. Prov. Ct.).

some rights to privacy. For example, in five provinces, legislation has been enacted to allow a person to seek a civil remedy for unjust invasion of privacy. But the laws are unclear and largely unused, and none of the other provinces have followed suit.

There are also provincial and federal laws protecting confidential personal or business information that is held by governments, such as reported earnings on income tax forms. The latter laws, however, are discussed in the chapter dealing with access to public information.

Naturally, journalists are concerned with the parameters of privacy laws. Questions about the "right to privacy" arise quite commonly, such as when a reporter secretly records conversations, digs through garbage cans for information or jumps over a fence to check out a story. This chapter sets out those areas where news gathering and "rights" to privacy often converge.

THE RIGHT TO PRIVACY IN FEDERAL LAW

Intercepting Private Communications

A common area of confusion for many journalists is whether one can listen in on conversations or secretly record them. The answer is yes, but some conditions must be met first.

Sections 183 to 196 of the Criminal Code[2] deal with the interception of private communications and contain the only references in criminal law to invasion of privacy. The unlawful interception of a private communication is a serious offence and is set out in section 184(1):

> Every one who, by means of an electro-magnetic, acoustic, mechanical or other device, wilfully intercepts a private communication is guilty of an indictable offence and liable to imprisonment for a term not exceeding five years.

Aside from the jail term, anyone aggrieved by an unlawful interception can also be awarded punitive damages of up to $5000.[3]

How to Stay Within the Law

A journalist or anyone else can lawfully intercept communications. But it's important to first understand some key definitions and elements of the offence.

To begin with, the communication in question must be private. A private communication is defined in the Code as:[4]

> any oral communication or any telecommunication made under circumstances in which it is reasonable for the originator thereof to expect that it will not be intercepted by any person other than the person intended by the originator thereof to receive it.

---

2 R.S.C. 1985, c. C-46.

3 S. 194.

4 S. 183.

Note that the law doesn't apply to situations where the "originator" of the communication cannot reasonably expect that it will be private.[5] For instance, if a camera crew is filming people talking during a break at a conference and people see the camera and microphone in front of them, they can't expect their conversations to be private. Similarly, people who use citizen band radios or send messages on telephone voice pagers can't expect their comments to be private.

The communication must also be oral or a telecommunication. The interception of a written note or other paper documents would not fall under this law.

The private communication must then be intercepted by an "electromagnetic, acoustic, mechanical or other device," which is defined as:

> any device or apparatus that is used or is capable of being used to intercept a private communication, but does not include a hearing aid used to correct subnormal hearing of the user to not better than normal hearing.

This includes any device ranging from an electronic telephone bug to a tape recorder left in a room to (theoretically) a glass placed against a wall. Interestingly, this definition excludes interceptions of communications made solely by the unassisted human ear. The offence is clearly only concerned with man-made devices.[6]

Finally, it's useful to know what it means to intercept a communication:

> "intercept" includes listen to, record or acquire a communication or acquire the substance, meaning or purport thereof

So, interception not only includes hearing or recording a message, it also includes finding out by any method the meaning, substance or purport of an unlawfully intercepted private communication. For example, if another person unlawfully heard or intercepted a communication and then told a journalist about it, the reporter could theoretically be found to have also unlawfully intercepted the communication.

The "Rule" for Lawful Interception

Understanding the limits of the offence, intercepting a private communication with some device is still permissible if it falls within one of four circumstances set out in section 184(2). Three don't apply to

---

5 In *R. v. Bengert* (1978), 47 C.C.C. (2d) 457 (B.C. S.C.), police investigating a narcotic offence told an airline to direct any call asking about a certain suitcase to a special police phone number. The police argued that this wasn't an unlawful interception because they were answering the phone and were therefore a consenting party to any recording of the conversation. But the court declared the evidence inadmissible because the caller thought he was speaking to the airline and didn't intend to be speaking with the police.

6 See *R. v. Watson* (1976), 31 C.C.C. (2d) 245 at 249 (Ont. Co. Ct.), where evidence of a conversation overheard by a police officer by ear was deemed to be admissible and not an unlawful interception as defined by the Code because a mechanical listening device wasn't used to intercept the communication.

journalists. (A person may intercept a communication if: i) permission has been given by a judge (such as for police wiretaps); ii) someone supplying a telephone, telegraph or other communication service must intercept communications to repair the system; or iii) a person who is an officer or servant of the Crown intercepts a private communication during random monitoring for the management of the radio frequency spectrum.)

The "saving provision" or rule that can be used by journalists is subsection 184(2)(a). It says the offence of unlawfully intercepting a private communication doesn't apply to:

> a person who has the consent to intercept, express or implied, of the originator of the private communication or of the person intended by the originator to receive it.

Translating that into plain language: a journalist can secretly record or listen to a private communication, using an electronic or acoustical device, if he or she has the consent of anyone who is the sender or intended receiver of the communication.

It's that simple (but, as we'll see further on, broadcasters are limited in how they make use of secret telephone recordings).

If a journalist is one of the parties to the communication, the only consent needed is his or her own. If a journalist isn't directly involved, then one of the conversation's participants must agree. For example, a journalist electronically and secretly eavesdropping on a telephone conversation would need permission of one of the other people on the line. If more than one person originates the message or is intended to receive it, the consent of any one of those people is enough.[7]

However, if a journalist isn't party to the communication, it's important that the right person gives permission for the interception. The law states that the private communication must be directed at a person intended to receive it. For example, on one occasion a television newsmagazine arranged for someone to take a small tape recorder into a meeting. The person later left the room for a few moments and the recorder continued to run in his absence. As it turned out, the newsmagazine wanted to use comments recorded during this short time period, but could not because no one left at the meeting had given consent to the interception or was aware of it.

Other Dangers

As mentioned earlier, problems can also arise from the use of information gained by an unlawful interception. The Criminal Code makes it a separate offence to disclose any part of a private communication unless the person intercepting it has consent of one of the parties.[8] Disclosure includes divulging the substance, meaning and even the existence of a

---

7 R.S.C. 1985, c. C-46, s. 184(3).
8 S. 193(1).

private communication or the wiretap.[9] This is an indictable offence punishable with a sentence of up to two years in prison. An exception is provided for the publication of such information if it's revealed in an open judicial or court proceeding.[10]

The Criminal Code also makes it an indictable offence to possess, sell or purchase:[11]

> "any electro-magnetic, acoustic, mechanical or other device or any component thereof knowing that the design thereof renders it primarily useful for surreptitious interception of private communications."

Not all electronic devices are "primarily useful" for intercepting private communications. For example, this doesn't include radio receivers which intercept police communications.[12] It's also unlikely that it would include the sound recording equipment normally used by reporters during employment. But tape recorders and microphones are getting smaller and smaller and there may come a time when someone may suggest they are primarily designed for surreptitious interception, particularly if a reporter uses them as such.

An indication of that concern among law enforcers is a 1985 amendment (section 191(2)(b.1)) allowing police operatives to use "body packs" without violating the Code and without having to apply for a licence for the device.

It might also be noted here that the Criminal Code sections pertaining to the illegal interception of communications and invasion of privacy don't apply to film or video recordings without sound.[13] Only the interception of the words in a private communication violate the Code privacy provisions, not pictures.

Other Criminal Code Provisions

Trespassing at Night

Criminal Code section 177 protects individuals against people trespassing at night around their home:[14]

Every one who, without lawful excuse, the proof of which lies upon him,

---

9 *Ibid.*

10 S. 193(3).

11 S. 191(1).

12 *R. v. Gasper* (1976), W.W.D. 93 (Sask. Dist. Ct.).

13 *R. v. Biasi (No. 3)* (1981), 66 C.C.C. (2d) 566 (B.C. S.C.).

14 In *R. v. McLean* (1970), 75 W.W.R. 157 (Alta. Mag. Ct.), the court held it must be proven beyond a reasonable doubt that the accused was hunting in a stealthy manner for an opportunity to carry out an unlawful purpose. In other words, the simple act of trespass may not be enough to support a conviction under this section.

loiters or prowls at night on the property of another person near a dwelling-house situated on that property is guilty of an offence punishable on summary conviction.

Note that the offence only involves prowling around a residence. This provision is sometimes called the "peeping-tom section."

Intimidation

The Criminal Code also has a provision involving the watching, hounding or "besetting" of a person or place. Section 423(1) states:

Every one who, wrongfully and without lawful authority, for the purpose of compelling another person to abstain from doing anything that he has a lawful right to do, or to do anything that he has a lawful right to abstain from doing,

. . .

(c) persistently follows that person from place to place,

. . .

(f) besets or watches the dwelling-house or place where that person resides, works, carries on business or happens to be

is guilty of an offence punishable on summary conviction.

But section 423(2) offers this defence, which is particularly useful for journalists:

A person who attends at or near or approaches a dwelling-house or place, for the purpose only of obtaining or communicating information, does not watch or beset within the meaning of this section.

Harassing Telephone Calls

The misuse of the telephone may constitute an invasion of privacy in certain circumstances set out in section 372 of the Code:

(2) Every one who, with intent to alarm or annoy any person, makes any indecent telephone call to such person is guilty of an offence punishable on summary conviction.

(3) Every one who, without lawful excuse and with intent to harass any person, makes or causes to be made repeated telephone calls to that person is guilty of an offence punishable on summary conviction.

Disrupting a Religious Service

Sections 176(2) and 176(3) of the Code apply to the privacy of religious worship and certain "benevolent" gatherings:

(2) Every one who wilfully disturbs or interrupts an assemblage of persons

met for religious worship or for a moral, social or benevolent purpose is guilty of an offence punishable on summary conviction.

(3) Every one who, at or near a meeting referred to in subsection (2), wilfully does anything that disturbs the order or solemnity of the meeting is guilty of an offence punishable on summary conviction.

Note that this section requires the disturbances to be of a willful nature. An accidental or unintentional interruption would be unlikely to support a conviction.

Federal Privacy Restrictions on Broadcasters
Radiocommunications

The Radio Act makes it an offence to divulge or make use of the substance of a "radiocommunication" without the consent of the originator.[15] In this case, a radiocommunication doesn't mean a commercial radio broadcast.[16] However, any other transmission (for example, police radio calls or cellular phone conversations) can't be divulged or broadcast. One could not then use such recordings on the air without permission.

Unfortunately, this section is quite vague and overly restrictive. For instance, in contrast to the Criminal Code wiretap law, it's not good enough to have the permission of the receiver of the radiocommunication. It must be the originator. It also appears to be an offence to make any use of information gathered, regardless of whether the communication is re-broadcast. A violation of the Act can result in a summary conviction and a fine not exceeding $2500 and/or 12 months in jail.

However, there are no recorded convictions for journalists under this section and it doesn't appear to be diligently enforced. The best advice is to seek out legal counsel when dealing with such communications.

Telephone Conversations

There is another broadcast law dealing with privacy. The Canadian Radio-television and Telecommunications Commission's Radio Regulations, 1986 state no licensee shall broadcast any telephone interview or telephone conversation, or any part thereof, with any person unless the person's oral or written consent to the interview or conversation is obtained before the broadcast.[17] The only exception, is when the person telephoned the station for the purpose of participating in a broadcast.[18]

---

15 R.S.C. 1985, R-2, s. 11(2).
16 *Ibid.*
17 C.R.C. 1978, c. 379, s. 5(1)(*k*). A challenge of this section failed in *R. v. CKOY Ltd.* (1976), 70 D.L.R. (3d) 662 (Ont. C.A.). The appeal court held that a trial judge was wrong in declaring the section invalid and stated that the CRTC is empowered to make such regulations so as to ensure programming of high standards.
18 *Ibid.*

THE RIGHT TO PRIVACY IN PROVINCIAL LAW

As at the federal level, provincial laws dealing with privacy are spotty and inconsistent between jurisdictions. Five provinces do have laws that speak directly to an individual's right to privacy. The Privacy Acts in British Columbia, Saskatchewan, Manitoba and Newfoundland create a civil remedy for invasions of privacy. Québec's Civil Code also can be applied to violations of privacy. As with any civil matter, the law requires a plaintiff to initiate a court action and the laws don't create any criminal or provincial offences.

These laws have yet to be fully tested in the courts. For example, one would expect the news media to be frequent targets of civil suits with such laws. But there have been few lawsuits because precisely what the laws cover is vague and there are broad exemptions for news gathering. At the time of writing, no other provinces have indicated they will follow suit with their own privacy legislation.

The provincial privacy laws are based on similar legislation in the United States. South of the border, privacy laws have been used to protect individuals in a wide variety of circumstances. For example, some states protect people against publications of defamatory, yet true, statements, the unauthorized use of personal letters, harassing phone calls or photos that single out an individual in a public place for no valid reason. The news media have also had to watch how they use old or dated "file" pictures of people who were in accidents or were grief-stricken at some tragedy.

Although the U.S. legislation has been far-reaching in some states, actions for invasion of privacy are uncommon in Canada, perhaps because most people don't know about the Acts and because of the statutory defences for those involved in news gathering.

While Privacy Acts in four of the provinces are similar, there are subtle differences and each province will be dealt with separately.

British Columbia

The Privacy Act in this province states under section 1(1):[19]

It is a tort, actionable without proof of damage, for a person, wilfully and without claim of right, to violate the privacy of another.

That would seem to be a fairly widesweeping prohibition against any violations of privacy. But to decide whether there has been an invasion of privacy, the statute directs courts to look at more than the simple fact that someone's privacy has been violated.

---

19 R.S.B.C. 1979, c. 336.

A court must examine the nature, incidence and occasion of the alleged invasion, and the relationship between the parties. For example, the relationship between a journalist and a public figure will be different from the relationship between a reporter and the average citizen.

The offended person doesn't have to prove that any damage was suffered by the invasion. But he or she does have to prove that the invasion of privacy was intentional and without a lawful right. For example, a police officer with a search warrant would have a lawful right to enter a specific property. According to the B.C. Act, an invasion of privacy can occur with:

1) eavesdropping or surveillance, whether or not accomplished by trespass,
2) misappropriation of a person's name or portrait for the purpose of advertising or promoting the sale or trading of property or services, without consent, or
3) anything the court feels constitutes an invasion of privacy within the ambit of the Act.

Note that the first provision protects citizens against eavesdropping or surveillance even when there has been no act of trespass. For example, an invasion of privacy may occur if you take a photograph of someone while peering over the edge of their fence. There have been few cases to test these subsections and their potential is uncertain. For example, does eavesdropping include surreptitious recordings in which one of the participants to the private conversation consents to the taping? If so, someone may be able to sue for civil invasion of privacy even though such an invasion of privacy is lawful under the Criminal Code.

The second provision incorporates the general common law position on misappropriation of personality.

And the third provision gives the court a very wide latitude in deciding what's a violation of privacy.

The Defences

An act is not a violation of privacy, under section 2(1), where:

(a) it is consented to by some person entitled to consent;
(b) the act or conduct was incidental to the exercise of a lawful right of defence of person or property;
(c) the act or conduct was authorized or required by or under a law in force in the Province, by a court or by any process of a court; or
(d) the act or conduct was that of . . . a peace officer . . . or a public officer . . . in the course of his duty . . . [and the violation of privacy is not] disproportionate to . . . the matter [being investigated] nor committed in the course of a trespass.

One other defence, set out in section 2(2), is particularly useful to reporters:

A publication of a matter is not a violation of privacy if

(a) the matter published was of public interest or was fair comment on a matter of public interest; or
(b) the publication was, in accordance with the rules of law relating to defamation, privileged;

but this subsection does not extend to any other act or conduct by which the matter published was obtained if that other act or conduct was itself a violation of privacy.

Deciding what is a matter of public interest will be up to the judge or jury. It would have to be a matter of public interest in the eyes of the "reasonable man" and it's irrelevant that the reporter felt it was a matter of public interest.

A reporter may also be able to prove that the matter published was in a situation of absolute or qualified privilege as defined in defamation law. For example, information brought out in court may be published without concern over a violation of privacy lawsuit under this Act. Note, however, that this defence only applies to invasions of privacy which fall within the ambit of the public interest or privilege subsections. For example, any other act by a reporter which amounts to an invasion of privacy, but doesn't fall under the two subsections, could be successfully pursued in court.

For the most part, this Act doesn't appear to have interfered with the normal activities of the B.C. news media. In 1985, the owner of a store involved in a bitter labour dispute sued a BCTV reporter and cameraman for invasion of privacy under the Act.[20] The journalists had approached the store owner for an interview and he told them to leave and stay off the store property, including the parking lot.

The cameraman and reporter went across the street and started filming. At one point, they moved back on to the parking lot for some shots and a fight broke out between the news crew, the owner and his security staff. The cameraman recorded the fight and it was later shown on television.

The court held there was not an invasion of privacy on either of two counts. First, the judge felt the act of filming the fight on the plaintiff's property was not a violation of privacy because it took place on a site that wasn't shielded from the public. While the property itself was private, anyone passing by could see what was happening there. Second, the

---

20 *Silber v. B.C. Broadcasting System* (1985), 25 D.L.R. (4th) 345 (B.C. S.C.).

broadcast of the fight also wasn't a violation of privacy because section 2(2) of the Act permitted publication of any matter of public interest. In this case, the labout dispute was certainly within the public interest.

Saskatchewan

As in B.C., the Privacy Act in this province states:[21]

It is a tort, actionable without proof of damage, for a person, wilfully and without claim of right, to violate the privacy of another person.

Again, the offended person doesn't have to prove that any damage was suffered by the invasion of privacy. But he or she does have to prove that the invasion of privacy was intentional and without a lawful right. The Saskatchewan Privacy Act is similar to the British Columbia Act because it directs the court to consider the circumstances of the alleged violation of privacy.

But the Saskatchewan law does appear to give a reporter more freedom to gather the news than is extended to journalists in other provinces, as will be discussed below.

However, section 3 of the Saskatchewan law is more specific than the B.C. law as to what violates privacy:[22]

Without limiting the generality of section 2, proof that there has been:

(a) auditory or visual surveillance of a person by any means including eavesdropping, watching, spying, besetting or following and whether or not accomplished by trespass;

(b) listening to or recording of a conversation in which a person participates, or listening to or recording of messages to or from that person passing by means of telecommunications, otherwise than as a lawful party thereto;

(c) use of the name or likeness or voice of a person for the purposes of advertising or promoting the sale of, or any other trading in, any property or services, or for any other purposes of gain to the user if, in the course of the use, the person is identified or identifiable and the user intended to exploit the name or likeness or voice of that person; or

(d) use of letters, diaries or other personal documents of a person; without the consent, expressed or implied, of the person or some other person who has the lawful authority to give the consent is *prima facie* evidence of a violation of the privacy of the person first mentioned.

As in British Columbia, the Act protects citizens against eavesdropping or surveillance even when there has been no act of trespass. For example,

---

21 R.S.S. 1978, c. P-24, s. 2.
22 R.S.S. 1978, c. P-24, amended S.S. 1979, c. 69, s. 19.

an invasion of privacy may occur if you take a photograph of someone while standing on the edge of their property. However, the Saskatchewan Act is more specific about other acts that constitute eavesdropping and surveillance (for example, following someone).

This Act also has a much more detailed definition of misappropriation of personality. A violation of privacy can occur not only with the unauthorized use of someone's name or likeness, but also their voice. The plaintiff must be identifiable and the defendant must have intended to exploit the name, likeness or voice of someone for either commercial purposes or "any other purposes of gain."[23]

The Defences

According to section 4(1), an act or publication is not a violation of privacy in these cases where:

   (a) it is consented to, either expressly or impliedly by some person entitled to consent thereto;
   (b) it was incidental to the exercise of a lawful right of defence of person or property,
   (c) it was authorized or required by or under a law in force in the province or by a court or any process of a court; or
   (d) it was that of
       (i) a peace oficer acting in the course and within the scope of his duty; or
       (ii) a public officer engaged in an investigation in the course and within the scope of his duty.

There are two other defences of importance to reporters, also stated in section 4(1):

An act, conduct or publication is not a violation of privacy where:

   (e) it was that of a person engaged in a news gathering:
       (i) for any newspaper or other paper containing public news; or
       (ii) for a broadcaster licensed by the Canadian Radio-Television Commission to carry on a broadcasting transmitting undertaking;

   and such act, conduct or publication was reasonable in the circumstances and was necessary for or incidental to ordinary news gathering activities.

And, as set out in section 4(2):

A publication of any matter is not a violation of privacy where:

---

23 R.S.S. 1978, c. P-24, s. 3(c).

(a) there were reasonable grounds for belief that any matter published was of public interest or was fair comment on a matter of public interest; or

(b) the publication was, in accordance with the rules of law relating to defamation, privileged;

but this subsection does not extend to any other act or conduct whereby the matter published was obtained if such other act or conduct was itself a violation of privacy.

As in B.C., deciding what is a matter of public interest will be up to the judge or jury. It must be a matter of public interest in the eyes of the "reasonable man" and it's irrelevant that the reporter felt it was a matter of public interest.

A reporter may also be able to prove that the matter published was in a situation of absolute or qualified privilege as defined in defamation law. For example, information brought out in court may be published without worry of a violation of privacy lawsuit under this Act.

But note that this defence only applies to invasions of privacy which fall within the ambit of the public interest or privilege subsections. For example, any other act by a reporter which amounts to an invasion of privacy, but doesn't fall under the two subsections, could be successfully pursued in court.

Manitoba

Manitoba's Privacy Act is somewhat different from the other two Western provinces.[24] It has this strongly-worded definition of invasion of privacy:

A person who substantially, unreasonably, and without claim of right, violates the privacy of another person, commits a tort against that other person.

As in the other provinces, the offended person doesn't have to prove that any damage was suffered by the invasion. But the plaintiff does have to prove that the invasion of privacy was substantial, unreasonable and without claim of right. The Manitoba law gives examples of violations of privacy in section 3 that are similar to those set out in the Saskatchewan Act.

The Defences

The defences to violations of privacy are also similar to those in the Saskatchewan law. But the provision about news gathering (as found in

---

24 R.S.M. 1987, c. P125, s. 2(1).

the Saskatchewan Act) isn't included. The only defence particular to journalists is set out in section 5:

> In an action for violation of privacy of a person, it is a defence for the defendant to show
>
> > (f) where the alleged violation was constituted by the publication of any matter
> > > (i) that there were reasonable grounds for the belief that the publication was in the public interest; or
> > > (ii) that the publication was, in accordance with the rules of law in force in the province relating to defamation, privileged; or
> > > (iii) that the matter was fair comment on a matter of public interest.

Newfoundland

The Newfoundland Privacy Act states:[25]

> It is a tort, actionable without proof of damage, for a person, wilfully and without a claim of right, to violate the privacy of an individual.

As in the other provinces, the offended person does not have to prove that any damage was suffered by the invasion. But he or she does have to prove that the invasion of privacy was intentional and without a lawful right. The Newfoundland legislation gives detailed examples of violations of privacy similar to those set out in the Saskatchewan Act.

The Defences

The defences are similar to those in the Saskatchewan law. But the provision about news gathering (as found in the Saskatchewan Act) isn't included. The only defence available to reporters is set out in section 5(2):

> A publication of any matter is not a violation of privacy if
>
> > (a) the matter published was of public interest or was of public interest or was fair comment on a matter of public interest; or
> > (b) the publication was, in accordance with the rules of law relating to defamation, privileged;
>
> but this subsection does not extend to any other act or conduct whereby the matter published was obtained if such other act or conduct was itself a violation of privacy.

---

25 S.N. 1981, c. 6, s. 3(1).

Québec

In Québec, Article 1053 of the Civil Code is the rule followed in cases involving invasion of privacy:

Every person capable of discerning right from wrong is responsible for the damage caused by his fault to another, whether by positive act, imprudence, neglect or want of skill.

To succeed in court, the plaintiff must prove three elements. Each element must be proven on the balance of probabilities.[26]

The plaintiff must first prove the *fault* of the defendant.[27] Fault can be shown by negligence, incompetence or want of skill or the direct action of the defendant.[28]

The plaintiff must then prove he or she suffered damage. In Québec, even proof of hurt feelings or sensibilities can be enough.[29]

Then, the plaintiff must prove the causal link between the fault of the defendant and the damage suffered.[30] Therefore, ruthlessly intruding into the private life of an individual in pursuit of a story could be enough to sustain an action for invasion of privacy.

In one invasion of privacy case brought under this section, a broadcaster received a letter of complaint from a man. The broadcaster told his audience about the letter and then proceeded to read out the person's telephone number and address, and suggested everyone should call the complainant to give him their opinions.

The man received many phone calls, some threatening and harassing.[31] The lawsuit against the broadcaster was successful.

In addition, Québec's Charter of Human Rights and Freedoms bolsters the privacy protections.[32] Section 5 promises every person "respect for his private life." Section 6 protects against trespass and ensures the "peaceful enjoyment . . . of . . . property." Section 9 states "Every person has a right to non-disclosure of confidential information."

GENERAL ISSUES IN PRIVACY

Visual Invasions of Privacy

Can you take someone's picture and use it as you wish? There are

---

26 *Thibeault v. Porlier Transport,* [1971] C.A. 518.

27 See Nicholls, *Offences and Quasi-Offences in Quebec* (Toronto: Carswell, 1938), p. 38.

28 *Ibid.*

29 *Ibid.*

30 *Ibid.,* p. 21.

31 *Robbins v. CBC,* [1958] Qué. S.C. 152.

32 R.S.Q. 1977, c. C-12.

few laws dealing with visual invasions of privacy other than what's noted in the provincial Privacy Acts. The common law is also spotty in this area.

Generally, you can take anybody's picture without their permission. The crucial question, though, is whether you need consent to publish it. For day-to-day news reporting, where a person is photographed as part of an event or in a public place, consent isn't needed. And despite popular misconceptions, it's no different with children or minors and the consent of the parent is not needed.

But what about crowd shots or the use of "file" photographs to illustrate or accompany a story? Again, there's no need to worry about getting consent for news or feature stories. However, journalists should watch for potentially defamatory comments accompanying any pictures which might unintentionally suggest that an identifiable or particular person in the picture is the subject of the remark.

If someone isn't in a public place when photographed (for example, at home or on a private beach) and is not aware the picture has been taken, there's a chance they could sue for invasion of privacy in one of the five provinces with privacy laws or maybe try a common law action in the other provinces. In this case, consent might be needed.

If a photograph is for commercial purposes (that is, for promotional or financial gain or profit), a signed consent from the subject of the photograph is usually required. For example, a company placing a person's picture on a product is basically stating that the person endorses the product. If he or she didn't authorize it, an action for *misappropriation of personality* can be pursued in the civil courts.

The subject of a commercial photo should also be told of the end use of a photo. For example, a model who signs a general release or consent may not expect her picture to end up on the cover of a book about hookers. The commercial use of a person's likeness can also be defamatory if their profession is one which requires members to steer away from commercialism (for example, an amateur athlete endorsing a product). News and current affairs programs are not generally considered commercial programs.

Finally, it's worth remembering that the Criminal Code sections about interceptions of private communications don't apply to film or video recordings without sound.[33] This may seem unusual to point out, but it may someday be useful to know. An American network used this "twist" in the law to its advantage several years ago. While investigating a story in a state where privacy laws barred secret audio recordings, the journalists effectively used a hidden camera (without sound recording) to record the subject of the story completing a shady deal on a street corner. The pictures said it all and no law was violated.

---

33 Note 14, above.

Trespass to Land

Laws against trespass are forms of ensuring the privacy and enjoyment of a person's property.[34] Generally, a trespass is any invasion of another individual's property.[35]

Trespass to land can be an offence under provincial trespass laws or a distantly related Criminal Code offence. It may also be the subject of a private civil action even though the intrusion may have caused no damage at all. A person commits a trespass by simply going onto property without express or implied permission,[36] causing something to go onto the property[37] or, after being allowed to enter, refusing to leave when asked.[38]

But there are limits to what is considered a trespass. For example, flying over property (for example, to take pictures) doesn't constitute trespass, unless it's so low that it interferes with the ordinary use of the land.[39]

Journalists often encounter situations in which someone orders them to leave a property or warns them not to enter. The law has recognized that anyone who is in lawful possession of the property can enforce his rights against an act of trespass. That person doesn't have to own the property. He or she only has to be in possession of it.[40] For example, someone leasing a property can protect it against trespass. In addition, any agent, representative or employee of that person can order you off the property.[41]

There's no general criminal offence of trespassing. But, as mentioned above, the section 173 of the Criminal Code deals with the act of trespassing at night. The Criminal Code also gives a person in possession of property the right to defend it. Section 41(1) states:

---

34 The oft-quoted phrase in the famous *Semayne's Case* (1604), 77 E.R. 194 at 195 (K.B.), is: "That the house of every one is to him as his castle and fortress. . . ."

35 *Entick v. Carrington* (1765), 95 E.R. 807.

36 *Ashby v. White* (1703), 87 E.R. 810 at 816 (H.L.).

37 *Campbell v. Reid* (1857), 14 U.C.R. 305 (C.A.).

38 In *R. v. Peters* (1970), 16 D.L.R. (3d) 143 (Ont. C.A.), a boycott picket was ordered out of a shopping mall by management. The Supreme Court of Canada upheld the decision without comment in (1971), 17 D.L.R. (3d) 128 (S.C.C.).

39 See the English case of *Bernstein of Leigh (Baron) v. Skyview and General Ltd.*, [1977] 3 W.L.R. 136 (Q.B.). Here, an English nobleman was unsuccessful in proving a case of trespass after a plane flew over his land and took a picture of his estate.

Although flying over property may not be an act of trespass in Britain or Canada, it may be considered an invasion of privacy in provinces with Privacy Acts.

40 *Gidney v. Bates* (1862), 10 N.B.R. 395 (S.C.). In *Penney v. Gosse* (1974), 6 Nfld. & P.E.I.R. 344 at 346 (Nfld. S.C.), the court said anyone has "possession" who displays a clear and exclusive intention to possess the property.

41 *Ibid.*

> Every one who is in peaceable possession of a dwelling-house or real property, and every one lawfully assisting him or acting under his authority, is justified in using force to prevent any person from trespassing on the dwelling-house or real property, or to remove a trespasser therefrom, if he uses no more force than is necessary.

If the trespasser resists any attempt to prevent his entry or to remove him, he commits an assault "without justification or provocation."[42]

Provincial Trespass Laws

Most provinces have some form of legislation offering protection against trespass. The penalties range from fines to, in some provinces, the right to seize motor vehicles used in the trespass. Only Saskatchewan and the two territories have no Trespass Act. These jurisdictions rely on the common law.

Charges of trespass are usually prosecuted as summary conviction offences in provincial courts. However, an individual may also sue for trespass in the civil courts for damages suffered by the intrusion. As mentioned at the beginning of this section, the damage may be nominal or non-existent, but the action will still succeed.[43]

In addition, if the trespass is done in an arrogant or high-handed manner, the courts may award punitive damages to the plaintiff.[44] The motive of the trespasser is irrelevant at common law and it's no defence to say you made a mistake.[45]

As noted above, a person must have express permission to enter the property or there must be an implied invitation to enter (for example, a business which is open to the public). For instance, the pathway leading to a home's door is an implied invitation to walk up to the house (that is, unless signs state otherwise). But once the occupier, owner or agent of either says you must leave, you have no choice and can't stay. A "No Trespassing" sign, a fence or a natural boundary is clear evidence there is no implied invitation to enter a property.

The provincial laws vary from detailed prohibitions to short Acts setting out a basic offence and penalty. Some provinces provide a statutory defence that no trespass will have occurred where the accused has a fair and reasonable supposition that he or she can traverse the property or believed they had title to the land. Most provinces also spell out the requirements for notices prohibiting trespassing. Normally, signs must be

---

42 S. 41(2).

43 *Demers v. Desrosier (No. 2)*, [1929] 2 W.W.R. 241 at 244 (Alta. S.C.).

44 *Townsview Properties ltd. v. Sun Construction and Equipment Co.* (1974), 56 D.L.R. (3d) 330 at 334 (Ont. C.A.).

45 *Turner v. Thorne* (1959), 21 D.L.R. (2d) 29 at 31 (Ont. H.C.).

prominently displayed at normal access points. Some provinces authorize the occupant of land to arrest the trespasser and immediately take the offender to a judge or justice of the peace.

Public vs. Private Property

An oft-asked question is whether there are any special rights of access attached to public property or private property which is open to the general public, such as a shopping mall.

As a rule, private property which is open to the public may regularly allow or even invite public access. But at any time, a lawfully authorized person (for example, shopping mall manager) could exclude everyone or only one individual.[46] Even though members of the general public were invited onto the property, that invitation can be withdrawn at any time by a person with the proper authority.

The same applies to public property. Any lawfully authorized person can order a person out of a government building or even off a public street, if there's a lawful reason. For example, a peace officer or a public officer can require people to stay out of an area if he or she is administering or enforcing the law.

But the courts may start adopting the rationale of some American cases which give the public a broader right of access to public property. A 1986 Federal Court case ruled that Canadians have a constitutional right to engage in political activity or pass out pamphlets to passersby in airports. The judge said expelling the political activists was an infringement of their freedom of expression and said the public corridors of the airport were to be considered extensions of the streets.[47] This decision, however, was overturned on appeal.[48]

At least one other court has recognized that the media have a job to do, despite a clear trespass. In a 1984 case, seven members of the news media were each fined $200 under Ontario's provincial trespass law after they climbed over a fence at Toronto's international airport to investigate an aircrash. A provincial court judge rejected a Crown request for the maximum $1000 fine, saying he was aware of the conflict between the news media trying to serve the public and airport officials maintaining security and safety. In the end, the judge imposed the smaller fine to stress the need to maintain airport security.

---

46 In *Harrison v. Carswell* (1975), [1976] 2 S.C.R. 200, the Supreme Court of Canada upheld the right of a shopping mall manager to order peaceful picketers off the property.

47 *Comité Pour La République du Canada v. The Queen* (1986), 25 D.L.R. (4th) 460 (Fed. T.D.).

48 (1987), 36 D.L.R. (4th) 501 (Fed. C.A.).

How to Handle Trespass Situations

Unless there's some sort of fence, boundary or warning sign, a journalist may wander into any area without immediate concern about trespass laws. However, once someone in authority says the journalist must leave, there is no sense resisting.

If a journalist is caught trespassing by the occupier of the property, it's important to note that he or she isn't required to hand over any of his or her belongings, notes or equipment.

The act of trespassing doesn't entitle the occupier to confiscate or destroy any tapes, notes or film. If you have film or video tape, even a policeman or other law enforcement officer cannot seize it, unless you're being arrested. If you are arrested, the film or tape may be seized to prove the trespass happened. But the police don't have the authority to destroy any belongings.

A PRIVACY CHECKLIST

1. In Canada, there is no general right to be protected against invasion of privacy. However, there are laws protecting privacy in select areas.
2. The Criminal Code prohibits the unlawful interception of private communications (such as by wiretap). However, a person can secretly record or listen to a private communication, using an electronic or acoustical device, if he or she has the consent of anyone who is the sender or intended receiver of the communication.
3. The Criminal Code indirectly protects privacy rights with sections concerning trespassing at night, intimidation, harassing telephone calls and disrupting a religious service.
4. Other federal laws affecting broadcasters guard against the unauthorized use of radiocommunications and recordings of telephone conversations.
5. British Columbia, Saskatchewan, Manitoba and Newfoundland have enacted Privacy Acts which create a civil remedy for invasions of privacy. Québec's Civil Code can also be used to assert privacy rights.
6. Generally, photographs of people in public places or at public events can be used freely in news reports. However, when using crowd or "generic" shots, journalists should guard against associating pictures of identifiable individuals with potentially defamatory remarks.
7. Trespassing is a form of invasion of privacy and can be pursued in civil or criminal courts. A fence, boundary or sign can serve as sufficient warning to potential trespassers. Even without a warning sign, once a person is told to leave private property he or she must go. Even in public places, such as government offices or shopping malls, someone in authority can order individuals to leave the property.

6

Contempt

Any conduct which tends to undermine or bring into disrepute the authority and administration of justice or interfere with someone's right to a fair hearing before a court or other quasi-judicial body could be considered an act of contempt. Common examples of contempt are disobeying a court order, disrupting a hearing or publishing damaging information about someone involved in a trial.

For journalists, committing a serious act of contempt can have staggering consequences. In theory, the penalty could be a jail term and/ or a large fine. In practice, however, the courts are quite lenient and often ignore minor acts that don't pose a significant threat to a proceeding.

Therein lies much of the difficulty with contempt. One judge may ignore a contemptuous act, while another may punish it. There are no hard and fast rules. Still, the "danger zones," particularly for journalists, are well defined. In recent years, there have been suggestions that contempt of court is an obsolete concept and should be done away with. Some argue, for instance, that scathing criticisms of judges or the justice system shouldn't be punishable acts of contempt.[1] However, contempt in all its forms has been around for hundreds of years for good reason. In many ways, it not only protects the individual, but also society.

Many of us rely on the news media for fair and objective reports of events, such as court proceedings. Writing a story and selecting facts or comments involves judgment calls on the part of the journalist. As a result, the courts are particularly mindful of the interpretation journalists give to happenings in the judicial system. But the power to punish for contempt shouldn't be seen to constitute a censor of the news or an instrument to stifle public discussion. The primary concern of any judge is that the trial he or she presides over is fair and recognized by all to be fair. It's this concern which often takes precedence over the rights of the news media and even the public, and invokes the use of contempt powers.

THE CATEGORIES OF CONTEMPT

Historically, a court's ability to punish contempt comes from an inherent power to preserve the sanctity of proceedings, to protect the reputation of the justice system and to ensure the public abides by the law. Over the years, statutes have even extended limited contempt powers to quasi-judicial bodies, such as public inquiries. However, not all bodies

---

1 In *R. v. Kopyto* (1987), 3 W.C.B. (2d) 263 (Ont. C.A.), where a lawyer was cited for contempt for saying the courts and police were stuck together "like Krazy Glue," a majority of the appeal judges held that the common law offence of contempt by "scandalizing the court" is an unjustified infringement of the guarantee of freedom of expression in section 2(b) of the Canadian Charter of Rights and Freedoms [Part I of the Constitution Act, 1982, being Schedule B of the Canada Act 1982 (U.K.), 1982, c. 11 (hereinafter, Charter)]. However, the judges went on to say the problem lies in the loose definition of scandalizing the court and to suggest the offence would be valid if it were re-defined to require the Crown to prove there was an intention to bring justice into disrepute and to prove there was a serious or real risk to the administration of justice. The remaining appeal judge dissented, saying the offence is not an infringement of the Charter right.

can punish all types of contempt.

At its simplest level, there are two basic categories of contempt. First, there is contempt *in facie curiae* (that is, "in the face of the court"). Such direct acts of contempt include witnesses refusing to testify, someone throwing an egg at the presiding official or creating a disturbance in the courtroom. The second type of contempt is the indirect act which happens outside the actual proceeding, or contempt *ex facie curiae* (that is, "away from the face of the court"). This is also called "constructive" contempt and journalists are most prone to this category. For example, it's constructive contempt when a journalist publishes stories that unfairly attack the court or adversely affect a hearing.

Not all tribunals can punish both types of contempt. As a rule, most quasi-judicial tribunals and inquiries only have authority to deal with direct acts of contempt. Courts, as a rule, can punish both types. However, as will be discussed below, there are exceptions.

There are two other further categories of contempt. *Civil contempt* is the disobedience of a civil court judgment or civil court order. A common act of civil contempt is the failure of an ex-spouse to make child support payments. Technically speaking, a civil contempt is not considered to be an affront against the court, but rather an offence against the person to whom the dishonoured obligation or duty was owed under the civil judgment or order.

The other category is *criminal contempt*, which is any behaviour which prejudices or unjustly insults the administration of justice in either civil or criminal proceedings. This is an offence against society and the justice system. For example, it's an act of criminal contempt for a news reporter to refer to an accused as a "mafia boss" before or during a trial.

In practice, the distinctions between criminal and civil contempt have become blurred. For example, the willful and blatant disobedience of a civil court order, such as an injunction prohibiting broadcast of a defamatory news report, is considered just as much an act of criminal contempt as it is civil contempt.[2]

WHAT JOURNALISTIC BEHAVIOUR OFFENDS A COURT?

Within the class of criminal contempt are two sub-categories that often involve journalists:[3]

---

2 This was discussed in *Poje v. A.G. British Columbia*, [1953] 1 S.C.R. 516. More recently, in *R. v. Clement*, [1981] 6 W.W.R. 735 (S.C.C.), the Supreme Court of Canada held that while an offence may constitute an act of civil contempt (such as disobeying a civil court order), it can still be prosecuted in a criminal proceeding under section 127(1) of the Criminal Code.

3 Actually, courts have traditionally set out three categories of contempt: i) Scandalizing the court itself, ii) Abusing the parties to an action, and iii) Prejudicing mankind against persons in a trial. These divisions go back hundreds of years, as can be seen in the early English case of *Re Read and Huggonson* (1742), 2 Atk. 469. For the purposes of this

Scandalizing the Court

Scandalizing the court involves any accusation of bias, perverted justice or improper motives on the part of the court or the judge in the discharge of a judicial duty.[4] It's irrelevant there was no intention to scandalize the court.[5]

This doesn't mean courts, judges or decisions can't be criticized. Still, any criticism of the administration of justice or judges must be within the limits of fair comment[6] or based on provable facts. A reporter can comment on a judgment or a judge's public actions, but shouldn't accuse a judge of improper motives or personally attack the judge without cause or proof.[7] Believe it or not, most judges would encourage reporters to point out errors in fact or law in their judgments.[8]

Generally, the courts have looked for some form of malice in the attack on the court. Evidence of malice can be found in an improper motive, ill will on the part of the journalist or carelessness or negligence in the publication of the statement.[9]

---

chapter, though, the latter two categories will be dealt with under the heading of "prejudicing someone's right to a fair trial."

4 The case of *R. v. Murphy*, [1969] 4 C.C.C. 147 at 153 (N.B. C.A.), is a good example of why the offence of scandalizing the court will likely always be around. The accused, a writer for a student newspaper, testified at a trial and then wrote a story that lambasted the hearing. He called the court (at pp. 148-149) "a mockery of justice," accused the judge of bias and stated that New Brunswick courts "are simply the instruments of the corporate elite."

Some other examples: In *Re A.G. Canada and Alexander* (1976), 27 C.C.C. (2d) 387 (N.W.T. S.C.), a cartoon accused a judge of a double standard of justice, while the accompanying editorial alleged a cover-up by the judge in the trial of some public figures. In *Re Borowski* (1971), 3 C.C.C. (2d) 402 at 405 (Man. Q.B.), a Manitoba cabinet minister criticized a magistrate in an interview by saying "if that bastard hears the case I will see to it that he is defrocked and debarred." He also said the magistrate's court decision "is so blatant and so improperly judicially improper that I can only come to one conclusion, that it was based on political considerations, rather than on the facts. . . ." The court had no trouble finding this an obvious case of scandalizing the court.

5 See *R. v. Larose et al.*, [1965] Que. S.C. 318. However, in most cases, the motive or intention may be considered in sentencing.

6 See *Re Nicol*, [1954] 3 D.L.R. 690 at 699 (B.C. S.C.). In *R. v. Fotheringham*, [1970] 4 C.C.C. 126 (B.C. S.C.), the famed columnist criticized a coroner's inquest for its lack of sympathy toward the mother of a dead child. The coroner asked the court to punish Fotheringham for his comments. The court found that, although there were inaccuracies in the story, the comments were not made in bad faith or maliciously; all efforts had been made to ascertain the facts and that justice had not actually been impaired.

7 For example, in *R. v. Glanzer* (1963), 38 D.L.R. (2d) 402 (Ont. H.C.), judges were accused of perverting justice and breaching their oaths.

8 *R. v. Wilkinson; Re Brown* (1877), 41 U.C.Q.B. 47 (Ont. C.A.). The court said a judge's errors can be pointed out, but said it is improper to impute base motives to a judge, attack his honesty or say he is a liar. It might be added that the truth is a legitimate defence in circumstances such as this.

9 See *R. v. Murphy*, note 4, above.

Prejudicing Someone's Right to a Fair Trial

While section 2(b) of the Charter recognizes "freedom of the press and other media of communication," no court or judge can allow what has been called "trial by newspaper" or "trial by press."[10] The principle is finely embodied in this quotation from an Ontario case:[11]

> . . . no judge or juror should be embarrassed in arriving at his decision in a judicial proceeding by an expression of opinion on the case by any one unless he is before the Court as a party to the proceedings . . . . [N]either a judge nor a juror should be put in such a position that if he decides in accordance with the opinion expressed or the popular sentiment existing it can be said he has been influenced thereby, nor should he be put in a position where it can be said that he is antagonistic to any opinion or popular sentiment.

The court can also use its contempt powers to discourage the news media from "abusing the parties" involved in a court action. For example, if a journalist writes an editorial chastising someone for taking an issue to court such that it might discourage them from pursuing the issue or prejudices that person in the minds of prospective jurors, it could be considered an act of contempt. The court will look carefully at any comments that defame a party to an action. The key question is whether the abuse poses a serious and real threat to the trial.[12]

WHEN DOES THE DANGER OF CONTEMPT ARISE?

The courts have a great reluctance to seriously impair the freedoms of the press and the power to punish for contempt of court is exercised very carefully.[13] Generally speaking, the danger of contempt for journalists begins from the time the courts become involved in a case and lasts until it ends. However, the degree of danger varies depending on what stage a proceeding is in and the circumstances involved.

Because judges have such broad and far-reaching powers to punish contempt, a judge will take many things into account when considering whether a hearing has been prejudiced by a news report. The judge will try to determine exactly what effect the report will tend to have on the hearing or the reputation of the court itself. The judge will also consider

---

10 In *R. v. Vairo and CFCF Inc.* (1982), 4 C.C.C. (3d) 274 (Que. S.C.), a man awaiting trial was referred to in a news report as a "mobster" and member of the "French Mafia." The court reiterated that a fair trial is paramount to the freedom of the press.

11 *R. v. Thomas; Re Globe Printing Co.*, [1952] O.R. 22 at 24-25 (H.C.).

12 In *Staples v. Issacs and Harris*, [1939] 2 W.W.R. 540 (B.C. S.C.), the court said every instance of defamation of a person about to be tried is not necessarily a contempt of court, but it could be found contemptuous if the accused can prove the trial has been prejudiced. In this case, an editorial was found not to be an act of contempt because the trial was still several months away.

13 In *Brown v. Murphy*, [1972] 6 W.W.R. 331 at 338 (B.C. S.C.), the court cautioned that the power to punish for contempt should be used sparingly and only in obvious cases that can be proven beyond reasonable doubt.

whether there is any sensationalism in the reporting, the story's prominence in the newspaper or broadcast, the story lead or headline, whether the trial has a jury and the timing of the article in relation to the trial.[14]

It's also no secret that the type of judicial proceeding involved has a bearing on whether an act of contempt is punished. Juries can be more easily swayed by public opinion than judges sitting alone[15] or hearings in the courts of appeal.[16] Although courts of appeal and judges sitting alone are less likely to be influenced by contemptuous publications, a journalist must still exercise care in discussing the merits of a case. If an editorial comment urges a court to reach a certain result, the "professional judge" will probably disregard the opinion. But the judge might be concerned that the public will think he has been influenced by the editorial comment.[17]

The moment a court becomes involved in a criminal or civil proceeding, the matter is said to be *sub judice*, or "in the course of trial," and reports about pending or current court cases must be carefully considered. That said, it may be difficult at times to tell when a court is "formally" involved. For example, in criminal proceedings, the court could be said to be formally involved in a case once it issues a search warrant during an investigation.

As a rule, however, the danger of contempt begins for journalists with any of the following: arrest without a warrant, issue of a warrant for arrest, issue of a summons to appear or service of an indictment or other document (for example, laying an information) specifying the charge. The danger of contempt in a criminal proceeding does not end until the appeal or appeal period has ended.

It's been held in some English cases that a matter can be *sub judice* even before criminal charges are laid and, particularly, when someone knows that a criminal charge is "imminent." For example, in England, the publication of the criminal record of a person who had barricaded himself into a house and was holding hostages was found to have prejudiced a later trial.[18] Canadian

---

14 Some of these same points were mentioned in *Zehr v. McIssac* (1982), 39 O.R. (2d) 237 at 246 (Ont. H.C.).

15 In *Re Depoe and Lamport* (1967), 66 D.L.R. (2d) 46 (Ont. H.C.), the court held a trial by judge alone was unlikely to be affected by a story urging a guilty verdict. But in *R. v. McInroy, Re Whiteside* (1915), 26 D.L.R. 615 at 619-620 (Alta. S.C.), the court held the mere fact a trial is by judge alone does not give a journalist the licence to publish any comment.

16 In *A.G. v. Times Newspapers Ltd.*, [1973] 3 All E.R. 54 at 65 (H.L.), the court said, "it is scarcely possible to imagine a case where comment could influence judges in the Court of Appeal."

17 In *R. v. Carocchia* (1973), 15 C.C.C. (2d) 175 at 184 (Qué. C.A.), the judge was concerned that the publication of a police press release could have been construed as influencing a non-jury criminal trial.

18 This happened in *R. v. Beaverbrook Newspapers*, [1962] N.I. 15 (Q.B.D.). In another English

courts haven't taken a position on this issue to date.

However, even in Canada there are times when there could be a danger of prejudicing a trial before charges are laid. It's a wise and common practice when publishing a police photograph or sketch of a suspect to simply state the suspect is being sought for questioning about the crime, instead of declaring him or her as the villain.[19] Quite apart from the contempt risk, there's a danger of being sued for defamation if an innocent person is shown.

For civil proceedings, the danger of contempt begins with the service of the writ or notice required by law to start an action and the danger doesn't end until the appeal or appeal period has passed.

The courts have held it is irrelevant that there was no intention to commit an act of contempt, but the judge can take the lack of motive into consideration when sentencing.[20] It's also irrelevant that a journalist didn't make the contemptuous statement. The court will punish the publisher of the statement as quickly as the author or originator.

Since contempt of court can happen unintentionally, the courts are generally quite tolerant of comments in the news media. In fact, minor acts of contempt in our daily news media often go unpunished because judges feel no real harm has been done.

It's important to note that an act of contempt won't be ignored simply because the statement is made outside the court's physical jurisdiction. The courts know no boundaries, particularly when a contemptuous act or comment attacks the court itself. In one case, a Federal minister in Ottawa made a contemptuous statement about a Québec court.[21] Although the Québec judge cited other grounds for his decision, he held that the court had the authority to go anywhere to punish contemptuous remarks

---

case, *R. v. Savundranayagan*, [1968] 3 All E.R. 439 at 441 (C.A.), the court strenuously objected to a television interview with the accused that was conducted just prior to the accused's arrest with full knowledge that charges were imminent. But the court felt it was not necessary to punish the contempt because the interview was done well before the trial and there was such strong evidence against the accused that no jury could have reasonably found the accused not guilty.

19 In the English case of *R. v. Daily Mirror; Ex parte Smith*, [1927] 1 K.B. 845, a photograph of a suspect was published before charges were laid. The aggravating factor was that the identification of the perpetrator was in question. The court felt the publication of the photograph could influence witnesses in the trial.

20 See *A.G. Manitoba v. Winnipeg Free Press Co.*, [1965] 4 C.C.C. 260 at 263 (Man. Q.B.). In *R. v. Murphy*, note 4 above, the court held it must consider only the effect of the contemptuous act and not what was intended. The court in *R. v. Aster (No. 1)* (1980), 57 C.C.C. (2d) 450 (Qué. S.C.), held that intention is irrelevant and it considered an indifferent attitude or disregard of the consequences of a contemptuous act to be malicious. But in *Re Depoe*, note 15, above, the court decided the remarks in question did not actually interfere with the trial and, in dismissing the contempt charge, took into consideration that the accused clearly did not intend to influence the trial.

21 *Re Ouellet; R. v. Atlantic Sugar Refiners Co.* (1976), 34 C.R.N.S. 234 at 243-245 (Qué. S.C.).

attacking the court itself, regardless of the court's jurisdiction.

The courts have also punished contemptuous publications affecting a trial which, while not originating in the court's jurisdiction, are distributed in the area of the trial. The concern is that prospective jurors will hear or read details about the trial that are inadmissible or which prejudice the accused's right to a fair hearing. In these cases, the court will punish anyone they can find who is responsible for the contemptuous publication.[22]

WHAT IS THE PUNISHMENT FOR CONTEMPT?

For now, no law or statute sets out a maximum penalty for the general offence of contempt of court.[23] In theory, the potential penalties are unlimited and at the complete discretion of the judge. The historical and inherent nature of the courts' power to punish contempt is at the root of the reluctance to set limits. For example, even the Criminal Code pays homage to the court's common law power to punish contempt. Section 9 of the Code states that no one shall be convicted of a criminal offence under the common law, but specifically goes on to add that this isn't intended to interfere with the court's power to punish contempt.

Anyone, including a judge or a lawyer for one of the parties, can bring an act of contempt to the attention of the court and start proceedings. The method by which allegations of contempt are handled is unlike any normal court process. It's called a "summary process" and you won't find its procedure set out in the Code. The general aim of the summary process is to bring the offender before the court as quickly as possible to avoid further damage to the justice system. But some people believe it borders on an infringement of our fundamental rights to a fair trial.

For serious contempts, for instance, a judge can immediately cite an offender for contempt and punish him on the spot. In most cases, however, a judge will issue a summons to the offender directing him or her to later appear in court to "show cause" as to why he or she shouldn't be punished. At the show cause hearing, the accused's lawyer can make out a case and call any evidence to support the accused's actions.

There have been several attempts in recent years to challenge the summary process and have it declared an unconstitutional infringement on our Charter rights. Courts have rejected the argument, noting that a

---

22 In *R. v. Bryan*, [1954] O.R. 255 (H.C.), a U.S. magazine was distributed in a small Ontario town containing lurid details of a murder case about to tried by a jury there. The court found the distribution of the magazine to be a serious contempt of court and issued a large fine against the local distributor of the magazine; the judge also warned he would fine the U.S. company and its editors if they ever came into his jurisdiction.

23 There are some sections of the Criminal Code which do set out penalties for certain direct acts of contempt such as the refusal of a witness in a preliminary hearing to testify (that is, s. 545). Also see s. 708 which makes it an offence for a witness required to attend a court hearing to fail to show up or remain at the hearing.

person tried in a summary process does have a right to a lawyer, to offer an explanation and to call witnesses. However, the courts have also held that it doesn't include the right to a jury. Though there's no theoretical limit to a contempt penalty and Charter section 11(f) guarantees jury trials for offences involving jail terms of five years or more, courts have rejected the position that jury trials are a right. The courts have noted that an act of contempt rarely draws a penalty of more than a few months and therefore doesn't come under the Charter section.[24]

If convicted, the judge may simply want ample expressions of remorse and apologies in court. Jail sentences are usually only handed out to witnesses who refuse to testify. Journalists are rarely sentenced to jail for their contempts and more often are fined. In some cases, though, this can be expensive. Judges have ordered news media outlets to pay the costs of a mistrial caused by the contempt.

WHO CAN PUNISH FOR CONTEMPT?

As mentioned above, the ability to punish contempt is available to bodies other than courts. But not all official or government bodies that hold hearings have such a power. As a matter of public policy, the law has restricted the power to punish for contempt to bodies which act judicially, making decisions which affect an individual's rights.

The power is usually only found in judicial, quasi-judicial and legislative bodies. For example, Parliament, legislative assemblies and public tribunals (such as utilities boards and public inquiries) have a statutory and even inherent right to maintain the sanctity and order of their proceedings.[25]

But the scope of this power isn't the same for all bodies (including the courts). Although they all can deal with direct acts of contempt (such as expelling a raucous spectator), only a limited few can punish both direct and indirect acts of contempt, such as those committed by journalists.

From a jurisdictional standpoint, our judicial system is divided into federally-appointed Superior Courts and provincially-appointed Inferior Courts. Only the Superior Courts (for example, Supreme Courts, Courts of Queen's Bench, Appeal Courts and Federal Courts) have the broad common law power to punish direct and indirect acts of contempt. The Inferior Courts (for instance, Justices of the Peace, Magistrate's Courts

---

24 In *R. v. Cohn* (1984), 15 C.C.C. (3d) 150 (Ont. C.A.), the Ontario Court of Appeal dealt with whether a witness who refused to testify has a right to a jury trial in a contempt proceeding under section 11(f) of the Charter. The court held the actual penalties are never beyond two years and the Charter right cannot be invoked. See also *R. v. Kopyto*, note 1, above. Similar themes can be found in *A.G. Qué. v. Laurendeau* (1982), 3 C.C.C. (3d) 250 (Qué. S.C.) and *Re Layne and R.* (1984), 14 C.C.C. (3d) 149 (Alta. C.A.).

25 See, for example, *Hamilton v. Anderson* (1858), 6 W.R. 737 (H.L.).

and Provincial Courts) are limited to punishing acts of direct contempt.[26]

This doesn't mean a journalist is free to say what he or she wants about proceedings in Inferior Courts. As the common law has evolved, Superior Courts can punish acts of constructive contempt directed against Inferior Courts. All a judge in an Inferior Court has to do is ask a higher, Superior Court to punish the contempt on his or her behalf. So, all courts, one way or another, can punish a direct or constructive act of contempt.

Some public tribunals have the same powers as courts to punish acts of direct contempt, such as the refusal of a witness to testify. Often it's set out in the legislation that created the body. Examples are compensation boards, coroners' inquests, utilities boards, labour boards, police commissions, municipal boards and public inquiries.

But it's rare for legislation creating any administrative tribunal or inquiry, even a federally-appointed one, to allow for punishment of constructive contempt. However, there is precedent for tribunals, such as coroners' inquests, to also ask a Superior Court to punish someone who is seriously undermining the authority of the proceedings.[27] It is, however, very rarely done.

Although bodies other than courts may punish a contemptor, the vast majority of cases involve the courts. For that reason, much of this chapter will concern itself with court-related incidents. Keep in mind, though, the same rules can be applied to quasi-judicial tribunals.

THE DANGER ZONES

While any act of contempt is to be avoided if possible, the fact is the degree of danger for journalists varies depending on the stage of a judicial proceeding — that is, before, during and after a trial. The closer a civil or criminal action gets to trial, particularly when a jury is involved, the more cautious a journalist must be in his or her reports. When a case moves on to the appeal courts, the danger of contempt often lessens and freer comments can usually be published.

Many common problem areas in contempt fall within one of these three periods and being aware of the danger zones can help prevent a nasty encounter with a judge.

---

26 In *CBC v. Cordeau*, [1979] 2 S.C.R. 618, a police commission inquiry into organized crime activity in Québec issued a direct order that the identity of a witness (that is, a police informer) not be published. The CBC published a picture of the witness and the commission tried to cite the network for contempt. The Supreme Court of Canada held that the statute which gave the commission the power to punish contempt applied only to acts of direct contempt, such as the refusal of a witness to testify. The court also made it clear the provinces have no constitutional power to grant a body the ability to punish acts of indirect contempt.

27 *Ibid.*, at 638. Also, see the case of *Levesque v. Rawley*, [1955] Qué. S.C. 36.

1. Before Trial

In the period preceding a trial, the standard of care required by a journalist will increase as the trial date gets closer. Conversely, the further away the trial is the less chance exists of influencing potential jurors. That said, there are still areas to be wary of.

Civil Pleadings

Pleadings are the statements of claim and defence from the parties to an action and include the affidavits, transcripts and other documents filed with the court before trial. Publishing pleadings, though they are court documents, invokes no special protection from defamation or contempt actions, unless they have already been read out or entered as evidence in open court.

One province, Alberta, imposes a partial-restriction on the publication of proceedings. In that province, a journalist can only publish the names and addresses of the parties and their solicitors and a concise statement of the "nature" of the claim (for example, "the party is seeking damages for personal injuries caused by negligent operation of a car"). The restriction is in effect until the end of the trial in Alberta or, if there is no trial, the proper determination of the proceedings.[28]

Although there's no similar statutory restriction in the other provinces, at least one case has held that media reports of information in pleadings can be contemptuous. In that case, a newspaper published the amount of damages the plaintiff was seeking while the jury trial was going on. The court dismissed the jury and ordered a new trial. The judge said pleadings contain allegations which ought not to be known by a jury. He noted that pleadings are invariably wrong and, when they reach trial, are often greatly changed.[29]

The publication of the amount of damages sought in civil jury actions is a danger in all provinces, except Québec, where there are no civil jury trials. The judge and jury should be free to come to their own decision about how much should be awarded. Often the claims are over-estimated by each side and must be substantiated in court. It's generally accepted, however, that a journalist may publish the amount of damages sought when an action is first filed. But the current thought is that the amount shouldn't be published once the date of trial is set, so as to avoid influencing jurors.

Contemptuous Statements in Other Proceedings

Sometimes, a statement may be made in a court proceeding which could prejudice the outcome of a pending trial or one which is being heard in another court. While defamation legislation protects journalists giving

---

28 See the Judicature Act, R.S.A. 1980, c. J-1, s. 30(2).

29 *Bielek v. Ristimaki*, unreported, June 21, 1979 (Ont.). Judgment reprinted in Stuart Robertson, *Courts and The Media* (Toronto: Butterworths, 1981), at App. A, pp. 287-292.

fair and accurate reports of judicial proceedings, that protection extends only as far as the publication of defamatory matter. The publication of any contemptuous statements or information isn't protected by any privilege, even when the contemptuous remark is made in another court.[30]

Describing Criminal Charges

Care must be taken in describing the charges the accused is facing.[31] It may be considered a contempt of court if an accused is reported as being charged with a more serious offence than the one actually laid. The proper title of the charge should be used where possible.

Evidence from Coroners' Inquests and Public Inquiries

An inquest or inquiry is not a formal "court" and can't determine criminal or civil guilt or innocence in most cases. The coroner and his jury or the inquiry board usually can only report on the facts or circumstances surrounding an event and make recommendations. The evidence garnered from the inquest (particularly admissions or confessions) shouldn't be re-published once criminal charges are laid or a civil jury trial begins. Evidence which was admissible at the inquest or inquiry could be inadmissible at trial.[32]

Hypothetical Cases

Sometimes, a journalist will want to discuss an issue that's before the courts and, hoping to avoid punishment for contempt, will pose the issue in the frame of a hypothetical case with no mention of the actual case trial. You should be very careful in discussing hypotheticals, particularly those relevant to high-profile cases. Any discussion favouring one

---

30 *Ibid.*, Robertson, p. 22.

31 In practice, the courts are quite tolerant of innocent errors in describing charges. In *R. v. Hamilton Spectator; R. v. Globe and Mail*, [1966] 4 C.C.C. 375 (Ont. C.A.), the court took into consideration that an honest mistake was made in reporting a charge and that it was made without negligence by a journalist who was acting in good faith. In the case of *Westman v. Southam Inc.* (1984), 34 Alta. L.R. (2d) 189 (Q.B.), the use of the word "rape" in a news report instead of "sexual assault", was held not to be an act of contempt and did not endanger a fair trial. But in the English case of *R. v. Hutchison; Ex parte McMahon*, [1936] 2 All E.R. 1514, the court found that a newspaper photo of an man being arrested during a parade and captioned with the words "Attempt on the King's life" implied that the man would be charged with attempted murder. In actual fact, he was only charged with unlawful possession of a firearm, and the newspaper was found to be in contempt.

32 In *Re Editions MacLean and Fulford; R. v. Dion* (1965), 46 C.R. 185 (Qué. C.A.), an article was published three weeks prior to a trial that reviewed the accused's life and his own testimony at a coroner's inquest, along with confessions he had made. The court said, at 185, that this was contempt and it did not matter that the inquest's testimony had been well publicized.

side over the other or calling for a certain verdict, could be considered contemptuous depending on the timing and whether the discussion could incite public opinion one way or the other on issues involved in the case.

Interviewing Witnesses Prior to Trial

The courts frown on amateur investigations of crimes by reporters. But a factual presentation of the events can still be produced. In a contempt case where the court said it was done properly, the journalist had interviews with witnesses explaining what had happened without any expression of opinion by the reporter or any statement of facts other than those gleaned from the witnesses. At no point was the accused mentioned as actually being the perpetrator. The court said if the witnesses' statements were proved wrong in court, the accused could always sue for defamation.[33]

The danger in interviewing witnesses is that inadmissible evidence will be published and the fairness of the trial will be destroyed. The timing of this type of report is crucial. The closer it is to trial, the more dangerous it becomes to interview witnesses.

Other Court Proceedings Involving the Accused

When an accused is facing more than one criminal trial over a period of time or is involved in a concurrent civil proceeding, a journalist shouldn't link the proceedings together in a single story. It could prejudice either of the individuals' trials, particularly any proceeding with a jury.[34]

---

33 See *Fortin v. Moscarella et al.* (1957), 11 D.L.R. (2d) 606 (B.C. S.C.). English courts have also condemned independent inquiries by the press. See *R. v. Evening Standard* (1924), 40 T.L.R. 833 (D.C.), where a newspaper systematically investigated a crime while the accused awaited trial and published play-by-play accounts of their investigation, including stories about the accused's troubled life and the suffering of his wife. The court held the newspaper would have no way of knowing what facts could become an issue at trial and was committing a serious contempt by conducting the amateur investigation.

34 In *R. v. Bochner and Ruby*, [1944] 3 D.L.R. 788 (Ont. H.C.), a newspaper published an account of concurrent divorce proceedings involving the accused just before his criminal trial. The article said he was a "notorious local underworld character" and brought up his criminal record. The court said it did not matter that the newspaper was unaware that the other trial was about to take place, since the paper knew charges were pending. In *Bédard v. Laviolette* (1981), 22 C.R. (3d) 230 (C.S. Qué.), the annual report of a professional society related that an action was being taken against one of its members and mentioned the result of another trial involving the member. Although technically an act of contempt, the court refused to punish the society because the offended party waited too long before bringing the complaint to court. In the English case of *R. v. Astor*

Police Comments

The police are no different from other individuals. Once charges have been laid, any comments from them suggesting guilt, admissions or confessions could endanger a fair trial, until presented as evidence at the trial in open court.[35]

Previous Criminal Record of Accused and Witnesses

As soon as criminal charges are laid (or perhaps even known to be imminent), a journalist should not make reference to the criminal record of an accused or a potential witness until it is brought out in open court.[36]

One common scenario that troubles many news rooms is what to do about someone who is arrested while on parole. Do you mention the person's record? Generally, it's permissible to mention this fact at the time of the arrest. But as the trial date approaches, the person's record shouldn't be mentioned until it's brought out in court. A less problematic situation involves the prison inmate who murders a prison guard or commits some other crime while escaping custody. When he or she is brought to trial,

---

(1913), 30 T.L.R. 10 (D.C.), a story reported the outcome of a case and then went on to tell of another upcoming case against the man, something the court felt might prejudice the second trial.

35 In *R. v. Carocchia* (1973), 15 C.C.C. (2d) 175 (Qué. C.A.), a police press release that announced an arrest implied the accused was guilty by listing other charges which police said were yet to come and which said the accused was linked to organized crime. The police were found to be in contempt. In *Steiner v. Toronto Star Ltd.* (1955), 1 D.L.R. (2d) 297 (Ont. H.C.), a journalist wrote a story before a trial in which a senior police officer was quoted as saying the accused had admitted his guilt. In the story, the reporter tried to cushion the impact of the police comment, by saying the accused had "allegedly" confessed. Still, the court cited the reporter and editors of the newspaper for contempt. It said the use of words like "alleged" are of no protection since the story would lead any reasonable person to assume the accused was guilty.

36 While publishing the criminal record of someone involved in a trial is usually a cut and dried case of contempt, in *Re Murphy and Southam Press Ltd.* (1972), 9 C.C.C. (2d) 330 at 335 (B.C. S.C.), the court held that the publication of the criminal record of a witness prior to his appearance was not contempt because the community knew of his record, the jury would have been told anyway and the trial was still some time off. But the court recognized that, generally, the criminal record of an accused or witness should not be brought out before it is tendered as evidence in the trial.

Also, see *R. v. CHEK TV Ltd.* (1987), 33 C.C.C. (3d) 24 (B.C. C.A.), where a broadcaster was found to have committed the offence of contempt after broadcasting information about the accused's criminal background during a trial. This case is notable because the court found it was contemptuous despite the fact the criminal record of the accused was placed before the jury. The appeal court felt that while there was no real risk of an unfair trial of the accused, the broadcast interfered with the justice process and created a perception of unfairness.

it is certain the jury will be told the accused was in jail.

As an aside, consider whether it's really important to mention a criminal record. For example, is it fair to report that a person arrested for a petty theft is on parole from a murder charge?

In civil cases, any references to the criminal record of an individual involved in the trial should also be avoided, particularly in jury trials, unless the record is brought out in open court.

Reporting Foreign Proceedings or Arrests

Sometimes, a person will be arrested in another country for a crime committed in Canada or there may be proceedings, such as an extradition hearing, to bring the person back to this country for trial. A reporter should be careful of sensational details reported in another country's media or from foreign authorities, particularly suggestions of confessions or admissions. Evidence that's admissible in another country may not be here.

Re-Trials

A court may order a new trial of a matter or a mistrial could be declared which would require a re-trial. When a jury is involved in the second trial, a journalist must not make any reference to the fact that it is a re-trial or publish any details of the evidence, representations made or results of the original trial until after the second trial.[37]

Stories Relevant to a Case, Sidebars

The publication of features or related stories that are linked to a case being tried could theoretically be contemptuous. For instance, it could be considered an act of contempt to publish a story on the increasing use of illegal drugs by children alongside a court story about a jury trial of a major drug dealer. This doesn't mean to say that everyday news and features can't be published. A journalist should simply be careful in the line-up or placement of stories so that nobody could reasonably think the related story is a comment on the case before the courts.

Visuals

In some trials, the ability of witnesses to identify the accused is an

---

37 For example, the June 24, 1982 edition of the *Whitehorse Star* reports that the staff was fined a total of $1000 for writing stories noting that a current trial was a retrial and comparing evidence from the first trial with testimony in the second.

important factor in proving the charge. A newspaper or broadcasting outlet could endanger a trial if it publishes a picture of the accused when identification is an issue.[38]

As mentioned above, police-supplied photographs for manhunts can also endanger a fair trial if the suspect is portrayed as the perpetrator. It's advisable to say the suspect is "sought for assistance" or "questioning" by the authorities in connection with a certain crime.

2. During Trial

The standard of care which a journalist must exercise before a trial begins is raised to a higher level as the court action goes to trial.[39] While the court may allow a contemptuous act or publication to go unpunished in the period leading to the trial, any contempt of court during the trial is less likely to escape judicial notice. Most of the "danger" areas listed above continue to apply during the trial. These problem areas can be added:

Audio and Visual Recording in Courts

Generally, all courts in Canada prohibit journalists from making visual or audio recordings of courtroom proceedings. In most jurisdictions, individual judges have the discretion to allow cameras or tape recorders into the courtroom, but it's rarely allowed. In some jurisdictions, journalists aren't even allowed to take pictures or record an interview with someone in the hallways of the court building. The policy regarding photographs can usually be obtained through the court clerk. Any violations of the rule will be punished as acts of direct contempt of court.

In Ontario, a statute has established a formal offence for unauthorized audio and visual recordings in court buildings. Section 146 of Ontario's Courts of Justice Act, 1984 prohibits the taking of photographs, motion pictures, audio recordings or other records capable of producing visual or aural representations by electronic means or otherwise:[40]

    (i) at a court hearing,

---

38 See the English case of *R. v. Daily Mirror; Ex parte Smith*, [1927] 1 K.B. 845, where a newspaper published a photograph of a suspect arrested in a case where the identification of the culprit was in question. The photo appeared in the paper on the same morning as witnesses viewed a police line-up. Although the court was told no witnesses saw the picture and identification turned out not to be a crucial issue in the trial, the court still held it was an act of contempt because the newspaper knew at the time of publication that identification could have been an issue.

39 This was noted in *A.G. Manitoba v. Winnipeg Free Press Co. Ltd.*, [1965] 4 C.C.C. 260 at 262 (Man. Q.B.).

40 S.O. 1984, c. 11, ss. 146(1), (3).

    (ii) of any person entering or leaving the room in which a court hearing is to be or has been convened, or

    (iii) of any person in the building in which a court hearing is to be or has been convened where there is reasonable ground for believing that the person is there for the purpose of attending or leaving the hearing. . . .

Recently, the Ontario law was amended to permit reporters to use audio tape recorders to assist them in taking notes. The prohibition still exists on using the recordings in a broadcast.

The only other exceptions in Ontario are where the judge presiding at a court hearing authorizes the pictures or audio recording for the presentation of evidence or where solicitors use a tape recorder as a substitute for their notes or if the pictures or audio recordings are in connection with ceremonial proceedings with the permission of the judge or in connection with educational or instructive purposes with the permission of the judge, parties and witnesses.

The Ontario legislation also states that this law doesn't prohibit someone from "unobtrusively" making handwritten notes or sketches at a court hearing.[41]

In 1986, the CBC unsuccessfully challenged a charge laid under this section after an Ottawa camera operator shot pictures of a participant in a trial within the precincts of the courtroom. The court held the section wasn't an infringement on the freedom of the press.

End of the Trial

Determining when a proceeding has ended may seem obvious, but it has been a troublesome point sometimes. In criminal cases, the trial doesn't formally end until the judge passes sentence. Therefore, comments urging a particular punishment before the sentence is actually handed down could be viewed as attempts to influence the judge's decision.[42] In a civil court action the jury verdict usually signals the end of a trial, but a trial by judge alone will not be over until the decision is handed down.

Further to this, though, the courts have decided that a factual presentation of evidence brought out in court and published before the sentence is pronounced, with no comment on the jury verdict or what sentence should be rendered, would be unlikely to have any effect on a judge's final decision.[43]

---

41 *Ibid.*, s. 146(2).

42 In *R. v. Panrucker* (1961), 34 W.W.R. 94 (B.C. Mag. Ct.), the accused pleaded guilty to his crime and a public outcry erupted prior to sentencing, prompting the judge to warn the public about comments urging a particular sentence.

43 Such was the case in *Bellitti v. CBC* (1973), 44 D.L.R. (3d) 407 (Ont. H.C.).

Evidence and Exhibits

Any document or evidence which is read into open court or filed as an exhibit can be included as a part of a report of judicial proceedings. Evidence which has been declared to be inadmissible or is not entered as evidence in open court has no place in a report of judicial proceedings and may be contemptuous.[44] Of course, the documents and their contents can be published after the trial and appeal period has passed, but won't be privileged in a defamation action.

Headlines or Captions

A headline or caption is considered a part of the story and can be contemptuous, even if the main story itself is fair and accurate.[45] While this is a problem area that can crop up at any time, it most frequently happens when the news media report on an on-going trial or proceeding. For example, headlines shouldn't state opinions as facts. A headline blaring "Jones is a thief" is more likely to influence a juror or the public than one saying "Jones is a thief, Crown tells court."

In-Camera *Proceedings*

Sometimes, a court will hold a hearing *in camera* or behind closed doors, perhaps to allow a nervous witness to testify. Occasionally, reporters are allowed to stay in the court while the general public is ordered out or transcripts of the *in camera* hearing may be made available after the trial. The common law rule is that a fair and accurate report in good faith and without malice, of proceedings held *in camera* isn't contemptuous, unless the court has ordered a ban on publication during the trial.[46] One province makes specific reference to this. In Ontario, the Courts of Justice Act, 1984 expressly states that the publication of proceedings held *in camera* isn't a contempt of court, unless the judge has issued a ban on publication.[47]

However, a word of caution. Since the *in camera* proceedings aren't held in public, any news reports of the closed door hearings aren't privileged under defamation law.

---

44 In *R. v. Dorion* (1953), 10 W.W.R. 379 (Man. Q.B.), a newspaper was found to be in contempt for publishing the contents of a document declared inadmissible during a *voir dire* conducted while the jury was excluded from the courtroom.

45 See *Hatfield v. Healy* (1911), 3 Alta. L.R. 327 (S.C.).

46 The seminal case is *Scott v. Scott*, [1913] A.C. 417 (H.L.), in which the House of Lords said a hearing can be held *in camera* under the common law only in proceedings involving wards, the mentally-disordered, trade secrets or where holding the trial in public would defeat the whole object of the proceeding. Statutes may set out some other exceptions to the "open court" rule.

47 S. 145(3).

Interviews with Lawyers

The professional conduct codes for lawyers caution them about speaking to the media and "touting" themselves.[48] However, the strict rules of the past are loosening and most law societies accept lawyers as media representatives. Still, many lawyers are careful not to appear unprofessional.

For example, the professional conduct code for New Brunswick lawyers is very detailed in outlining how to deal with the media. It says any comments by lawyers during a trial shall be of a non-confidential nature with factual information based on public records or evidence already given at a public hearing or in open court. The character or credibility of a party to the action or a witness shouldn't be commented upon. No statements should be made by lawyers as to the evidence yet to be offered or any other matter which could interfere with a fair trial.[49]

Despite the suggested guidelines for lawyers, it's important to note that law societies don't have a right to order lawyers not to contact the news media,[50] and it's not contemptuous to ask a lawyer to repeat outside the courtroom what he or she said to the court.[51] Judges may, however, be disturbed by lawyers who first tell the news media what they plan to tell the court before the judge actually gets to hear it. But usually it's the lawyer who is cited for contempt, and not the journalist, in these cases.

Interviews with Judges

Judges aren't untouchables, but they do see their position in society as one which should remain impartial. One federal Department of Justice book gives judges the following advice. A judge shouldn't comment on current trials or actions that are before the courts or issues which have a potential to become court actions. The same goes for comments on new

---

48 For example, see the *Code of Professional Conduct*, Canadian Bar Association.

49 See the New Brunswick *Code of Professional Conduct*, Part F.

50 In *Re Klein and L.S.U.C.; Re Dvorak and L.S.U.C.* (1985), 50 O.R. (2d) 118 (H.C.), the court said a lawyer has a moral, civic and professional duty to speak out in the news media where he sees an injustice. A Law Society of Upper Canada rule restricting contact with the media infringed the Charter's guarantee of freedom of expression and impaired the right of the lawyer, client and public to disseminate information. The court said the public has a constitutional right to know about pending cases and the legal profession.

51 See *A.G. Ontario v. CBC* (1977), 39 C.C.C. (2d) 182 (Ont. H.C.). In this case, a motion was made to stay proceedings and during the subsequent break, a lawyer repeated the essence of the motion before a television camera. The court found no contempt because the lawyer was only repeating what was already said in court. A similar decision was made in *Residential Tenancy Commission v. Toronto Apartment Buildings Co. Ltd.* (1983), 42 C.P.C. 314 (Ont. Div. Ct.).

legislation or judicial decisions. If a judge feels there's a lack of public understanding of some part of the proceedings before him, he should make his comments in open court from the bench.[52]

Multiple Accused

A reporter should be careful when several people are charged in connection with the same incident and tried separately. After the first trial and sentencing, comment may have to be restricted if any of the accused are still awaiting trial or sentence. For example, the judge may think an editorial comment about the lax sentence given to one of the accused is urging him to impose a different sentence on the remaining accused.[53]

3. During the Appeal Period or Appeal

The court's jurisdiction over a matter doesn't end with the completion of the trial. Each province has legislated the time period within which appeals must be launched (usually 30 to 45 days).

In theory, comments on trial decisions during the appeal period or appeal must be guarded and shouldn't be seen as an attempt to influence the court of appeal's decision. In practice, though, courts are quite generous in allowing fair comment upon cases during the appeal period and even during the hearing of appeals.

But what is fair comment is somewhat unpredictable. For example, in 1985, an Alberta judge issued an injunction banning the showing in that province of a CBC drama loosely based on the controversial case of James Keegstra, a schoolteacher accused of inciting racial hatred. The court felt the "thinly-guised characterization of . . . Keegstra"[54] would endanger an upcoming appeal of his conviction and a possible re-trial. However, on appeal, this injunction was ordered set aside.[55] The court noted that the appeal had yet to be held when the program was to air and that a re-trial would have been at least two years away. The court held there were no grounds for the injunction because the risk to the accused was neither real nor substantial.

There are really only two common areas of concern after a trial.

---

52 The Hon. J.O. Wilson, *A Book for Judges*, (Ottawa: Ministry of Supply and Services, Government of Canada, 1980), pp. 57-59.
53 This was the case in *R. v. Thomas; Re Globe Printing Co.*, [1952] O.R. 22 (H.C.).
54 Quoted in *CBC v. Keegstra* (1986), 35 D.L.R. (4th) 76 at 77 (Alta. C.A.).
55 *CBC v. Keegstra* (1986), 35 D.L.R. (4th) 76 (Alta. C.A.).

Criticism of Decisions

During the appeal period or before the appeal, a journalist may wish to comment upon a decision. As mentioned, in theory, the courts dislike any attempt to influence the decision-making process. But public interest usually demands discussion of the decision before the appeal is heard and appeal courts are unlikely to be influenced by such discussion.[56]

The courts seem to be very tolerant and an important question to the court in cases of serious contempt, is whether there's a real chance of a re-trial of the matter which could be prejudiced by the report or comment.

Criticism of Juries

Any statements criticising jury members after the trial should be within the limits of fair comment. For instance, to brand jury members as "murderers," as one newspaper did, is beyond fair comment.[57] The personal virtues of the jury members shouldn't be attacked and a journalist may also run the risk of being sued for defamation. The court may be concerned that an unjustly critical comment on the jury could impede justice by making other people reluctant to serve on juries.

CONTEMPT AND LEGISLATIVE BODIES

As mentioned at the beginning of this chapter, provincial legislatures and Parliament are among the recognized bodies which can punish acts of contempt. Contempt proceedings involving a legislative body are rare, but do occur from time to time. Aside from the possibility of being accused of contempt by a legislature or Parliament, many journalists may not be aware that contempt proceedings can also arise from reporting contemptuous remarks made in a government proceeding.

Contempt of a Legislative Body

Legislative bodies have the power to punish both direct and indirect

---

56 In *Re O'Brien; R. v. Howland* (1889), 16 S.C.R. 197, an article criticized a judgment on purely legal grounds. Despite inaccurate views on the law, it was not considered contemptuous because the comments were made in good faith and without malice. In *R. v. Thomas Sophonow* (1983), 2 C.R.D. 525.70-03 (Man. C.A.), the court held that a lawyer's request for a ban on the publication of "extra-judicial comment" until after the appeal is heard, is neither practical nor appropriate. The court said it would amount to censorship and a denial of a public hearing.

57 *Re Nichol*, note 6, above.

acts of contempt affecting their members or proceedings, and ultimately can send an offender to jail. The only legislative bodies which do not have a full power to punish for contempt are those in the Northwest Territories and the Yukon.[58]

Any act which a court of law would find objectionable, a legislative body could too. Among the examples of punishable acts against legislative forums are false or perverted reports of debates, bribery of members of the legislative body, defamatory reflections on members or the body itself, and the wide-sweeping category of "disrespect to that which is entitled to legal regard."[59]

Parliament and the provincial legislatures rarely exercise this power against the news media. But it has happened, and recently legislative bodies have shown they are at least willing to consider punishing contemptuous acts. For instance, on April 1, 1985 several news outlets published the recommendations of a confidential House of Commons committee report the day before it was to be tabled. A ban had been placed on the publication of the report by the committee and a Member of Parliament accused the news outlets of contempt. The Speaker of the House agreed it was a serious issue and undertook to decide whether the news outlets should be made to appear before a special Commons committee. He decided the news outlets were not in contempt, despite the publication ban on the report, and cited three Parliamentary precedents in support of the decision. The Speaker held that before an alleged act of contempt can be acted upon there must be some proof that the privileges of M.P.s were violated. In this case, there was no such proof.

Although punishment for legislative contempt is rare, the power has been exercised on occasion. In most of the cases, the reporter or publisher of the contemptuous statement was called before the House to answer the charges and then made to apologize.

Reporting Contemptuous Remarks Made in the House

Members of our legislative bodies have always taken comfort in the fact that they can speak freely and even maliciously about any person or subject that concerns them without fear of a defamation action while they conduct their business in the House, Senate or legislative assemblies

---

58 See Joseph Maingot, *Parliamentary Privilege in Canada* (Toronto: Butterworths, 1982), p. 175. Another excellent book on this topic is *Beauchesne's Parliamentary Rules and Forms*, 5th ed., (Toronto: Carswell, 1978).

59 *Ibid., Parliamentary Privilege*, p. 196. For a list of examples of legislative contempt, see the Legislative Assembly Act of any province. For instance, in Alberta, see R.S.A. 1980, c. L-10.

of the country. And journalists take comfort in the knowledge that they too enjoy a privilege for fair and accurate reports of even the most defamatory remarks made during these public debates.

The members debating in our legislative bodies enjoy this absolute privilege even when their remarks might constitute an act of contempt against the courts. But the court's respect of such privilege stops at the doors of the proceedings. While reports of defamatory matter arising from the proceedings of a legislative forum are privileged, a journalist is not protected from being punished for contempt for reporting a contemptuous remark made in the House, Senate or a legislative assembly.[60]

This includes statements in reports, papers, votes or proceedings of the legislature or Parliament. The "proceedings" include those in connection with the formal transaction of business or those necessarily incidental to a House or committee.[61] Therefore, if a Member of Parliament scandalizes the court or says something which could endanger the fair trial of an individual, the publication of the statement by reporters is not protected from contempt proceedings. It should be noted that case examples of the use of this type of power by the courts are rare.

POSSIBLE REVISIONS TO CONTEMPT LAW

There are very few references to contempt in statutory law. As noted, section 9 of the Criminal Code preserves the common law right of courts to punish acts of contempt, but the Code sets out no maximum penalty and doesn't specify the procedure to be followed by a court to punish contempt.

This is seen by some people as too broad a power and in some cases not a specific enough power. In 1984, the Liberal government of the time proposed some major changes to the Criminal Code, including provisions dealing with contempt of court. The amendments would have done away with the common law power to punish acts of indirect contempt and replaced it with a formal offence of criminal contempt and an offence of scandalizing the court.

The proposed amendments would have preserved the common law power of the courts to punish acts of civil contempt (for example, disobedience of a civil court order), as well as the power to maintain order in the judicial proceedings (such as expelling a raucous spectator). Since the proposed amendments died on the order paper in 1984, little more has been said by the federal government. A new Criminal Code is in the

---

60 *Re Clark and A.G. Canada* (1977), 81 D.L.R. (3d) 33 at 56 (Ont. H.C.).
61 *Ibid.*, pp. 69-72.

works and chances are no further movement will be seen in the area of contempt until that work is completed.

It is interesting, however, to note what might have been changed. In 1984, the following criminal contempt offence would have been created:

131.11 (1) Every one who knowingly makes or causes to be made any publication that creates a substantial risk that the course of justice in any particular civil or criminal judicial proceeding pending at the time of the publication will be seriously impeded or prejudiced is guilty of

(a) an indictable offence and is liable for imprisonment for a term not exceeding two years; or
(b) an offence punishable on summary conviction.

If placed into law, the offence would have been prosecuted under the summary conviction process, thus enabling Inferior Courts to deal with the offence. This is a departure from the common law rule that only Superior Courts can punish indirect contempt. The phrase "knowingly makes or causes to be made" would require the Crown to prove that the contempt was intentional, which is another change from the common law which holds a person responsible for unintentional interferences with justice.

The proposed reforms also would have formally set out when the *sub judice* rule would be in effect. For criminal proceedings, the rule would begin upon arrest, issuance of a summons, warrant or appearance notice, or a preferred indictment. It would end after all appeals. For civil proceedings, it would be in effect from the time of setting down a trial date until the end of the appeal process. Note the change from the present approach for civil proceedings. Under the proposed law, the *sub judice* rule would not have begun until a date had been set down for trial. The proposed reforms also would have specified that when a new trial is ordered after an appeal, the *sub judice* rule would continue to apply up until the new trial was properly adjudicated and new appeals were over.

The reform also would have set out two defences:

(i) the publication was a fair and accurate report of a legal proceeding held in public and was published contemporaneously and in good faith.
(ii) the publication was made as or as a part of a discussion in good faith of public affairs or other matters of general public interest and the risk of impediment or prejudice was merely incidental to the discussion.

The defences would not have applied where a court order banned publication of evidence or information, nor would the defences apply to publications of the details of *in camera* proceedings.

The proposed amendments also would have created a specific offence for scandalizing the courts:

Every one who, without lawful justification or excuse, willfully makes or causes to be made any publication of a false, scandalous or scurrilous statement calculated to bring into disrepute a court or judge in his official capacity is guilty of

    (a) an indictable offence and is liable to imprisonment for a term not exceeding two years; or

    (b) an offence punishable on summary conviction.

The statutory defence would be that the publication was for the public benefit at the time of the publication and that the statement was true. There is no telling when these amendments or ones like them could be re-introduced. Journalists should keep an eye open for any new enactments concerning the Criminal Code and contempt.

SOME FINAL THOUGHTS

The law which has developed around "contempt of court" might be seen by some as judicial muzzling of the news media. But that is not the intention. The principles of contempt law seek to preserve the reputation of justice and guarantee a fair trial for the accused. On the other hand, the courts recognize the value of a free press and often quote this phrase from the 18th-century philosopher Jeremy Bentham:

Where there is no publicity, there is no justice.

A CONTEMPT CHECKLIST

1. Any conduct which tends to undermine or bring into disrepute the authority and administration of justice or interfere with someone's right to a fair hearing before a court or other quasi-judicial body could be considered an act of contempt. Common examples of contempt are disobeying a court order, disrupting a hearing or publishing damaging information about someone involved in a trial.

2. Two types of contempt most often involve journalists: *scandalizing the court* and *prejudicing someone's right to a fair trial.* Scandalizing the court involves any accusation of bias, perverted justice or improper motives on the part of the court or the judge in the discharge of a judicial duty. The second type of contempt is concerned with what is usually called "trial by press."

3. Generally speaking, the danger of contempt for journalists begins from the time the courts become involved in a case and lasts until it ends. However, the degree of danger varies depending on what stage a proceeding is in and the circumstances involved.

4. Among the potentially contemptuous areas for journalists to watch are:

civil pleadings, describing criminal charges, interviewing potential witnesses, reporting criminal records of accused or witnesses, police comments, multiple accused, foreign court proceedings and criticizing judges or juries.

5. Legislative bodies can also punish journalists for contemptuous stories. However, it is rare. It should also be noted that journalists are not protected from being cited for contempt if they report contemptuous remarks made in a legislative proceeding.

7

Publication Bans and Restraining Orders

The courts have always recognized and supported the news media's role in reporting what goes on in the halls of justice. However, there are times when the ends of justice may be better served by restricting the flow of information to the public.

To do this the courts have at their disposal a variety of inherent common law and statutory powers to temporarily, and sometimes permanently, restrain the publication of certain information arising from hearings.

For example, the publication of evidence tendered in a preliminary hearing is usually banned until after a full trial can be held before an unbiased jury. Or a judge may want to ban the publication of a rape victim's name to lessen her trauma.

Publication bans have also been incorporated into some federal and provincial laws. For example, a provincial family law act may prohibit the publication of the names of children and family members involved in a child abuse hearing.

Although most publication bans have a laudable goal, sometimes the public interest in the information is greater. The news media have been fairly successful in recent years in challenging unreasonable restrictions on the public's right to know. For instance, some statutory restraints have been declared invalid because they're absolute, allowing a judge no discretion in issuing the ban. However, this area of the law is unsettled and many more court challenges lie ahead.

RESTRAINTS ON PUBLICATION IN CRIMINAL PROCEEDINGS

The present Criminal Code was designed to govern society a hundred years ago and contains many outdated ideas and laws.[1] For example, most of the sections applicable to journalists pre-date electronic media and only mention newspapers. As well, many sections restricting activities of the news media are poorly-worded. For a few sections, no charges have been laid in recent memory and, in the near future, it's likely some will be wiped off the books.

Most of the Code's restraints on publication reflect the common law. However, it's clear that judges can still use their inherent discretionary powers to issue bans or court orders in the interests of justice.

This section looks at the interaction of both Code provisions and the inherent powers of courts in the various stages of criminal proceedings.

Common Law Bans on Publishing Names of Accused

The common law indicates that a judge has the discretion to ban the publication of evidence, names of witnesses and crime victims, and even the fact that a court proceeding is happening. However, the common law also suggests there must be extenuating circumstances for such an order, such as concern over a threat to a witness' life or the possibility of compromising the fairness of another trial.

In the vast majority of cases, these are temporary bans. But the courts do appear to also have a common law authority to permanently ban the publication of certain information, usually the names of witnesses, children or victims.

However, with very few exceptions, courts have agreed that a judge shouldn't ban the publication of the name of the accused.[2] This is in keeping

---

1 R.S.C. 1985, c. C-46.

2 In *R. v. Several Unnamed Persons (Orillia Opera House)* (1983), 44 O.R. (2d) 81 (H.C.), the court rejected a request to ban the publication of names of individuals charged with gross indecency and tossed out the argument that pre-trial publicity about the accused would

with the principle of an open justice system. The only cases where such a ban does tend to be ordered is in sexual assault trials where the accused is related to the victim or closely associated with the victim (such as a school teacher). The concern here would be identifying the victims by virtue of naming the accused.

Bail Hearings

Section 517 gives a justice the authority during a bail hearing to ban the publication of evidence where a prosecutor or the accused intends to "show cause" as to whether the accused should be detained until further proceedings. If the request for the ban comes from the accused, the justice is obliged to grant the request. A request from the prosecutor may or may not be granted at the justice's discretion.

If the ban is ordered, a journalist can't report on the evidence taken, the information given, the representations made and the reasons for the decision or conditions of bail. The ban is in effect until the accused is discharged after a preliminary hearing or the accused is committed to trial and the trial has ended. This doesn't mean a journalist can't report the accused's name, the charges, the fact that a bail hearing is being held

---

prejudice a fair trial and the presumption of innocence. In *R. v. Robinson* (1983), 5 C.C.C. (3d) 230 (Ont. H.C.), a man accused of murder asked for a court order banning the publication of his name prior to trial also on the basis that pre-trial publicity could prejudice his hearing. The court refused the order and rejected the argument that he was being denied the right to be presumed innocent. In *Re R. and Unnamed Person* (1985), 22 C.C.C. (3d) 284 (Ont. C.A.), a young woman charged with infanticide at the provincial court level applied to a Superior Court for an order to permanently ban the publication of her name to avoid embarrassment to herself and her family, and damage to her employment opportunities. The order was issued by the court, but the Ontario Court of Appeal later held there was no authority to make such an order. The court did note the inherent authority in a Superior Court to lend necessary assistance to an Inferior Court, such as a Provincial Court, but said there was no need for help in this case because there was no problem with the process of the court, only a problem of embarrassment for the accused.

But in *R. v. P.* (1978), 41 C.C.C. (2d) 377 (Ont. H.C.), a judge *did* grant a ban on the publication of the name of a man accused of soliciting. The accused feared for his ill wife and the embarrassment of his children. The court took this into consideration and also noted that because the soliciting charge against the man was a test case, his name wasn't important. It should be noted that when the soliciting charge was appealed, another judge who was asked to continue the ban on publication refused because he felt that while he had the authority, mere embarrassment was not enough justification: *R. v. P.; R. v. DiPaola* (1978), 43 C.C.C. (2d) 197 (Ont. H.C.).

Another exception was made in *R. v. Southam Inc.* (1987), 40 C.C.C. (3d) 218 (Ont. H.C.), where the court held that a trial judge properly issued an order banning publication of the name of the accused. Here, the accused was a schoolteacher accused of gross indecency and sexual assault involving a pupil at the school. The order was issued under s. 486(3), the Code section dealing with sexual assault charges.

and the actual decision as to whether bail is granted.[3]

A judge also cannot ban the publication of information obtained outside the bail hearing. In a 1987 Québec case, the police participated in media interviews after the arrest of several individuals. When the accused later appeared for their bail hearing, the judge issued an order that the media not publish the names of the accused or any of the information they had obtained from the police. Another court quashed the order, saying the judge exceeded his jurisdiction.[4] The court went on to state that the temporary ban in section 517 is a reasonable limit on the press and if the publication of other information by police or the media endangers the fair trial of the accused, the court can always resort to its contempt power.

Preliminary Hearings

Bans on Publishing Evidence

Section 539 allows the accused to request a ban on the publication of evidence heard at the preliminary hearing.[5] The justice is obliged to grant the request and the evidence given cannot be published until the accused has been discharged after a preliminary hearing or the accused has been committed to trial and the trial has ended. If the prosecutor requests the ban, the justice has a discretionary power to order it.

The ban only applies to evidence, so a journalist can still report the non-evidentiary matters, such as that a preliminary hearing is being held and a publication ban has been ordered. It also appears the accused's right to a publication ban can be granted part of the way through the hearing and, moreover, can be withdrawn owing to the accused's own behaviour.[6]

Although the section clearly refers to preliminary hearings, some lawyers have tried unsuccessfully to apply it to collateral pre-trial proceedings, such as a motion to quash a subpoena ordering a witness to attend a preliminary hearing.[7]

---

3 In *Re Forget and R.* (1982), 65 C.C.C. (2d) 373 (Ont. C.A.), the appeal court said the actual decision as to whether to grant bail can be published and the restrictions set out in s. 517 apply only to those things listed (for example, representations made or reasons given).

4 *Re Southam Inc. and R.* (1987), 38 C.C.C. (3d) 74 (Qué. S.C.).

5 In *R. v. Banville* (1983), 3 C.C.C. (3d) 312 (N.B. Q.B.), it was held on appeal from a provincial court's decision that s. 539 is constitutionally valid under the Canadian Charter of Rights and Freedoms, Part 1 of the Constitution Act, 1982, being Schedule B of the Canada Act 1982 (U.K.), 1982, c. 11 (hereinafter, Charter).

6 In *R. v. Harrison* (1984), 14 C.C.C. (3d) 549 (C.S.P.), a ban imposed by the court in the middle of a preliminary hearing was revoked the day after because the accused had conducted a news conference outside the court to discuss the evidence just after the ban was issued, leaving the impression that the court was being manipulated by the accused. The court felt any prejudice to the accused caused by the revocation was his own fault.

7 In *R. v. Stupp* (1982), 2 C.C.C. (3d) 111 at 118 (Ont. H.C.), a Superior Court judge held he had no statutory power under s. 539 to ban publication of the details of a hearing

Bans on Publishing Confessions

Section 542 absolutely prohibits the publication of any admission or confession that is "tendered" (that is, offered) in evidence at a preliminary hearing. For example, the Crown or a police witness at the preliminary hearing may tender evidence that the accused told them he committed the crime or did something that would suggest he committed the crime (for example, showed the police where the body was). Section 542 applies even if there's no ban issued by the judge on the publication of evidence.

On rare occasions, the accused himself will testify at the preliminary hearing and testimony of this kind isn't considered to fall under this section. The prohibition on publishing evidence of confessions continues until the accused is discharged or has been committed to trial and the trial has ended, or the confession is admitted as evidence in an open trial.

In addition, there's a common law rule that once charges are laid, no information should be published which would amount to a confession or admission or directly confirm the guilt of the accused until the evidence is brought out in an open trial.[8]

Restrictions on Details of Search Warrants

A 1985 amendment to the Code made it an offence to publish certain information related to search warrants where charges hadn't been formally laid. Soon after the amendment came into force, it was struck down by a court.[9] While the section is considered to have no legal force, it has not yet been repealed. The government may refashion the section to conform to the court's ruling, so it's included here, at least for reference.

Section 487.2(1) states that anyone who publishes any information with respect to:

(a) the location of the place searched or to be searched, or
(b) the identity of any person who is or appears to occupy or be in possession or control of that place or who is suspected of being involved in any offence in relation to which the warrant was issued,

without the consent of every person referred to in paragraph (b) is, unless a charge has been laid in respect of any offence in relation to which the warrant was issued, guilty of an offence punishable on summary conviction.

Note that only details of executed search warrants which find

---

of a motion brought by a witness to quash a subpoena ordering him to testify to solicitor-client matters.

8 In *Steiner v. Toronto Star Ltd.* (1956), 1 D.L.R. (2d) 297 (Ont. H.C.), a newspaper was found to be in contempt after a reporter spoke with a policeman and then published the statement that a senior police officer "alleged" that the accused had admitted to committing the crime. The publication occurred before the trial began and the court felt the news report would lead any reasonable person to consider the accused guilty. The use of the word "alleged" was held to be of inconsequential value in clearing the contempt.

9 *Canadian Newspapers Co. Ltd. v. A.G. Canada* (1986), 32 D.L.R. (4th) 292 (Ont. H.C.).

something can be published and that a relevant charge has to be laid before the information as to place and identity can be published. If no charge is laid, the amendment stated that the information as to identity and the place searched can only be published with consent of all the parties who were the subject of the search.

Other Pre-Trial Proceedings

The courts must resort to inherent discretionary powers to prohibit the publication of details of any other pre-trial proceedings. For example, one court issued a ban on the publication of evidence on the mental fitness of the accused submitted in a hearing held before the accused was actually arraigned (that is, charges read and plea taken). A newspaper was held in contempt when it disobeyed the order.[10]

In another case, a judge temporarily banned the publication of details of a change of venue proceeding and even that there had been an application for a change of venue, until after the trial was held. The court felt publishing the fact that an accused wanted a trial in another jurisdiction could taint the accused in the mind of prospective jurors.[11]

Trials

Bans on Publishing Names

The courts may use section 486(1) of the Code as an authority to ban the publication of names of witnesses in special circumstances.[12] Normally, this section is only used to exclude the public from hearings "in the interests of justice." But the courts have held it also allows judges to make special orders banning the publication of certain information where the interests of justice will be better served. The special circumstances required to justify this extreme restraint on the news media must be substantial. The order may not be granted if the only concern of the witness

10 In *R. v. Southam Press (Ont.) Ltd.* (1976), 31 C.C.C. (2d) 205 (Ont. C.A.), the appeal court held the story containing a summary of evidence given by experts on the mental fitness of the accused while this ban was in effect, was indeed a contempt of court. The court felt the publication of the experts' statements could prejudice the accused in the minds of prospective jurors.

11 See *Re Southam Inc. and R. (No. 2)* (1982), 70 C.C.C. (2d) 264 (Ont. H.C.), where the court held on an appeal that this ban didn't violate the freedom of the press. The court distinguished this case from the situation in *Forget*, note 3 above, which held that a decision of a judge in a bail hearing can be reported despite a ban on representations made before the judge and the reasons for his decision. The court here held that reporting the fact that a bail decision had been made would not have any effect on the trial of the accused. But it said reporting the fact that a change of venue hearing was held could prejudice the minds of prospective jurors.

12 *R. v. McArthur* (1984), 13 C.C.C. (3d) 152 (Ont. H.C.). The special circumstances in this case involved the risks of repercussions against prison inmates who were testifying in a murder trial against fellow inmates.

is embarrassment, humiliation or even financial loss.[13] The order is likely to be granted where physical safety is at risk or a witness is likely to be put through extreme suffering because of the publicity.

However, it seems that the right of a judge to exclude the public under this Code section can't be used to create a select courtroom audience having no journalists present, and thus preventing the publication of witnesses' names. In 1979, the Manitoba Court of Appeal quashed a trial judge's order under section 486(1) which allowed the general public to stay, but sent a reporter out of the courtroom so he couldn't publish the names of witnesses found in a bawdy-house.[14] The appeal court held this was an abuse of the Code section and was being used to censor the news. The court said the exclusion of any person must be on the basis that their presence is objectionable. In this case, the appeal court said the reporter was only doing his job and wasn't disrupting proceedings.

It would also appear that Superior Courts (with federally-appointed judges) have an inherent power to issue a court order against the publication of names of witnesses or victims without resorting to section 486(1). For example, one court permanently banned the publication of the names of patients who were sexually abused by a doctor who was under investigation by a medical body.[15] The former patient who applied for the ban argued that her professional reputation would be damaged by the publicity. The court held that nothing would be gained by allowing the media to publish names of former patients and noted that the patients had suffered enough.

Bans on Publishing Evidence

In addition to the Code sections, there is another statutory authority for banning the publication of evidence arising during trials. The Canada Evidence Act grants Superior Courts a discretionary power to ban the disclosure of information affecting national security or international relations, confidential cabinet records or anything that shouldn't be disclosed "on the grounds of a specified public interest."[16] The court will consider issuing such a ban only if a specific objection to disclosure is made to the court.

The common law has also permitted courts to issue permanent bans on the publication of other confidential information, such as trade secrets. The rationale is that parties to the action would be discouraged from taking

---

13 *Ibid.*, p. 155.
14 *Re F.P. Publications (Western) Ltd. and R.* (1979), 51 C.C.C. (2d) 110 (Man. C.A.).
15 In *Hirt v. College of Physicians and Surgeons of B.C.* (1985), 60 B.C.L.R. 273 (C.A.).
16 Canada Evidence Act, R.S.C. 1985, c. C-5, ss. 37, 38 and 39.

their dispute to court if the secret were publicized through the hearing.[17]

The Charter's guarantee of freedom of the press may further limit judges' inherent powers to ban publication during trials. In a 1988 Québec case, a Superior Court judge considered a defence counsel request to question a police officer who had worked with a police informant.[18] After a *voir dire*, the judge allowed the request on the condition that the defence not ask any questions that would disclose the informant's identity. While no such questions were asked, the judge also ordered a ban on the publication of the officer's testimony.

The news media asked another court to set the order aside on the basis that it was an unreasonable infringement on freedom of the press.[19] The appeal court judges said there was no justification for the ban since the trial judge had already decided that the identity of the informer wouldn't be disclosed. The court stated that the general rule as to openness of trials should prevail.

Bans Involving Multiple Accused

On rare occasions, the courts have resorted to their inherent powers to temporarily ban the publication of details of trials and even the verdicts in cases where more than one person is accused of crimes arising out of the same incident.[20] There's disagreement in this area, however, and at least one court has refused to ban publication of the details of trials of multiple accused.[21]

---

17 *Scott v. Scott*, [1913] A.C. 417 (H.L.).

18 *R. v. Southam Inc.* (1987), Barrette-Joncas J. (Qué. S.C.).

19 *R. v. Southam Inc.* (1988), 42 C.C.C. (3d) 333 (Qué. C.A.).

20 In *R. v. Dolan* (1983), 2 C.R.D. 525.70-01 (Ont. Co. Ct.), the court placed a temporary ban of a few days on the publication of a guilty plea by a co-accused because it would have tainted the other accused's trial. The court said it was not a serious infringement to delay reporting the evidence, decision or plea until the other case on the same facts is heard. This happens rarely. One of the few cases like this goes back to 1821 (*R. v. Clement* (1821), 4 B. & Ald. 218).

More recently, in *Re Church of Scientology of Toronto v. R. (No. 6)* (1986), 27 C.C.C. (3d) 193 (Ont. H.C.), the court held that a provincial court judge has the power to issue a temporary publication ban on details and result of a proceeding when other co-accused are awaiting a trial or preliminary hearing.

21 In a 1983 British Columbia case involving a group of alleged terrorists known as the Squamish Five, the trial judge considered the scanty case law on this subject and then refused to grant a temporary ban on the publication of details of all the accuseds' trials. The judge felt that an impartial jury could still be found for each trial despite the intense publicity surrounding the case. As it turned out, there was only one trial before the others pleaded guilty.

Restrictions in Sexual Assault Trials

Section 486(3) places this restriction on the publication of the name of the complainant (victim) or a witness under the age of 18 in a sexual assault trial:

> Where an accused is charged with an offence under section 151, 152, 153, 155, or 159, subsection 160(2) or (3), or section 170, 171, 172, 173, 271, 272, 273, 346 or 347, the presiding judge or justice may, on his or her own motion, or shall, on application made by the complainant, by the prosecutor or by a witness under the age of eighteen years, make an order directing that the identity of the complainant or a witness and any information that could disclose the identity of the complainant or witness shall not be published in any document or broadcast in any way.

A 1985 Ontario Court of Appeal decision declared part of a predecessor of this section (which was similarly worded) to be in violation of the freedom of the press guarantee in the Charter.[22] The court held that the portion making it mandatory to ban the publication of the identity of the complainant on the application of the complainant or the prosecutor, is not a reasonable limit on the freedom of the press. However, in 1988, the Supreme Court of Canada overturned the lower appeal court decision and said that although the wording does infringe on freedom of the press, it does so justifiably.[23]

In a sexual assault trial, the introduction of evidence by the accused about the sexual activity of the complainant is limited by section 276. To introduce such evidence, the accused's lawyer must apply to the court for permission to present it. The justice will hold a hearing to determine if the evidence is admissible. Under section 276(4), the public and jury must be excluded from the hearing and this publication restriction is placed on reporters:

> The notice given under subsection (2) and the evidence taken, the information given or the representations made at a hearing referred to in subsection (3) shall not be published in any newspaper or broadcast.

Restrictions in Jury Trials

Bans on Evidence in a Voir Dire

Section 648 prohibits the publication of any evidence or information concerning any portion of the trial at which the jury was not present (that is, a *voir dire*). The section only applies to juries permitted by the court to "separate" (to go home during a long trial, for example). If a jury is

---

22 *Canadian Newspapers Co. Ltd. v. A.G. Canada* (1985), 49 O.R. (2d) 557 (Ont. C.A.).
23 (1988), 43 C.C.C. (3d) 24 (S.C.C.).

sequestered during the trial, this prohibition doesn't apply. However, few juries today are sequestered for the length of a trial.

The prohibition continues only until the jury retires to consider its verdict and then the details of the *voir dire* can be published.

In a 1985 case, a judge tried to permanently ban publication of evidence in a *voir dire*. The *voir dire* had heard wiretap evidence which could be embarrassing to people not involved in the trial. The attempted ban happened when the accused decided to plead guilty and the judge ordered the jury to retire and return a verdict of guilty. The judge then told the news media they couldn't publish the details of the wiretap evidence since it had never been placed before a jury.

The Alberta Court of Appeal held that section 648 doesn't extend past the point where the jury retires to consider its verdict. However, while the court allowed publication of the wiretap, it used its inherent powers to prohibit publication of the names and any facts identifying the people who were taped in the wiretap.[24]

Bans on Jury Deliberations

Section 649 prohibits any member of a jury from ever disclosing information relating to the deliberations of the jury when it was absent from the courtroom. Only details about the jury's deliberations which are disclosed in open court can be published. If a reporter urges a juror to tell what went on in the jury room, the reporter could be charged with aiding in the commission of the offence.

It's possible to interview a member of the jury if you carefully restrict the interview to matters which happened in open court and you don't try to get the juror's comments about jury deliberations. For example, the CBC in 1984, interviewed one of the jurors in a case involving alleged illegal abortions by a well-known doctor. The trial was unique in many ways, but one interesting element was the use of jury selection experts from the United States. The interview with the juror confined itself to what the juror thought about the use of these experts. The interview stayed away from comments about jury deliberations and was consequently not in contravention of the Code section.

It should be noted that in 1984 the federal government of the time proposed several amendments to the Criminal Code, some of which dealt with the reporting of court proceedings involving jurors. Although, the amendments were never enacted, it's very likely that they'll be proposed again soon. At the time, an offence would have been created for intimidating or harassing jurors. Another offence would have prohibited journalists from

---

24 *Toronto Sun Publishing v. A.G. Alta.* (1985), 39 Alta. L.R. (2d) 97 (C.A.).

publishing any information about jury selection or the identities and addresses of jurors during the trial. It also would have prohibited the publication of anything showing a likeness of a juror (for example, a sketch) until after the trial.

Restrictions on Publishing Immoral Details

Indecent Matters

Section 166 prohibits anyone from printing or publishing any indecent matter or indecent medical, surgical or physiological details heard in judicial proceedings, which would tend to injure public morals. The Criminal Code offers no guidelines as to what indecent material would violate the section and nowadays it would be difficult to know where to draw the line in some of the more bizarre court cases heard today. There have been no recorded convictions under this section in Canada.

Divorces

Section 166 also partly-restricts the publication of details of judicial proceedings for dissolution of marriage, nullity of marriage, judicial separation or restitution of conjugal rights. Only the following details can be published by the media:

    (i) the names, addresses and occupations of the parties and witnesses,

   (ii) a concise statement of the charges, defences and countercharges in support of which evidence has been given,

  (iii) submissions on a point of law arising in the course of the proceedings, and the decision of the court in connection therewith, and

  (iv) the summing up of the judge, the finding of the jury, the judgment of the court and the observations that are made by the judge in giving judgment.

This section is intended to prevent the publication of embarrassing details of couples' love lives or their marital indiscretions. In practice, there are no recorded charges under this section in recent times. It should also be noted that the ban on the publication of indecent matters is still in effect despite the details permitted for divorces.[25] Alberta's Judicature Act has a similar provision, with a maximum fine of $1000 for a person and up to a year in jail for default on the fine and a fine of up to $5000 for a corporation.[26]

---

25 S. 166.
26 R.S.A. 1980, c. J-1, ss. 30(1) and 31(1).

A 1985 court challenge of this prohibition in Alberta, suggesting it was an infringement on the freedom of the press, was unsuccessful.[27]

Young Offenders

The Young Offenders Act[28] replaces the Criminal Code provisions and the Juvenile Delinquents Act which dealt with the trials of juveniles. The object of the restrictions on reporters in this Act is to protect the identity of a young person who has committed a crime and any other young person involved in the proceedings either as a witness or a victim.[29]

A *young person*, within the definition of the Act, is someone who is or, in the absence of evidence to the contrary, appears to be 12 years of age or more, but under 18 years of age.[30]

Section 38 states:

[N]o person shall publish by any means any report

    (a) of an offence committed or alleged to have been committed by a young person, unless an order has been made under section 16 with respect thereto, or

    (b) of any hearing, adjudication, disposition or appeal concerning a young person who committed or is alleged to have committed an offence

in which the name of the young person, a child or a young person who is a victim of the offence or a child or a young person who appeared as a witness in connection with the offence, or in which any information serving to identify such young person or child, is disclosed.

The reference to section 16 involves the procedure for applications

---

27 The decision in *Edmonton Journal v. A.G. Alta.* (1985), 40 Alta. L.R. (2d) 326 (Q.B.), held that section 30(1) of the Judicature Act was necessary to protect public morals. The court said the section protects the right of families to privacy in such intimate matters. The court held the section is not an infringement on the rights of the press because it allows the publication of some details and isn't a complete ban. The court also held it applies to the electronic media, as well as newspapers.

28 R.S.C. 1985, c. Y-1.

29 This protection existed in the now-repealed Juvenile Delinquents Act as well. In *A.G. Man. v. Radio OB Ltd.* (1976), 70 D.L.R. (3d) 311 (Man. Q.B.), the court found an interviewer for an open-line radio program to have violated s. 12(3) of the Act after the mother of a juvenile delinquent appeared on the program to talk about inadequate facilities for mentally disturbed youths. The interviewer knew there was soon going to be an application to transfer the son to adult court. The court found that several comments in the interview suggested the woman's son was guilty of his crime and, despite the use of a false name by the mother, the well-publicized nature of the case allowed listeners to identify the youth being talked about as the same youth who was the subject of the application for transfer to adult court.

30 S. 2(1).

to transfer the young person to adult or ordinary court. The statutory prohibitions against publishing the identity of young people in both the Young Offenders Act and the now-repealed Juvenile Delinquents Act have been challenged unsuccessfully on several occasions. The prohibition against identifying the young person is felt to be a reasonable limit on the press.[31]

In most situations, a reporter can mention the age and sex of the young offender unless otherwise ordered by the youth court judge. One case further clarified the section recently by determining that section 38's ban on publishing the name of a "young person aggrieved by the offence" does not apply to someone who is dead.[32]

Section 17 also places this restriction on journalists reporting on applications for transferring a youth to adult court:

Where a youth court hears an application for a transfer to ordinary court under section 16, it shall

(a) where the young person is not represented by counsel, or

(b) on application made by or on behalf of the young person or the prosecutor, where the young person is represented by counsel, make an order directing that any information respecting the offence presented at the hearing shall not be published in any newspaper or broadcast before such time as

(c) an order for a transfer is refused or set aside on review and the time for all reviews against the decision has expired or all proceedings in respect of any such review have been completed; or

(d) the trial is ended, if the case is transferred to ordinary court.

The Young Offenders Act only applies to Criminal Code and federal statute offences.[33] It doesn't apply to federal commissions or inquiries involving young people. It also doesn't apply to provincial or municipal offences, but most of the provinces and territories have enacted companion

---

31 This section was unsuccessfully challenged in *Southam Inc. v. R.* (1984), 14 D.L.R. (4th) 683 (Ont. H.C.). After hearing extensive psychological testimony from the defence, the court held the prohibition against publishing the identity of the young offender was a reasonable limit on the press. The Ontario Court of Appeal later affirmed the trial judge's decision ((1986), 25 C.C.C. (3d) 119 (Ont. C.A.); leave to appeal to Supreme Court of Canada refused on May 22, 1986).

A challenge of a similar provision in the Juvenile Delinquents Act was also unsuccessful. The court in *R. v. T.R. (No. 1)* (1984), 10 C.C.C. (3d) 481 (Alta. Q.B.), held the provision is consistent with the Charter and for the better good of the child.

But a similar provision in Ontario's Child Welfare Act, R.S.O. 1980, c. 66, s. 57(4) (Now Child and Family Services Act, S.O. 1984, c. 55), was held to be unconstitutional and an infringement on the freedom of the press in the case of *R. v. M.C.* (1984), 4 C.R.D. 525.70-02 (Ont. Prov. Ct.).

32 *R. v. Les Publications Photo-Police Inc.* (1986), 31 C.C.C. (3d) 93 (Qué. C.A.).

33 See s. 2(1), "offence" of the Act.

legislation similar to the Young Offenders Act to enforce provincially-created offences and the sections banning publication of evidence are usually included.

Under section 46 of the Act, it is also an offence to possess a copy of a youth court or police record relating to an offence alleged to have been committed by a young person, unless the copy has been properly released under the provisions of the Act. It's also an offence under this section for anyone who has been given permission to have a copy of such records, to disclose their contents to anyone else unlawfully.

Appeals and Eternity

Bans on publishing names of individuals or confidential information are generally intended to be for eternity.[34] While appeal courts rarely issue a ban on the publication of their own proceedings, it's within their inherent jurisdiction.[35]

RESTRAINTS ON PUBLICATION IN CIVIL PROCEEDINGS

Publication bans in civil court trials are the same in certain respects as those in criminal trials. For instance, any evidence considered in a *voir dire* cannot be published to a civil jury during the trial.

Due to the structure of our court system, civil trial courts and criminal trial courts are often one and the same. As a result, civil courts have the same inherent powers to ban the publication of the names of witnesses or evidence in exceptional cases.

Statutory bans on publication are less common in the civil sphere (with the exception of family law matters discussed below). One province has legislated publication restrictions on reporting the details of pleadings in civil court proceedings. Alberta's Judicature Act partly-restricts the publication of civil pleadings of lawsuits heard in that province.[36] The restriction is in effect until the end of the trial or, if there's no trial, until

---

34 In *R. v. T.R. (No. 1)* (1984), 10 C.C.C. (3d) 481 (Alta. Q.B.), the appeal court held that the statutory ban on publishing the identity of a juvenile delinquent (now referred to as a young offender) continued at the appeal level and is not an unreasonable infringement of the Charter's guarantee of freedom of the press.

35 See *R. v. Sophonow* (1983), 21 Man. R. (2d) 110 (C.A.), where the Manitoba Court of Appeal refused to issue a ban on the media's discussion of a murder case while it was being appealed to the court. While the judges said they had the authority to issue the ban, they felt it would amount to censorship of the news.

36 R.S.A. 1980, c. J-1, s. 30(2). Pleadings include statements of claim, statements of defence, examinations for discovery, affidavits or any other document. In practice, there appear to have been no charges laid against journalists for many years under this section.

the proper determination of the proceedings within Alberta. The Act only allows the publication of the names and addresses of the parties and their solicitors and a concise statement of the "nature" of the claim (for example, "the party is seeking damages for personal injuries caused by negligent operation of a car"). A court challenge of this provision in 1985 was unsuccessful.[37]

The publication of pleadings in other provinces isn't restricted. However, reporters should note that pleadings can be one-sided, inaccurate in fact and law, and defamatory. Besides the risk of defamation, the publication of pleadings can be contemptuous, particularly when a report close to the start of a trial mentions the amount of damages being sought.

PUBLICATION BANS IN FEDERAL STATUTES

Most offences in federal statutes are prosecuted using Criminal Code procedures in criminal justice courts. Examples are the Food and Drugs Act,[38] the Narcotic Control Act[39] and the Fisheries Act.[40] Unless a law specifically opts out of Code procedures, the same publication ban authority can be exercised, such as the ban on publishing evidence in a preliminary hearing.[41]

PUBLICATION BANS IN PROVINCIAL STATUTES

Coroners

Some provinces have placed statutory restrictions on the publication of details heard in *in camera* coroners' hearings and at least one province has given coroners the authority to ban publication of evidence and the identities of people testifying at the inquiry.

---

37 In *Edmonton Journal v. A.G. Alta.* (1985), 7 C.R.D. 525.70-01 (Alta. Q.B.), the court held that section 30(2) didn't violate the freedom of the press and was enacted to ensure a fair trial without the risk of sensationalized reporting based on the pleadings. The court noted that the ban isn't complete and does allow publication of some details of the claims before trial and complete details of the pleadings after the matter is dealt with.

38 R.S.C. 1985, c. F-27.

39 R.S.C. 1985, c. N-1.

40 R.S.C. 1985, c. F-14.

41 In *Re Global Communications Ltd. and A.G. Can.* (1983), 5 C.C.C. (3d) 346 (Ont. H.C.), a county court judge conducting an extradition hearing under the Immigration Act, 1976 ordered a ban on the publication of evidence and representations at a bail hearing using s. 517(1) of the Criminal Code. On appeal, the Ontario High Court judge said the ban was within the rights of the extradition court which used Criminal Code procedures and it was a reasonable limit because it was temporary and protected the fair hearing of the accused.

For example, in Alberta no one may publish the details of oral testimony of documentary evidence heard *in camera* unless the evidence is contained in a public finding or official report of the proceeding.[42]

The legislation affecting coroners in Québec outlines several restrictions on the news media.[43] The legislation prohibits the publication of: a coroner's photograph of a dead body which is the subject of an inquest without the permission of the coroner; the name, address or any information identifying anyone under 18 years old who is implicated or is a witness in the proceedings; arrest warrants, bail decisions, transcripts of notes or recordings or a copy of the order issuing the publication ban; and photographs, sketches, or recordings of the inquest proceedings.

Where criminal proceedings are started in Québec against someone implicated in the same death as is the subject of the inquest, the law forbids the publication of evidence presented at the inquest until the end of the criminal trial and appeals. A Québec coroner also has the authority to issue a ban on the publication of any information where it is in the public's interest or to protect the right to privacy or the right to a fair hearing. Any violation of the various prohibitions is considered a contempt of court.

In one Ontario case, a court said a coroner had exceeded his authority when he promised a witness that he could testify anonymously.[44] But the court refused to grant a media application to have the witness' name disclosed, primarily because the judges felt it would bring the administration of justice into disrepute to renege on the coroner's promise. One judge noted that freedom of the press was not denied since reporters were still permitted to publish the testimony itself.

Family Law Acts

All the provinces and territories have provisions imposing either automatic or discretionary bans on the publication of the name or identity of people involved in family law matters before the courts, such as child welfare and custody issues, adoptions, proceedings involving children of unmarried parents and family service matters.[45]

---

42 See the Fatality Inquiry Act, R.S.A. 1980, c. F-6, s. 40.6(1); S.A. 1985, c. 26, s. 5.

43 See An Act respecting the determination of causes and circumstances of death, S.Q. 1983, c. 41, ss. 141-148.

44 *Re Canadian Newspaper Co. Ltd. and Isaac* (1988), 48 D.L.R. (4th) 751 (Ont. Div. Ct.).

45 In *R. v. M.C.*, note 31 above, an Ontario court found the ban against identifying children and family in the Child Welfare Act to be an unreasonable limit on the press because it is absolute, instead of discretionary. However, the same provision continues in the Child and Family Services Act, S.O. 1984, c. 55, s. 41(8) and (9), which replaced the old Act. There have been no challenges of the absolute ban in the present Act and a 1988 decision on the rights of the media covering a wardship hearing did not question the validity

The restrictions are generally on the publication of the name or identity of any child witnesses, the child who is the subject of the proceedings, the parents, foster parents, guardian, any member of the family, or any person charged with an offence at the hearing.[46]

Venereal Disease Prevention Acts

Most provinces still have old acts on the books that aim to control the spread of venereal disease. They also may prohibit the publication of the identity of anyone with such a disease or the fact that anyone who was examined for a venereal disease is being treated (even if it is true).[47] In some provinces, it's an offence to publish the details of any *in camera* hearings held under the Act.[48]

Provincial Offences

All the provinces have either adopted the Criminal Code procedure for their Summary Conviction Acts, which enforce provincially-created offences, or as a few provinces have done, they have their own procedure. In either case, a ban on the publication of evidence is usually within the provincial court's authority.[49]

Provincial Young Offenders Acts

Most jurisdictions have adopted special legislation to handle young offenders who violate provincial laws. Most have also adopted provisions similar to the federal legislation in regard to prohibiting the publication

---

of the relevant section. See *Re Children's Aid Society and L.* (1988), 49 D.L.R. (4th) 440 (Ont. U.F.C.).

Some other provinces give a presiding judge a discretionary power to issue a ban. For example, see Nova Scotia's Children's Services Act, S.N.S. 1979, c. 8, s. 59(2) which prohibits the publication of the identity of a child, parent or guardian involved in a child abuse proceeding, unless otherwise ordered by a family court judge.

46 For example, see Ontario's Child and Family Services Act, S.O. 1984, c. 55, s. 41, which automatically prohibits publication of such details.

47 See Prince Edward Island, R.S.P.E.I. 1974, c. V-2, s. 13 [rep. S.P.E.I. 1980, c. 42]; Alberta Public Health Act, S.A. 1984, c. P-27.1, s. 65; Saskatchewan, R.S.S. 1978, c. V-4, s. 21; Newfoundland, R.S.N. 1970, c. 389, ss. 13, 14; amended by S.N. 1981, c. 85, s. 17(2); British Columbia, R.S.B.C. 1979, c. 422, s. 15; and Ontario, R.S.O. 1980, c. 521, ss. 13(1).

48 For example, see Saskatchewan's s. 29, P.E.I.'s s. 12(2) and Newfoundland's s. 13.

49 For example, see Newfoundland's Summary Proceedings Act, S.N. 1979, c. 35, s. 26, in which it states that hearings must be held in public, but that a judge can order a ban on the publication of evidence.

of the identity of an offender or any other young person involved in the offence.[50]

Victim Compensation Boards

Most provinces and both territories allow victims of crime or their families to apply for compensation from a specially created provincial tribunal. The victim compensation boards may have either a discretionary or absolute authority to ban the publication of the name of a victim and evidence given at the hearing.[51]

A PUBLICATION BANS CHECKLIST

1. Courts have a variety of inherent common law and statutory powers to temporarily, and sometimes permanently, ban the publication of information arising from hearings, such as names of victims or witnesses, evidence and even the fact that a proceeding happened.
2. With very few exceptions, a court will not ban the publication of the name of a person accused of an offence.
3. The following Criminal Code sections may be used by a judge during criminal proceedings to issue publication bans:
   • Section 517 (bail hearings)
   • Section 539 (preliminary hearings)
   • Section 542 (absolute ban on publishing confessions during preliminary hearings)
   • Section 486(1) (general authority to ban publication of names)
   • Section 486(3) (ban on publishing names of victims and witnesses under 18 in a sexual assault trial)
   • Section 648 (*voir dire* evidence in jury trials)
   • Section 649 (absolute ban on publishing jury deliberations)
4. Section 38 of the Young Offenders Act bans publication of the identity of a young person who has committed or is alleged to have committed an offence, as well as the publication of the identity of a child or a young person aggrieved by the offence or a child or young person who

---

50 Such provisions can be found in Newfoundland, S.N. 1984, c. 2, s. 20; Prince Edward Island, S.P.E.I. 1985, c. 47, s. 16(1); Alberta, S.A. 1984, c. Y-1, s. 20, amended by S.A. 1987, c. 41, s. 12; British Columbia, S.B.C. 1984, c. 30, s. 4; Nova Scotia, S.N.S. 1985, c. 11, s. 23; Québec, S.Q. 1984, c. 4, s. 56; Northwest Territories, O.N.W.T. 1984, c. 2 (1st), s. 59. Also see Ontario's Provincial Offences Statute Law Amendment Act, S.O. 1983, c. 80, prohibiting the publication of any information which could tend to identify a child charged with a provincial offence who is between 12 and 16 years old.

51 For instance, see legislation in Nova Scotia, Criminal Injuries Compensation Act, S.N.S. 1975, c. 8, s. 16 and the Yukon, R.O.Y.T. 1978, c. C-10.1, s. 15.

appeared as a witness in connection with the offence. Section 17 permits a ban on evidence heard at a hearing to transfer a youth to adult court.

5. Provincial statutes may contain provisions banning the publication of certain information or names of individuals involved in proceedings. Such bans may be found in acts dealing with coroners' inquests, family law matters, provincial offences, venereal disease and victim compensation boards.

8

Gaining Access to Public Hearings
and Meetings

There is a general, but unwritten, presumption in law that the public should have access to meetings or hearings of official bodies which act on behalf of the public and deal with matters of public interest. But that's just a presumption, and there are a variety of circumstances in which it is quite lawful for the public, and consequently the news media, to be excluded from hearings or meetings.

DOES THE PUBLIC HAVE ANY RIGHTS OF ACCESS?

The greatest chance of finding any rules or laws generally ensuring public access is within the court system. The courts have long cultivated the idea of an open justice system, as in this comment from a Supreme Court of Canada judgment on the topic:[1]

> [C]urtailment of public accessibility can only be justified where there is present the need to protect social values of superordinate importance.

In some provinces, the procedural and administrative laws for the courts (for example, Queen's Bench Acts or Rules of Court) expressly state hearings shall be held in public, except in extreme circumstances.[2] In other provinces, courts operate on the general common law presumption that the justice system should be open.

While each province may or may not expressly state that its courts are open, it's clear that courts in all jurisdictions have inherent common law powers and certain statutory powers to limit public access in some situations.[3]

For administrative tribunals, quasi-judicial bodies and public forums (for example, public utilities boards, worker's compensation boards or municipal council meetings), the "right" of public access is less certain. If the statute that created the tribunal doesn't set out the public's right of access then it's usually up to the discretion of tribunal officials. The general principle with such bodies is that the public should have access to public proceedings except where it's in the interest of the public and the administration of justice to have a closed hearing.

Aside from statutory and common law statements on public accessibility, the Canadian Charter of Rights and Freedoms is having an increasing influence on the question of accessibility through its promise of "freedom of the press."[4]

The following are some statutory provisions and common law principles which set out guidelines for public access to the courts and other bodies.

---

1 *MacIntyre v. A.G. N.S.*, [1982] 1 S.C.R. 175 at 186-187.

2 For example, Ontario's Courts of Justice Act, 1984, S.O. 1984, c. 11 states at section 145(1), all court hearings shall be open to the public, except where there's a possibility of serious harm or injustice to any person.

3 Under the common law, the courts may only exclude the public in proceedings involving wards, the mentally disordered, trade secrets or where a public trial would defeat the whole object of the proceeding. This rule was set out in *Scott v. Scott*, [1913] A.C. 417 (H.L.). Of course, statutes can add further exceptions.

4 Part 1 of the Constitution Act, 1982, being Schedule B of the Canada Act 1982 (U.K.), 1982, c. 11, s. 2(b) (hereinafter, Charter).

FEDERAL LAWS
Criminal Code[5]
Generally

Section 486(1) sets out the court's general authority to exclude members of the public on certain occasions:

> Any proceedings against an accused shall be held in open court, but where the presiding judge, provincial court judge or justice, as the case may be, is of the opinion that it is in the interest of public morals, the maintenance of order or the proper administration of justice to exclude all or any members of the public from the court room for all or part of the proceedings, he may so order.

The exclusion of the public "in the interest of public morals" is in reference to the evidence to be presented, and not a reference to the charge against the accused.[6] The exclusion of a journalist from the courtroom must be for a valid reason. For example, to remove a journalist but not the general public, simply to prevent the names of witnesses found in a bawdy-house from being published, is not a valid reason.[7]

As noted above, courts also have an inherent jurisdiction to exclude the public from trials. In one case, the accused had pleaded guilty and the lawyer for the accused asked the court if the submissions on sentencing could be heard *in camera*. The lawyer said the accused had something important to say and it could only be said in private. The judge ordered the public out, citing his inherent right to preserve the administration of justice. He held that the accused couldn't get a fair hearing, in this case, if the public wasn't excluded. The court felt the rights of the accused were more important than public access.[8]

Applications for Search Warrants

In 1982, the Supreme Court of Canada held in *MacIntyre v. Attorney General of Nova Scotia* that the public has no right to attend a court proceeding where a search warrant is being issued.[9] Secrecy is crucial to the success of a warrant as an investigative tool and the court can't risk the chance that someone might destroy evidence if they knew a warrant was about to be executed.

---

5 R.S.C. 1985, c. C-46.

6 In *R. v. Warawuk* (1978), 42 C.C.C. (2d) 121 at 126 (Alta. C.A.), the court said an exclusion order could not be issued simply because a sexual offence was involved. The court said the purpose of the exclusion order is to protect public morals and the question is whether the evidence could reasonably be expected to offend or have an adverse or corrupt effect on public morals.

7 *Re F.P. Publications (Western) Ltd. and R.* (1979), 51 C.C.C. (2d) 110 (Man. C.A.).

8 *R. v. Parisian* (1985), 6 C.R.D. 525.70-03 (Alta. Q.B.).

9 [1982] 1 S.C.R. 175.

Hearings for Issue of Summons or Arrest Warrants

In 1987, an Ontario judge considered whether the public has a right to attend hearings held under section 507, where a justice receives sworn informations and issues summonses or arrest warrants.[10] Unless evidence were to be presented suggesting the accused may try to flee the jurisdiction, the judge held that conducting an *in camera* hearing under this section isn't a reasonable limit on the freedom of the press. The judge went on to note that the Charter's guarantee of freedom of expression and the press includes the right of free access to the courts.

Preliminary Hearings

Where an accused is charged with an indictable offence, section 537(1)(*h*) states that a justice holding a preliminary hearing may:

> Order that no person other than the prosecutor, the accused and their counsel shall have access to or remain in the room in which the inquiry is held, where it appears to him that the ends of justice will be best served by so doing.

The decision to bar the public from attending a preliminary hearing must be based on clear reasons.[11] In a 1982 case, a preliminary hearing involved an accused charged with manslaughter in a highly publicized killing. The judge was ready to begin proceedings when he was told that some American journalists who were present in the courtroom planned to publish the full details of the preliminary hearing contrary to section 539 of the Code. Upon determining that the reporters did indeed plan to publish the evidence (in the United States there's no such ban), he used section 537(1)(*h*) to bar the public from the hearing.[12] On a further application by Canadian journalists, the judge "reluctantly" refused to limit the exclusion order only to the American journalists. He held he didn't have the authority to make exceptions to the Code section and would have no way of knowing who in the court gallery might be acting for an American news outlet.[13]

Proceedings Involving Sexual Offences

Under section 276, the defence lawyer in a sexual assault trial must give notice to the court that he or she intends to enter evidence on the sexual activity of the victim. According to the Code, the judge, provincial court judge or justice must hold a *voir dire* (that is, trial within a trial) to determine if the evidence is admissible. Section 276(3) states that the *voir dire* can only be held after excluding the jury and other members of the general public from the courtroom. It should be noted that the notice

---

10 *Re Canadian Newspapers Co. v. R.* (1987), 38 C.C.C. (3d) 187 (Ont. H.C.).
11 *Re Vaudrin and R.* (1982), 2 C.C.C. (3d) 214 (B.C. S.C.).
12 *R. v. Sayegh (No. 1)* (1982), 66 C.C.C. (2d) 430 (Ont. Prov. Ct.).
13 *R. v. Sayegh (No. 2)* (1982), 66 C.C.C. (2d) 432 (Ont. Prov. Ct.).

given by the defence counsel and the evidence and representations made at the *voir dire* cannot be published (section 276(4)).

Young Offenders Act[14]

Section 39(1) states that a judge may exercise a discretionary power to exclude any person from all or any part of the proceedings under this Act if the court is of the opinion:[15]

(a) that any evidence or information presented to the court or justice would be seriously injurious or prejudicial to
    (i) the young person who is being dealt with in the proceedings,
    (ii) a child or young person who is a witness in the proceedings,
    (iii) a child or young person who is aggrieved by or the victim of the offence charged in the proceedings, or
(b) that it would be in the interest of public morals, the maintenance of order or the proper administration of justice to exclude any or all members of the public from the court room,

the court or justice may exclude any person from all or part of the proceedings if the court or justice deems that person's presence to be unnecessary to the conduct of the proceedings.

A *young person* is someone "who is or, in the absence of evidence to the contrary, appears to be twelve years of age or more, but under eighteen years of age."[16] Section 39(3) also allows a review board or youth court to exclude any outside parties during a later review of disposition (that is, the sentence), where any information presented to the court might be seriously injurious or seriously prejudicial to the young person.

Canadian Human Rights Commission

Preliminary investigations of complaints by the commission may be conducted *in camera*.[17] But formal hearings of the commission's tribunal must be held in public, unless it's in the public's interest to issue an exclusion order.[18]

---

14 R.S.C. 1985, c. Y-1.
15 A landmark decision involving the now-repealed Juvenile Delinquents Act, *Re Southam Inc. and R. (No. 1)* (1983), 41 O.R. (2d) 113 (C.A.), established that a provision requiring all juvenile trials to be held *in camera* was unconstitutional because it was an absolute ban on public access to the hearing and allowed for no judicial discretion.
    The court's power to exclude the public under the present Young Offenders Act has also been challenged. But in *Re Southam Inc. and R.* (1986), 25 C.C.C. (3d) 119 (Ont. C.A.), the appeal court held that an order to exclude the public is a reasonable limit on the guarantee of freedom of expression. Leave to appeal to the Supreme Court of Canada was refused on May 22, 1986.
16 S. 2(1).
17 This was confirmed in *McKenzie v. Canadian Human Rights Commission* (1985), 6 C.R.D. 525.70-04 (Fed. T.D.), where an M.P. wanted the public and reporters to be allowed into a commission meeting that was deciding whether to formally inquire into allegations made against the M.P.
18 Human Rights, Canadian Act, R.S.C. 1985, c. H-6, s. 52.

Canadian Security Intelligence Service Act

The Review Committee (that is, public watchdog) established under this Act to examine complaints against the Service, is required to conduct its hearings in private.[19] A report on the complaints explored is filed annually with Parliament.

Competition Act

Section 29(1) states that all preliminary inquiries into alleged offences under this Act[20] shall be in private, unless the Chairman of the Commission orders otherwise. But section 29(2) states that all proceedings, other than those in relation to a preliminary inquiry, may be held in public. The Chairman has the ultimate discretion to order that all or any part of the public proceedings be held in private.

Immigration Act

An adjudicator of an immigration inquiry has the discretion to allow observers into a hearing, but otherwise it should be conducted *in camera*.[21] But appeals to the Immigration Appeal Board shall be held in public, except where there's a request that the hearing be held *in camera*.[22]

Income Tax Act

A taxpayer has the right, upon request, to a hearing *in camera* when appealing assessments to the Federal Court and administrative bodies.[23] This right doesn't exist during prosecutions in criminal courts for income tax offences.

National Defence Act

A court martial is to be held in public except where the evidence or information would endanger public safety, defence or public morals. The presiding official may exclude the public for all or part of the proceedings.[24]

---

19 R.S.C. 1985, c. C-23, s. 48.
20 R.S.C. 1985, c. C-34.
21 R.S.C. 1985, c. I-2, s. 29, amended R.S.C. 1985, c. 31 (1st Supp.), s. 99.
22 *Ibid.*, s. 80, amended S.C. 1988, c. 35, s. 33.
23 S.C. 1970-71-72, c. 63, s. 179.
24 R.S.C. 1985, c. N-5, s. 180.

Official Secrets Act

Section 14(2) allows an application to be made to exclude all or any part of the public from a trial under this Act or proceedings on appeal, where evidence or statements to be made would be prejudicial to the interests of the State.[25] The sentencing of an individual, though, is to be held in public.

Canada Evidence Act

Anyone may object to the disclosure of any information in a court (or any body with the power to compel witnesses or the production of documents) on the grounds of "a specified public interest."[26] A judge will determine the validity of this "public interest." For example, this can include information about the Queen's Privy Council, international relations, national defence or confidential government information. If the information involves international relations, national defence or security, the application for non-disclosure and any subsequent appeals must be held *in camera*.[27]

Access to Information and Privacy Acts

Each of these Acts provides for court appeals of requests for access to information held by the Federal government. In each of these Acts, the Federal Court must, or may in some circumstances, hold the hearing *in camera*.[28] In addition, every investigation by the Information Commissioner must be conducted in private.[29]

PROVINCIAL LAWS

Court Proceedings Generally

Some provinces have expressly established the authority in statutes or court rules for judges to exclude the public from proceedings.[30]

---

25 R.S.C. 1985, c. O-5.

26 R.S.C. 1985, C-5, ss. 37-39.

27 S. 38(5)(a).

28 See ss. 47 and 52 of the Access to Information Act, R.S.C. 1985, c. A-1; ss. 46 and 51 of the Privacy Act, R.S.C. 1985, c. P-21.

29 See s. 35 of the Access to Information Act.

30 For example, see Québec's Code of Civil Procedure, R.S.Q. 1977, c. C-25 which allows judges in civil proceedings to exclude the public in the interests of good morals or public order. Also, see Québec's Charter of Rights and Freedoms, R.S.Q. 1977, c. C-12, s. 23 which speaks to the principle of an open court. In Ontario, see S.O. 1984, c. 11, s. 145(1). In Nova Scotia, see the Judicature Act, S.N.S. 1972, c. 3, s. 34, which provides for open hearings except where public morals, maintenance of order or the proper administration of justice requires an *in camera* hearing. In New Brunswick, see Judicature Act, R.S.N.B. 1973, c. J-2. For example, s. 11.3(1) (as amended S.N.B. 1978, c. 32) allows family court judges to hold hearings *in camera* in the interests of public order or to prevent potential harm or embarrassment to any person.

Generally, the legislation says the courts shall be open, except:

1. where public morals are endangered;
2. for the maintenance of order;
3. for the "proper administration of justice;" or
4. in child and family matters.

For example, Ontario's Courts of Justice Act, 1984 states that all court hearings shall be open to the public.[31] The only exception noted under the law is for hearings where the possibility of serious harm or injustice to any person justifies a departure from the general principle of an open court.[32]

However, the common law also gives courts an inherent power to exclude the public in certain circumstances.[33] But that same common law rule limits those circumstances. For example, an *in camera* hearing can't be held simply because both sides in a dispute want the hearing to be closed.[34]

Coroners

Ontario[35] and British Columbia[36] expressly allow coroners to exclude the public where evidence may endanger national security or where a witness is charged with an indictable offence under the Criminal Code. But the public can't be excluded where no criminal charges have been laid, even though the evidence given by a witness may be incriminating.

In Alberta,[37] all fatality inquiry hearings shall be public, except in matters of public security or where it's preferable to hear intimate or personal details in private. The Alberta statute says the public and private interests involved must be weighed against each other. The Act says the coroner's decision to bar the public cannot be reviewed by a court.

---

31 S.O. 1984, c. 11, s. 145(1).

32 *Ibid.*, s. 145(2).

33 See, note 3, above, in *Scott* at 436-438, where the court said judicial proceedings should always be open to the public except where it acts on behalf of wards or lunatics, where confidential information is concerned or where justice could not otherwise be done.

34 *Ibid.*

35 Coroners Act, R.S.O. 1980, c. 93, s. 32.

36 Coroners Act, R.S.B.C. 1979, c. 68, s. 29.

37 See the Fatality Inquiries Amendment Act, R.S.A. 1980, c. F-6, ss. 40.1 to 40.4, as amended S.A. 1985, c. 26, s. 5.. In a decision prior to this Act being proclaimed, *Edmonton Journal v. A.G. Alta.* (1983), 28 Alta. L.R. (2d) 369 (Alta. Q.B.), the court held the decision to exclude the public from an Alberta fatality inquiry was not a violation of the Charter's guarantee of freedom of expression because the inquiry isn't a court. The court said full access by the public must be set out in statute and by prior practice. That requirement has now been fulfilled in the present legislation.

Québec legislation says all inquests shall be held in public, but a coroner can ban the publication of evidence or information arising out of the hearing in the name of the public's interest, to protect someone's right of privacy or preserve the right to a fair trial.[38] In New Brunswick[39] and Nova Scotia,[40] coroners have the discretion to hold hearings in private.

Family Law Acts

All the provinces and territories have legislation which gives judges a discretionary power to exclude the public in matters involving children and family disputes. This can involve laws dealing with child welfare, adoption, children of unmarried parents and family services matters. Generally, an exclusion order will be issued where there's a potential for harm or embarrassment to any person related to the proceeding or where it's in the public's interest or the interest of justice. But one province does make a special concession for news media. Ontario's Child and Family Services Act, 1984[41] states that two or more members of the media may be allowed by the presiding judge to attend hearings even if the public is excluded.[42]

Where a presiding judge does exclude the public, there must be a good reason for it. For example, one court held the news media can't be excluded simply because they are media. The court held there must be some proof offered to show that the presence of a particular person in the courtroom (for example, a journalist) is a hindrance to the proceedings.[43]

Police Commission Hearings

British Columbia is the only province which specifically requires disciplinary hearings involving officers to be held in public. Other hearings of the police commission in that province may be held in private.[44] In

---

38 An Act respecting the determination of the causes and circumstances of death, S.Q. 1983, c. 41, ss. 140 and 146.

39 Coroners Act, R.S.N.B. 1973, c. C-23, s. 21.

40 R.S.N.S. 1967, c. 101, s. 10.

41 S.O. 1984, c. 55, s. 41(5).

42 In *R. v. M.C.* (1984), 4 C.R.D. 525.70-02 (Ont. Prov. Ct.), a court held a similar provision in the now-repealed Child Welfare Act was constitutional because it was a reasonable limit on the press allowing a judge to exercise discretion.

43 In *Re S.D.A.* (1982), 28 R.F.L. (2d) 121 (B.C. Prov. Ct.), the court was considering an exclusion order requested under the Provincial Court Act, R.S.B.C. 1979, c. 341, s. 3, which empowers a judge to exclude members of the public during family law matters.

44 Police Act, R.S.B.C. 1979, c. 331, s. 41.

Québec[45] and Nova Scotia,[46] inquiries into police matters are to be held in public, but may be heard *in camera* in certain instances (that is, public interest or security).

Provincial Offences Acts

Most of the provinces adopt the Criminal Code procedures in their Summary Conviction Act for enforcing provincially-created offences. Some Acts state that proceedings must be held in open court, while others don't say anything.

Some provinces, such as Ontario and Québec, have developed their own court procedure for provincial offences which allows the public to be excluded in special circumstances.[47] In Ontario, the public may be excluded for the maintenance of order, to protect the reputation of a minor or to remove an "influence" on a witness.[48]

Public Inquiries Acts

Despite their name, inquiries struck by the provinces don't necessarily have to be in public. Ontario is the only province which requires inquiries to be public.[49] Even in that province, the public may be excluded for reasons of public security, intimate financial or personal matters or when the benefit of an *in camera* hearing outweighs the public need for access.

Victim Compensation Board Hearings

Many provinces have established boards to compensate victims of crimes and other misfortunes. The compensation boards generally hold hearings in public, but some have the power to exclude the public. This may be done in circumstances where it's prejudicial to the trial of the person who caused the injury or death, in sexual offences where it is not in the interests of the victim or dependents or where it's in the public's interest.[50]

---

45 Police Act, R.S.Q. 1977, c. P-13, ss. 30 and 31, as amended, S.Q. 1979, c. 67, s. 16.
46 Police Act, S.N.S. 1974, c. P-17, s. 19(10).
47 For example, in Québec, see Summary Convictions Act, R.S.Q., c. P-15, s. 29, as amended S.Q. 1986, c. 95, s. 228.
48 Provincial Offences Act, R.S.O. 1980, c. 400, s. 53.
49 Public Inquiries Act, R.S.O. 1980, c. 411, s. 4.
50 For example, see the legislation in Alberta: Criminal Injuries Compensation Act, R.S.A. 1980, c. C-33, s. 4(1); Manitoba: Criminal Injuries Compensation Act, R.S.M. 1987, c. C305, s. 8; Yukon: Compensation for the Victims of Crime Ordinance, R.O.Y.T. 1976, c. C-10.1, s. 14; and Newfoundland: Criminal Injuries Compensation Act, R.S.N. 1970, c. 68, ss. 19 and 20.

Provincial Young Offenders Acts

Most jurisdictions have enacted legislation setting out the procedure to be used when dealing with young offenders who violate provincial laws. Some have adopted the same provisions as the federal Young Offenders Act, including the granting of a discretionary power to a judge to exclude the public.[51]

ACCESS TO ADMINISTRATIVE TRIBUNAL HEARINGS

When legislation creates a formal tribunal (for example, a labour board), but does not state whether its hearings or meetings are to be held in public, the decision as to public access is usually at the discretion of the tribunal members. Administrative tribunals, such as public boards, usually have the right to determine their own rules of procedure.

But the public has some limited rights of access to tribunal hearings. One Ontario case set out guidelines for access to statutory tribunals.[52] The case involved an arbitration board hearing of an allegation of wrongful dismissal against a newspaper. The tribunal participants were asked if the press and public could attend. One of the parties to the hearing objected and, on the strength of that one objection, the tribunal felt it therefore had to reject the request for public access.

The court, in reviewing the tribunal's decision, stated that the public has a legitimate interest in any hearing of a statutory tribunal. The court said it was an error in law for the tribunal to exclude the public simply because one party to the hearing objected. The court pointed to the English case of *Scott v. Scott*, which stands for the principle that a hearing of a judicial body, which has the potential of greatly affecting a person's rights, cannot be held *in camera* simply because the parties in a dispute consent to it.[53]

In the case of quasi-judicial bodies, such as this tribunal, the court held that while the tribunal has a discretionary power to allow public access, it's not compelled to bar the public merely because one party objects to the media's presence. The court went on to suggest that for public bodies which are purely administrative and don't act judicially, they need not,

---

51 This exclusion power can be found in Prince Edward Island: Young Offenders (P.E.I.) Act, S.P.E.I. 1985, c. 47, s. 17; Nova Scotia: Young Persons Summary Proceedings Act, S.N.S. 1985, c. 11, s. 24; British Columbia: Young Offenders (B.C.) Act, S.B.C. 1984, c. 30, s. 4; Alberta: Young Offenders Act, S.A. 1984, c. Y-1, s. 21, as amended S.A. 1987, c. 41, s. 13; Northwest Territories: Young Offenders Ordinance, O.N.W.T. 1984, c. 2 (1st), s. 61.

52 *Toronto Star v. Toronto Newspaper Guild* (1976), 73 D.L.R. (3d) 370 (Ont. Div. Ct.).

53 Note 3, above.

and perhaps should not, be held in public. The court said the board made a mistake and asked it to reconsider its decision in this case.

ACCESS TO PUBLIC, PRIVATE AND MUNICIPAL MEETINGS

Public Meetings

There's no law speaking to a general right of the public to attend a "public meeting." Presumably, a public meeting by definition invites any member of the public to attend. At anytime, however, someone can be ejected or asked to leave by the convenors of the meeting, particularly if it's held on property owned or controlled by the convenors. A journalist refusing to leave after being told to could be charged with trespassing under provincial law. Even public meetings in public places will have someone present (for example, a policeman) who can eject unwanted people.

Private Meetings

The news media has no legal right to demand access to a private meeting, even if its topic is one of intense public interest. If a journalist were to gain entry to such a meeting, the same rules apply as for public meetings and he or she would have to leave if asked.

Another type of private meeting that's sometimes of interest to journalists is corporate shareholders' meetings. Some journalists have been quite clever in their attempts to avoid getting tossed out of a meeting. On one occasion, a reporter who wanted to attend a shareholders' meeting for a company, bought some shares. But when the company officers discovered the reporter was present, he was kicked out. There was little the journalist could do, short of embarking on an expensive lawsuit alleging that minority shareholder rights were stomped on.

Municipal Meetings

A somewhat different set of rules apply to municipal council and committee meetings. Every province has a provision in their Municipalities Act that expressly states that regular municipal council meetings shall be held in public.

However, in many cases the law also permits a council to hold its other meetings or debates in private (such as committee of the whole meetings). What this can mean is that decisions from those closed-door meetings only have to be ratified in open council and the actual debate on the resolution may be in private. Only the final decision (that is, the vote) is required by law to be held in public and no province demands public debate.

Legislation in most provinces also allows committee meetings to be held in private. In Ontario, this right to *in camera* proceedings is extended to boards of commissioners of police and school boards (however, local bylaws may be passed to ensure public access).

In 1988, an economic development committee of Ontario's Hamilton-Wentworth Regional Council tried to get around a council bylaw that all council and committee meetings be held in public by calling an important meeting an "*in camera* workshop." The workshop was to review the committee's terms of reference and "directions for the future." The local newspaper felt it was really a full committee meeting and went to court. The Ontario Court of Appeal agreed with the newspaper and declared the meeting illegal.[54]

CAN YOU PUBLISH DETAILS OF CLOSED DOOR HEARINGS?

Sometimes, the general public is barred from a hearing to protect the interests of innocent parties or to allow a nervous witness to testify freely. Sometimes, journalists are allowed to stay, while the general public is shown out. Or a participant in a closed door hearing may decide to tell a journalist what went on.

The question that commonly arises then is, can you publish the details of a closed door hearing?

The common law rule is that there's no contempt of court when publishing details of *in camera* hearings unless a ban on publication has been issued by the court. Under the common law, a ban may be issued in cases involving wards of the State, trade secrets or national security information.[55] Indeed, this has been incorporated into the legislation of at least one province. Ontario's Courts of Justice Act, 1984 expressly states the disclosure of information relating to a proceeding heard in the absence of the public isn't a contempt of court, unless the court expressly prohibited the disclosure of the information.[56]

Of course, one shouldn't forget there may also be occasions in which a jury, but not the public, will be asked to leave the courtroom while lawyers debate points of law or admissibility of evidence. None of the details of these "closed" hearings may be reported until after the jury retires to consider a verdict (see section 648 of the Criminal Code).

---

54 *Southam v. Hamilton-Wentworth Regional Council* (1988), 12 A.C.W.S. (3d) 181 (Ont. C.A.).

55 *Ibid.*

56 Note 2, above, s. 145(3).

It should be noted there are risks of another kind in publishing details of *in camera* proceedings. For example, Québec's Press Act expressly states that reports of defamatory statements made in *in camera* hearings are not privileged.[57] The same rule is suggested in the common law provinces, where only reports of open court proceedings are protected from defamation actions.

There may also be statutory restrictions on publishing the details of closed hearings of bodies other than courts, such as coroners' inquests or criminal injuries compensation boards.

AN ACCESS TO HEARINGS AND MEETINGS CHECKLIST

1. There is a general presumption in law that the public should have access to meetings or hearings of official bodies which act on behalf of the public and deal with matters of public interest.
2. The following Criminal Code sections may be used to exclude the public from court hearings:
   i) Section 486(1) affirms a court's general right to exclude members of the public on certain occasions;
   ii) Section 537(1)(*h*) states that a justice holding a preliminary hearing may exclude everyone other than the prosecutor, the accused and their counsel; and
   iii) Section 276, which concerns sexual assault trials, contains a subsection stating that the public and jury must be excluded during a *voir dire* concerning the admissibility of evidence of the sexual activity of the victim.
3. Section 39(1) of the Young Offenders Act states a judge may exclude the public from all or any part of proceedings under this Act in certain circumstances.
4. Most federal and provincial judicial or quasi-judicial tribunals have the authority to exclude the public from hearings.
5. The public has limited rights of access to administrative tribunals. If legislation creating the tribunal does not state if its hearings or meetings are to be held in public, the decision as to public access is usually at the discretion of the tribunal members.
6. As a rule, a public meeting may be attended by anyone. At any time, however, someone can be ejected or asked to leave by the convenors of the meeting.
7. Every province has a provision in municipal laws stating that regular municipal council meetings are to be held in public. However, in many

---

57 R.S.Q., c. P-19, s. 10(*d*).

cases, the law also permits a council to hold its other meetings or debates in private (such as committee of the whole meetings).

8. The common law rule is that there is no contempt of court when publishing details of *in camera* or closed-door hearings unless a ban on publication has been issued by the court. Journalists should still be careful since publication of details of closed-door proceedings may not be protected under defamation laws.

9

Gaining Access to Court Documents

Generally, journalists have no general right of access to court documents unless the privilege is set out in a statute or a court rule. It's even been suggested that the public itself has no right of access to court documents.[1] As discussed here, "court documents" include exhibits, affidavits, transcripts of examinations for discovery, personal records or any documents submitted by the parties in a civil or criminal action.

There are several variables which will determine whether a person who is not a party to an action can gain access to court records. At the heart of the restrictions is the court's concern about prejudicing a fair trial or interfering with the course of justice. The rights of access vary from province to province and may be dependent upon what local

---

1 In *R. v. Thomson Newspapers Ltd.* (1984), 4 C.R.D. 525. 40-01 (Ont. S.C.), the court held the guarantee of freedom of the press in the Charter [Canadian Charter of Rights and Freedoms, Part 1 of the Constitution Act, 1982, being Schedule B of the Canada Act 1982 (U.K.), 1982, c. 11] gives the media and public no general constitutional right to compel the court to give access to any documents and no right to inspect, copy or photograph items before the court.

This protectionist attitude stretches back through the centuries. In a note to the English case of *Caddy v. Barlow* (1827), 1 Man. and Ry. K.B. 275 at 279, it said only "interested parties" (that is, litigants) may have access to court records for their "necessary use and benefit."

But, in recent times, some courts have said there is, at least, a limited presumption favouring a public right of access to court documents. In *Pacific Press Ltd. v. Vickers* (1985), 60 B.C.L.R. 91 (S.C.), the court held the public's right to know and have access to court documents takes precedence over the privacy of the litigants, particularly when a case has formally ended (that is, the appeal period has passed). The court granted a newspaper access to the court files on a case in which an "infant" sued the Crown for damages after being placed in a foster home. However, the court used its inherent authority to ban the publication of names, locations and particulars of abuse mentioned in the files.

legislation says, the stage of the court proceedings, the nature of the proceedings, the document requested, and to some degree, the working relationship between the journalist and the court.

CIVIL PROCEEDINGS

Pre-Trial Access

Most civil courts will allow anyone to see the "house-keeping" records which set out the names and addresses of parties involved in lawsuits, the remedy sought, the stage of proceedings and the coming date of trial or the result. Aside from these records, a court will keep a separate file for each case containing pleadings and other pre-trial documents, such as transcripts of examinations for discovery. However, not all documents may be examined by the public.

Only a couple of provinces have legislation setting out the public's rights of access to documents. Manitoba's Queen's Bench Act states in section 26(1) that everyone has the right to inspect court records and entries. It further notes that a person doesn't have to ask for any one particular case to gain access.[2]

Ontario's Courts of Justice Act, 1984 states that, on the payment of the prescribed fee, any person is entitled to see and copy any document filed in a civil proceeding, unless another statute or an order of the court provides otherwise.[3] The Ontario Act also states that any person can, on payment of the prescribed fee, see any list maintained by a civil court of proceedings started or judgments entered.

In one Ontario civil action by alleged victims of sexual assault, a judge ordered that all documents be kept confidential, sealed and not form part of the public record.[4] However, another judge set that order aside and said the press and public have a right of access to documents under the Courts of Justice Act that shouldn't be interfered with except in the clearest of cases. In this case, the judge held there wasn't enough evidence to justify barring public access to the documents.

Even with statutory references to public access like those above, the question may arise as to what is the definition of a "court record." In the eyes of some court officials, the definition may not go beyond the court books which register the names and addresses of parties to actions along with a short sentence on the remedy sought.[5]

---

2 R.S.M. 1987, c. C280.

3 S.O. 1984, c. 11, s. 147.

4 *Smith v. Crampton* (1987), 7 A.C.W.S. (3d) 128 (Ont. S.C.).

5 In *Howes v. Accountant of the Supreme Court of Ontario* (1984), 49 O.R. (2d) 121 (H.C.), the court held the Ontario section permitting access to documents doesn't apply to records

There are other situations in which the court or its officers (such as a court clerk) may bar access to a court record or document. For example, documents containing intimate personal or financial information, transcripts of examinations for discovery or solicitor-client fee agreements may be sealed by the court and taken out of the file available for public perusal.[6] Most jurisdictions statutorily bar public access to documents for family matters, such as disputes over the custody of children.

There's also a common law power in the courts to restrict access to documents to protect the rights of the innocent or in the interests of the administration of justice.[7] For example, in a British Columbia case dealing with complaints of unprofessional conduct against a doctor, the court agreed to order that the names of former patients be blacked-out from the transcripts kept in the file seen by the public. The court said the rights of the innocent were paramount, in this case, to the rights of the press.[8]

On one occasion, in Alberta in 1982, a man took a sheriff hostage as property foreclosure proceedings were being carried out. While the hostage-taking was going on, a journalist went to a court clerk to get a copy of the foreclosure documents, but was denied access. The Alberta Court of Queen's Bench held that the clerk's refusal to hand over the documents to the journalist was justified.[9] The protection of the sheriff's life was the primary concern and more important than the public's right to see the court document.

Although Alberta doesn't generally restrict access to court documents, it's the only province which partly-restricts the publication of civil pleadings until the end of the trial or, if there is no trial, until the proper determination of the proceedings.[10] Only the names and addresses of the parties and the solicitors, and the general nature of the claim can be published.[11] As a rule, the publication of details of civil pleadings in all provinces should

---

of moneys paid into court. The court said the right is restricted to records of writs issued and judgments entered. However, this may have been too restrictive an interpretation of the wording.

6 For example, see Alta. Rules of Court, Rules 199, 212(4) and 617, which contain some of these restrictions. In *Solomon and Southam Inc. v. McLaughlin* (1982), 37 A.R. 479 (Q.B.), the court said a clerk couldn't refuse access to documents without leave of the court. It was noted that while no Alberta statute compels public access, the public and news media do have a presumed right of access in most cases.

7 *Ibid., Solomon,* at 495-496.

8 *Hirt v. College of Physicians & Surgeons of B.C.* (1985), 60 B.C.L.R. 273 (C.A.).

9 Note 6, above, *Solomon.*

10 R.S.A. 1980, c. J-1, s. 30(2). Civil pleadings are defined as statements of claim, statements of defence or other pleadings, transcripts of examinations for discovery, affidavits or any other pre-trial documents.

11 In practice, it appears that no Alberta journalists have been charged with an offence

be carefully considered anyway because they are not privileged under defamation law. The pleadings can carry erroneous details and may be contemptuous, as well as being defamatory, if published before or during a trial.[12]

Access During Trial

Whether the public may have access to exhibits and evidence presented in open court is a more difficult issue. There is no law that such evidence must be accessible to the public and a journalist must seek out the permission of the presiding judge to examine or photograph evidence. Some judges may allow public access immediately after the evidence is presented in open court, while most others maintain that the fair trial of the issues would be endangered by the possibility of sensationalized reporting.

Access After Trial

After the case is over, most of the documents entered as evidence will be kept in the court record, where they may be examined by the public. But some evidence may not belong to the court. For example, personal or business records are usually returned to individuals after a court proceeding.

In one criminal case, the news media had been denied access during a trial to documents entered as evidence. After the trial was over, the CBC applied to the court for access to the documents and to determine if the court order was still in effect.

The court said the order was not in effect once the trial had ended and any appeal period had passed. However, the court noted that the documents in question were no longer the property of the court. It said they would normally be returned to the party that submitted them (the Crown, in this case) and permission to view the evidence would have to come from that party to the proceeding.[13]

That said, frequently, copies of the evidence remain with the court as a part of the court record and may still be viewed.

---

under this section in recent years even though journalists do publish more details than set out above. However, an attempt to have this section declared unconstitutional was unsuccessful in the case of *Edmonton Journal v. A.G. Alta.* (1985), 40 Alta. L.R. (2d) 326 (Q.B.).

12 In *Bielek v. Ristimaki*, June 21, 1979 (unreported), an Ontario trial judge dismissed the jury and ordered a new trial after a journalist published the amount of damages being sought by the plaintiff during the trial. The court held that the publication of the pleadings was an act of contempt because it could have released information to the jury which is not relevant or correct.

13 *Re CBC and Clerk of the Supreme Court of Alta.* (1977), 77 D.L.R. (3d) 621 (Alta. T.D.).

CRIMINAL PROCEEDINGS

Pre-Trial Access

The documents of most interest to journalists before a criminal trial are search warrants and "informations" (that is, sworn documents outlining offences police allege have been committed). The seminal case in this area is *MacIntyre v. Attorney General of Nova Scotia*, decided in 1982 by the Supreme Court of Canada.[14] In that case, a television reporter was refused access to search warrants and informations held by a justice of the peace. The Supreme Court of Canada ruled that:

> [A]fter a search warrant has been executed, and objects found as a result of the search are brought before a justice pursuant to s. 446 [now s. 490] of the Criminal Code, a member of the public is entitled to inspect the warrant and the information upon which the warrant has been issued pursuant to s. 443 [now s. 487] of the Code.

Note that not all search warrants are accessible. The court said the public has no right to see an executed search warrant which finds nothing and no right to a warrant which is yet to be executed. Unfortunately, the court was reluctant to deal with any other issues of the public's right to examine court documents. But the judges did say there is a strong presumption in favour of the public having access to court documents.

It must be noted that an amendment was made to the Criminal Code in 1985 that makes it an offence to publish certain information about search warrants where charges haven't been formally laid. Soon after this amendment was made, a court declared it unconstitutional since it infringed on freedom of the press.[15]

While the government didn't appeal the ruling, unfortunately the law is still on the books and hasn't been formally repealed. Since the court's decision there have been no charges laid under the amended section and it's considered to be of no legal force. However, the government has clearly indicated a desire to somehow limit the publication of details of search warrants, particularly where charges haven't been laid. It's possible the federal government will someday introduce a refashioned amendment to limit publication.

For interest's sake, at least, section 487.2(1) states that anyone who publishes any information with respect to:

(a) the location of the place searched or to be searched, or
(b) the identity of any person who is or appears to occupy or be in possession

---

14 [1982] 1 S.C.R. 175 at 190.
15 *Canadian Newspapers Co. Ltd. v. A.G. Canada* (1986), 32 D.L.R. (4th) 292 (Ont. H.C.).

or control of that place or who is suspected of being involved in any offence in relation to which the warrant was issued,

without the consent of every person referred to in paragraph (b) is, unless a charge has been laid in respect of any offence in relation to which the warrant was issued, guilty of an offence punishable on summary conviction.

The amendment reinforced the Supreme Court's prior ruling that only details of executed search warrants which find something can be published. But it went on to require that a charge also be laid before the details regarding place and identity could be published. Also, the charge had to be related to the offence for which the warrant was issued. A journalist would have had to call in legal advice in most cases to determine if the charge laid is the same as the one outlined in the warrant. For example, say police found illicit drugs using a warrant allowing a search for gambling machines. If the drug charges were the only ones arising from the search, a reporter would need legal advice.

If no charges were laid, a journalist would then have needed the consent of all people named in the warrant and the requirements for consent were quite complicated. Consent was required from every person named in the warrant as being suspected of an offence and anyone who was in possession or control of the places searched.

There have been other court decisions pertaining to access to pre-trial criminal documents. The 1959 case of *Southam Publishing Co. v. Mack*, which is noted in the *MacIntyre* case, held that the public can have access to "all informations and complaints" laid before a provincial court judge (that is, the charges laid before the court).[16] That access didn't extend to "all documents," only the informations and complaints.

Another case, decided in 1978, confirmed that all documents relating to informations and warrants should be available to the public on demand without prior approval from the Attorney-General or anyone else.[17] However, the court also recognized there would be cases where the administration of justice might be better served by not releasing a document.

Examples of such situations were noted in a 1982 Ontario case.[18] The court received a request from the Attorney General and the RCMP to restrict public access to eight sworn informations which were used to get search warrants. The judge said that to deny access to court documents it must be proven that access would be harmful to the ends of justice, such as in obstructing a police investigation, disclosing evidence of lawful electronic surveillance, disclosing the identity of a confidential informant

---

16 (1959-60), 2 Crim. L.Q. 119.
17 *Realty Renovations Ltd. v. A.G. Alta.* (1978), 44 C.C.C. (2d) 249 (Alta. S.C.).
18 *Re Yanover; Re Hill* (1982), 26 C.R. (3d) 216 at 228-231 (Ont. Prov. Ct.).

or revealing police investigative techniques. In other words, the release of such documents could allow an individual to avoid arrest, destroy evidence and discourage informants from giving information.

The court agreed that the release of the informations might interfere with an on-going police investigation and noted they contained details of wiretap evidence which had not yet been tendered as evidence in any trial. The judge also referred to several American cases suggesting other situations in which access should be denied. For example, court documents could be used for an improper or immoral purpose (for example, publishing disgusting details of a divorce case).

A recent case added another ground for keeping sworn informations out of the public eye. After a search warrant was executed pursuant to the Competition Act, the company that owned the seized documents applied to a court for an order to have the sworn information for the warrant kept confidential unless formal charges were laid.[19] The sworn information contained business secrets. The court agreed, noting that while there was a public interest in access to court documents, no public interest would be served in allowing the secrets to be revealed unless charges were laid.

Although the Criminal Code says little about access to warrants and informations, it does specifically limit access to one type of document. Section 187 of the Criminal Code states that a judge must seal applications for authorization for wiretaps in a "packet" and allow no public access.

Access During Trial

Requests for access to exhibits during a criminal trial should be addressed to the court clerk or the judge presiding over the case. If the release of a document would prejudice the fair trial of the accused or harm the innocent, the court may restrict access. As with civil actions, the right of access to evidence presented in open court is a difficult issue. You can't just walk up during a court recess and examine exhibits or make a few notes on their contents. A journalist must seek the permission of the judge to examine or photograph evidence. A few judges may allow public access immediately after the evidence is presented in open court, but most maintain that a fair trial of the issues would be endangered by the possibility of sensationalized reporting.

Access After Trial

After a case is over, some documents entered as evidence will be

---

19 *Re Dir. of Investigation & Research and Irving Equipment & Barrington Industrial Services Ltd.* (1986), 39 D.L.R. (4th) 341 (Fed. T.D.).

kept in the court record. But as mentioned in the above section on civil proceedings, access to some documents after a trial may no longer be within the control of the court. In the criminal case mentioned above, the court had denied a media request for access to exhibits during a trial. After it was over, the CBC again asked to see the documents. The court held the order wasn't in effect after the trial had ended and the appeal period had passed.[20] As noted above, the court said the documents would normally be returned to the party that submitted them (the Crown, in this case) and permission to view the evidence would have to come from the party which introduced it.

Again, though, in many cases, copies of the evidence remain with the court as a part of the court record and may still be accessible through normal channels.

OTHER PUBLIC PROCEEDINGS

Coroners' inquests, public inquiries and administrative tribunals allow the public no general right to inspect exhibits or evidence in their proceedings. As in the court system, it's up to the presiding official. In addition, if a journalist has been somehow able to gain access to documents used in the inquiry or proceeding, he or she should be cautious in reporting the contents of the documents if they aren't entered as evidence in open proceedings. The primary concern would be that reports of such documents wouldn't be protected under defamation legislation until they became a part of the public record of the proceedings.

A COURT DOCUMENTS CHECKLIST

1. Most courts will allow journalists to see "house-keeping" court records setting out the names and addresses of parties involved in lawsuits, the remedy sought, the stage of proceedings and the coming date of trial or the result. Courts keep a separate file for each case containing pleadings and other pre-trial documents, such as transcripts of examinations for discovery. However, not all these documents may be examined by the public.
2. Courts may bar access to a case file in accordance with statutes or where it contains intimate personal or financial information, solicitor-client fee agreements or family information in cases dealing with custody of children or abuse cases. There's also a common law power to restrict access to protect the rights of the innocent or in the interests of the administration of justice.

---

20 Note 13, above.

3. Alberta is the only province which partly-restricts the publication of civil pleadings until the end of the trial or, if there is no trial, until the proper determination of the proceedings. Only the names and addresses of the parties and the solicitors, and the general nature of the claim can be published. As a rule, the publication of details of civil pleadings in all provinces should be carefully considered because they are not privileged under defamation law.
4. The public's access to exhibits and evidence presented in open court is determined by the presiding judge or official in each case.
5. Journalists have a general right of access to executed search warrants which find something, and to criminal informations and complaints laid before a judge. The Criminal Code states that applications for wiretap authorizations must remain confidential.

10

Understanding Police Powers and Limits

News reporting often involves encounters with law enforcement officials. The police, other peace officers and even public officers wield broad powers and it's to the journalist's advantage to know the scope of law enforcement authority.

WHO HAS LAW ENFORCEMENT POWERS?

What may surprise some people is the great number of officials who hold law enforcement authority and the fact that such authority is not restricted to police. Even the average citizen has the authority to call upon law enforcement powers in limited circumstances. Generally, though, law enforcement powers are limited to those defined in the Criminal Code as "peace officers" and "public officers."

Section 2's definition of a "peace officer" illustrates the vast list of individuals with law enforcement powers:[1]

  (a) a mayor, warden, reeve, sheriff, deputy sheriff, sheriff's officer and justice of the peace,

  (b) a member of the Correctional Service of Canada who is designated as a peace officer pursuant to the Penitentiary Act, and a warden, deputy warden, instructor, keeper, gaoler, guard and any other officer or permanent employee of a prison other than a penitentiary as defined in the Penitentiary Act,

  (c) a police officer, police constable, bailiff, constable, or other person employed for the preservation and maintenance of the public peace or for the service or execution of civil process,

  (d) an officer or a person having the powers of a customs or excise officer when performing any duty in the administration of the Customs Act,

---

1 R.S.C. 1985, c. C-46.

chapter C-40 of the Revised Statutes of Canada, 1970 or the Excise Act,
(e) a person appointed or designated as a fishery officer under the Fisheries Act when performing any of his duties or functions pursuant to that Act,
(f) the pilot in command of an aircraft
  (i) registered in Canada under regulations made under the Aeronautics Act, or
  (ii) leased without crew and operated by a person who is qualified under regulations under the Aeronautics Act to be registered as owner of an aircraft registered in Canada under those regulations,
while the aircraft is in flight, and
(g) officers and non-commissioned members of the Canadian Forces who are
  (i) appointed for the purposes of section 156 of the National Defence Act, or
  (ii) employed on duties that the Governor in Council, in regulations made under the National Defence Act for the purposes of this paragraph, has prescribed to be of such a kind as to necessitate that the officers and non-commissioned members performing them have the powers of peace officers.

Section 2 also defines a "public officer" as:

(a) an officer of customs or excise,
(b) an officer of the Canadian Forces,
(c) an officer of the Royal Canadian Mounted Police, and
(d) any officer while the officer is engaged in enforcing the laws of Canada relating to revenue, customs, excise, trade or navigation.

These definitions of peace officer and public officer aren't exhaustive. For example, an animal control officer appointed under a municipal by-law pursuant to municipal legislation has been found by a court to be a "peace officer" within the definition of the Code and thereby entitled to exercise enforcement powers.[2] In another case, a court decided that an officer who reports to a provincial or municipal government, such as a municipal agriculture inspector, could be considered a "public officer."[3]

The territorial jurisdiction of peace officers is generally limited by the authority of the appointing body.[4] For example, a municipal police officer has no authority in another province. A peace officer's authority may also be limited by the "type" of individuals he or she comes in contact with. The best example is military police. In one case, it was held that a military police officer has no authority over a civilian who is not subject

---

2 *R. v. Jones* (1975), 30 C.R.N.S. 127 (Y.T. Mag. Ct.). The point in this case was that someone must be employed with the purpose of maintaining the public peace to be considered a peace officer.
3 *R. v. Cartier; R. v. Libert* (1978), 43 C.C.C. (2d) 553 (C.S. Qué.).
4 *R. v. Soucy* (1975), 23 C.C.C. (2d) 561 (N.B. C.A.).

to the Code of Service Discipline unless it involves the maintenance of law and order, such as traffic regulation on an armed forces base.[5]

WHAT IS THE EXTENT OF LAW ENFORCEMENT POWERS?

Use of Force

The Criminal Code protects the people administering and enforcing the law and, in appropriate circumstances, allows authorities to use whatever force is necessary. This authority can even extend beyond peace and public officers to the average citizen. For example, section 25(1) states:

> Every one who is required or authorized by law to do anything in the administration or enforcement of the law
> (a) as a private person,
> (b) as a peace officer or public officer,
> (c) in aid of a peace officer or public officer, or
> (d) by virtue of his office,
> is, if he acts on reasonable and probable grounds, justified in doing what he is required or authorized to do and in using as much force as is necessary for that purpose.

A person administering or enforcing the law isn't justified in using excessive force that is intended or is likely to cause death or grievous bodily harm unless he or she believes, on reasonable and probable grounds, that it's necessary to use it for self protection or to protect anyone else from serious harm or death.[6] An excessive use of force could be subject to criminal prosecution.[7]

Section 25(4) permits a peace officer to use as much force as is necessary to prevent a person who is about to be arrested from escaping, unless the escape could be prevented by reasonable means in a less violent manner.

The use of force isn't limited to peace officers. Section 27 permits any person to use as much force as necessary to prevent the commission of offences serious enough to allow arrest without a warrant or those that would be likely to cause immediate and serious injury to someone or their property.

Section 30 allows anyone who witnesses a breach of the peace to interfere with reasonable force so as to prevent the continuance of the breach. They may then detain the person involved in the breach of peace and must deliver the accused to a peace officer as soon as possible.

Section 32 allows a peace officer to use as much force as he or she

---

5 *Nolan v. R.* (1987), 34 C.C.C. (3d) 289 (S.C.C.).

6 S. 25(3).

7 S. 26.

believes, in good faith and on reasonable and probable grounds, is necessary to suppress a riot. For example, an officer might order camera crews out of an area if the crowd is reacting to the presence of the media.

Power of Arrest

An arrest is a serious act and one might reasonably assume that only duly-appointed peace officers have that power. But the Criminal Code does permit any citizen to make an arrest without a warrant within limited circumstances.

Under section 494(1), anyone may arrest without a warrant:

> (a) a person whom he finds committing an indictable offence; or
> (b) a person who, on reasonable and probable grounds, he believes
>   (i) has committed a criminal offence, and
>   (ii) is escaping from and freshly pursued by persons who have lawful authority to arrest that person.

It is important to note that a "citizen's arrest" can only be made under one of two conditions. First, the arrest may occur upon finding someone committing an indictable or "serious" offence. Note that summary conviction offences aren't included.

Second, a citizen may make an arrest after coming across someone whom he or she has "reasonable and probable grounds" to believe has committed either a summary conviction or indictable offence and who is at the same time running away from the police (that is, "freshly pursued").

So, the average citizen only has a limited power of arrest and certainly doesn't have the broad powers of the police. Once a warrantless arrest has been made, the citizen is required to deliver the accused to the nearest police officer as soon as is practicably possible.

A citizen's arrest doesn't entitle the citizen to interrogate, search a person or seize belongings. If a citizen (for example, a store security guard) has been found to have made an improper arrest, the "accused" could sue in the civil courts for false arrest or false imprisonment.

There are other instances in which average citizens can make arrests. Under section 494(2), anyone who is the owner of property or a person in lawful possession of property or a person authorized by the owner or person in lawful possession, can arrest someone without a warrant where he finds that person committing any criminal offence on, or in relation to, that property. Again, the accused must be found committing a criminal offence (in this case, either indictable or summary conviction). Merely having a suspicion that a crime has been committed is not good enough and could result in a civil action for false arrest. And again, the accused must be delivered to a peace officer immediately.

A peace officer can arrest anyone without a warrant whom he or she believes, on reasonable and probable grounds, has committed an indictable offence in the past or present. A peace officer can even make an arrest if he or she believes an indictable offence is about to be committed.[8]

What Constitutes an Arrest?

The Criminal Code does not set out exactly what constitutes an arrest. A person must be told that he or she is under arrest and the reason for the arrest unless it's obvious. Where possible, the peace officer must also go through the motion of seizing or simply touching a person with an intent to detain him or her.[9] The courts have also held that people are under "arrest" if they willfully accompany a peace officer, even though there has been no physical contact, such that they acknowledge they are in custody.[10]

But voluntarily going with a police officer simply for questioning or investigative purposes is not considered a form of custody or arrest.[11] Indeed, this little-known fact is a valuable investigative tool for police. Under section 10(b) of the Charter,[12] upon arrest or being detained you have a right to legal counsel and to be informed of that right by the police. But that right doesn't apply to situations where a person is merely accompanying an officer.

So, an investigator will often make a "request" that someone go with them to the police station to answer a few questions. Because most people don't know that they have a right to refuse to go along or are intimidated, they go along and may end up saying something incriminating without the advice of counsel.

This brings up another important question. When is a person actually in custody? In most cases, you'd know if you were arrested. But what if the police kept you in a room for 12 hours without telling you whether you're under arrest. Have you been "detained" such that you have a right to legal counsel?

A 1985 Supreme Court of Canada case discussed this very question.[13] The case involved a man's right to a lawyer upon being asked to go to the police station to take a breathalyzer test. The Court held that the person

---

8 S. 495(1).

9 *R. v. Whitfield* (1969), 9 C.R.N.S. 59 at 60 (S.C.C.).

10 *Ibid.*

11 *R. v. Acker* (1970), 9 C.R.N.S. 371 at 377-378 (N.S. C.A.).

12 Canadian Charter of Rights and Freedoms, Part 1 of the Constitution Act, 1982, being Schedule B of the Canada Act 1982 (U.K.), 1982, c. 11 (hereinafter, Charter).

13 *R. v. Therens*, [1985] 1 S.C.R. 613.

was "detained" when he accompanied a police officer back to the police station for the test. It held that to be considered "detained" for the purposes of the Charter's section 10(b), there must be some form of compulsion or demand from the peace officer, which if refused, could have a legal consequence (for example, a criminal charge for refusing to take a breathalyzer test).

Power of Search and Seizure

A peace officer may only perform a search of a person or a place in certain circumstances. Authorization for a search can come in the form of a warrant or it can be based on the inherent warrantless search powers granted law enforcers in statutes or common law. The use of search warrants is discussed in the chapter on "Search Warrants." This section focuses on the use of warrantless powers.

There is no general power allowing the search of a place or a person without a warrant, unless the search is incidental to the arrest of someone or if there is consent. There is also no general power to seize something unless it's in connection with the commission of an offence or under a warrant.[14]

So, a peace officer has no right to seize a journalist's notes, tapes, films or other personal property unless it's in connection with an offence or a search warrant.

The Supreme Court of Canada has recognized that individuals rightly have a reasonable expectation of privacy and occasions of warrantless searches should thus be limited.[15] There are times, however, when unauthorized searches will be allowed. For example, a person going through customs would not expect to be immune from questions or searches of their suitcases.

The Code also allows a search without a warrant in circumstances where a peace officer suspects violations of certain laws (for example, weapons or gambling offences).[16] At least a dozen federal laws ranging from dairy legislation to the Narcotic Control Act,[17] allow a peace officer to search a person or any place, other than in a dwelling-house, without a warrant.[18] But even in these statutes the use of the search power cannot

---

14 *R. v. Brezack* (1949), 9 C.R. 73 (Ont. C.A.).

15 *Dir. of Investigation and Research of the Combines Investigation Branch v. Southam Inc.*, [1984] 6 W.W.R. 577 (S.C.C.).

16 For example, see s. 101 which deals with weapons offences.

17 R.S.C. 1985, c. N-1.

18 For a discussion of this see Finkelstein, "Search and Seizure After Southam" (1985), 63 Can. Bar Rev. 193-199.

be arbitrary and the search must be based on a reasonable belief that an offence has been committed.

OBSTRUCTION OF JUSTICE AND JOURNALISTS

Section 129 of the Criminal Code makes it an offence to resist or willfully obstruct a public officer or a peace officer in the execution of his or her duty or any person lawfully acting in aid of such an officer.[19] It's this section that most commonly comes into play when journalists doing their jobs and police executing theirs, collide.

Generally, the courts have recognized that journalists have a job to do and have only punished serious acts of obstruction. In one case, a news photographer was taking pictures of a disturbed person who was being escorted away by a policeman under the authority of a Mental Health Act. The officer told the photographer to stop taking flash pictures because the patient was becoming hysterical. The photographer persisted and the charge of obstruction was laid. The court held that freedom of the press is not a right which is superior to the execution of a policeman's duty and found the photographer guilty.[20]

A Test for Obstruction

An important factor is that the obstruction must be willful. In other words, the accused must know what he or she is doing and must intend to obstruct the officer. In one case, an experienced photographer was covering a spectacular car accident.[21] Crowds of 250 to 300 people gathered and the police told everyone to stay on the sidewalk and keep off the street. The photographer was trying to get a good picture of the

---

19 This section also makes it an offence not to aid a public officer or peace officer, without a reasonable excuse, in the execution of his duty in arresting a person or in preserving the peace. You must be given a reasonable notice that you are required to help. It's also an offence under s. 129 to resist or obstruct any person in the lawful execution of a process against lands or goods, or in making a lawful distress or seizure.

20 *R. v. Kalnins* (1978), 41 C.C.C. (2d) 524 (Ont. Co. Ct.). Also see *Knowlton v. R.* (1973), 10 C.C.C. (2d) 377 (S.C.C.), where the Supreme Court of Canada said police were right to lay an obstruction charge against a press photographer who tried to push his way past a policeman guarding an area that had been cordoned off for a visiting dignitary. The court noted the dignitary had been assaulted several days earlier in another city and the photographer had inadequate identification.

21 *R. v. Sandford* (1980), 62 C.C.C. (2d) 89 (Ont. Prov. Ct.). This case and most obstruction cases are based on *R. v. Westlie* (1971), 2 C.C.C. (2d) 315 (B.C. C.A.), in which a man was charged with obstructing two plainclothes officers by pointing out to passersby that they were undercover cops. The court found the person guilty and said it was not necessary for the peace officer to be executing a specific duty at the time of the obstruction.

accident and stepped off the sidewalk. A charge of obstruction was laid. The court took a three step approach:

1. Was there an obstruction of a peace officer?
2. Was the obstruction affecting the peace officer in the execution of the duty he was then exercising?
3. If there was an obstruction, was it willful (that is, intentional) without lawful excuse?

The court found no willful obstruction in the photographer's actions and found him not guilty. The judge defined "willful" as being in the sense of having an "evil" intention to obstruct. He said the accused would have had to display an intention to actually obstruct the police in their duty.

YOUR RIGHTS WHEN DEALING WITH POLICE

The legal rights entrenched in the Charter are changing the shape of law enforcement powers and the methods of police investigation. Each right is important and can be expected to generate arguments and case law for generations to come. The following are some of your rights which pertain directly to the use of authority by the police:

1. You have the right to be secure against unreasonable search and seizure (section 8).
2. You have the right not to be arbitrarily detained or imprisoned (section 9).
3. You have the right on arrest or detention,
   i) to be informed of the reasons,
   ii) to retain and inform counsel without delay and to be informed of that right (section 10).
4. You have the right on being charged with an offence,
   i) to be informed without unreasonable delay of the specific offence,
   ii) to be tried within a reasonable time,
   iii) to be presumed innocent, and
   iv) not to be denied reasonable bail without just cause (section 11).
5. You have the right not to be subjected to cruel and unusual treatment or punishment (section 12).

The Right to Silence

There is one important right which everyone has which isn't expressly set out in the Charter or any other statute. In fact, there's nothing that compels any law enforcer to even mention this right to you (arguably, however, some officers do). It is the right to remain silent. Generally, there's no legal obligation on a person to give police any information, particularly during investigations. The only exceptions tend to be for identification purposes.

One Ontario Court of Appeal case examined the authority of police during an investigation.[22] The court noted that the police are entitled to ask any question of a person on the street, whether they are suspected of a crime or not. But the police have no lawful power to compel a person to answer. As noted elsewhere in this chapter, the police also have no power to detain someone against their will merely for questioning or investigation.

Still, there are some situations in which there could be a legal justification for police to ask for a person's identification. If a policeman is investigating an offence and believes you may have had a role in it, he or she may ask you to identify yourself. If you don't, the officer may take you into custody to establish your identity. At this point, you could be charged with obstructing justice.[23] But the officer must have reasonable grounds to believe you committed an offence and you're not required to give out any more than your identity. It should also be noted that a charge of obstructing justice cannot be laid if there is no evidence of a person having committed an offence.[24]

Some municipalities also have jaywalking by-laws which require a citizen to identify themselves to a police officer when caught. In addition, a driver of a motor vehicle is required to supply identification when stopped under provincial motor vehicle laws. Under the Criminal Code's section 252, any driver involved in an accident must stop and give police his or her name and address.

The police have wide-sweeping powers, some real and some imagined in the mind of the average citizen. When a policeman asks someone to come to the station for "some questions," few citizens are likely to ignore the request. Obviously, it's best to cooperate with police. But remember the police have limits too and if you're not under arrest or being detained for some legal reason, you have a right to leave.

If you're arrested or detained, simply identifying yourself doesn't mean you have to answer any other questions and you should not say anything else before speaking to a lawyer.

---

22 *R. v. Dedman* (1981), 32 O.R. (2d) 641 at 653 (Ont. C.A.).

23 In *Moore v. R.* (1978), 43 C.C.C. (2d) 83 (S.C.C.), the appellant committed a provincial offence while bicycling and refused to identify himself. While there was no provincial law requiring that a person identify himself, a court held that the bicyclist was obstructing the officer in the performance of his duties.

24 *R. v. Guthrie* (1982), 69 C.C.C. (2d) 216 (Alta. C.A.).

A POLICE POWERS CHECKLIST

1. Law enforcement powers are held by "peace officers" and "public officers," as defined in the Criminal Code. However, all citizens may use some law enforcement powers in limited circumstances.

2. A person enforcing the law isn't justified in using excessive force that is intended or is likely to cause death or grievous bodily harm unless he or she believes, on reasonable and probable grounds, that it's necessary to use it for self protection or to protect anyone else from serious harm or death.

3. The Criminal Code does not set out exactly what constitutes an arrest. A person must be told that he or she is under arrest and the reason for the arrest. Where possible, the peace officer must go through the motion of seizing or touching a person with an intent to detain him or her.

4. There is no general power allowing the search of a place or a person without a warrant, unless the search is incidental to the arrest of someone or if there is consent. There is also no general power to seize something unless it's in connection with the commission of an offence or under a warrant.

5. Conflicts between police and journalists may bring a Criminal Code charge of obstructing justice. The court may examine whether there actually was an obstruction of a peace officer, whether it affected the peace officer in the execution of his or her duty and whether it was willful. The accused must know what he or she is doing and must intend to obstruct the officer.

6. Aside from the protections in the Charter, a citizen's most important right in dealing with law enforcement authorities is the right to remain silent.

11

Court Orders: Search Warrants, Injunctions and Subpoenas

At some time, a journalist or a news outlet may become the subject of a court order. It could be a search warrant demanding tapes, an injunction blocking the publication of a defamatory story or a subpoena demanding that a journalist testify at a hearing. The first step when you get a court order is to call in legal counsel. There is nothing to be gained and much to be lost by resisting or ignoring a court order. In fact, a lawyer may be able to strike down a search warrant, injunction or subpoena through legal channels. Still, court orders demand respect and are increasingly being used in cases involving the news media. Thus, it's important to understand both their powers and limits.

SEARCH WARRANTS

The legal authority for a search can come in two forms. It can be in the form of a warrant or it can be warrantless. The authority to search a person or place without a warrant is covered in the chapter on police powers and this chapter will only deal with searches authorized by a warrant.

The Canadian Charter of Rights and Freedoms guarantees in section 8 the right "to be secure against unreasonable search or seizure."[1] The Supreme Court of Canada has made it clear that this fundamental guarantee isn't to be taken lightly. In one of its first Charter decisions, the Supreme Court set out the minimum acceptable standards needed

---

1 Part 1 of the Constitution Act, 1982, being Schedule B of the Canada Act 1982 (U.K.), 1982, c. 11 (hereinafter, Charter).

before a warrant can be authorized by a judge or other public official.[2] These standards have been summarized as follows:

1. There must be a belief based on reasonable and probable grounds, established upon oath, that an offence has been committed;
2. There must be a belief based on reasonable and probable grounds that the evidence of the offence is to be found at the place to be searched;
3. The area to be searched must be clearly described and the search must be limited to the probable area where the evidence is; and
4. The authorization for the search warrant must come from a neutral person who, if not a judge, is capable of acting judicially.[3]

In other words, the police or any other government agent can't go on a fishing mission and the issuance of the warrant must be based on reasonable grounds as determined by an independent third party. For example, a statute which gives the head of a government department the power to grant search warrants to his own employees would likely be found to be in violation of the Charter because of the lack of neutrality.

When is a Search Warrant Issued?

Generally, a search warrant is obtained from the courts. The Criminal Code sets out the general requirements for search warrants in sections 487 to 490.[4] To get a search warrant under the Criminal Code, the informant swears under oath to a justice in an information, that there are reasonable grounds to believe there is, in a building, receptacle or place:[5]

(a) anything upon or in respect of which any offence against this Act or any other Act of Parliament has been or is suspected to have been committed,

(b) anything that there is reasonable ground to believe will afford evidence with respect to the commission of an offence against this Act or any other Act of Parliament, or

(c) anything that there are reasonable grounds to believe is intended to be used for the purpose of committing any offence against the person for which a person may be arrested without a warrant.

For the search warrant to be valid, courts have held that it must be filled out properly and completely:[6]

---

2 *Dir. of Investigation and Research of the Combines Investigation Branch v. Southam Inc.*, [1984] 6 W.W.R. 577 (S.C.C.).

3 *Ibid.*, pp. 583-596.

4 R.S.C. 1985, c. C-46.

5 S. 487.

6 *Re McAvoy* (1970), 12 C.R.N.S. 56 at 65-66 (N.W.T. Terr. Ct.). The Criminal Code also now allows peace officers to request telewarrants, which are search warrants obtained

1. The warrant must disclose on its face the offence in relation to which the search is being conducted and the grounds of belief upon which the request for the warrant is made;
2. The place to be searched must be accurately described; and
3. The items to be searched for and seized must be reasonably described so they can be easily identified by the person at the premises and the officer executing the search.

Upon executing the search warrant the person conducting the search is required to meet certain standards:[7]

1. The warrant must be in his possession during the search;
2. The warrant must be exhibited for inspection upon request;
3. If the premises to be searched is a residence, there must be a demand to open before a forced entry is attempted (some exceptions allowed); and
4. The peace officer can only use the force which is necessary to enter the premises.

What Happens When a Search Warrant is Executed?

Criminal Code section 489 allows a peace officer to seize anything, in addition to things mentioned in the warrant, that on reasonable grounds he believes has been obtained by, or has been used in, the commission of an offence.

The granting of a search warrant or the exercise of a search power under other federal statutes must be executed judicially. That means the search must be based on reasonable grounds and the granting of the warrant must be within the power of the body or official.[8] There must also be a good reason to issue the warrant. The courts won't allow a search warrant to be used as an investigative arm of the state when other means are available.

In one case, the Department of Consumer and Corporate Affairs searched a news outlet for the notes of a journalist who covered a public demonstration.[9] The Department wanted the names of picketers who had stopped an inquiry from being held and knew that reporters had spoken with some demonstrators. The court considered the importance of the

---

over the telephone from a judge (s. 487.1) in circumstances where a personal appearance in a court is impractical.

7 *Wah Kie v. Cuddy (No. 2)* (1914), 23 C.C.C. 383 (Alta. C.A.).
8 Note 2, above.
9 *Pacific Press Ltd. v. R.*, [1977] 5 W.W.R. 507 (B.C. S.C.). The reasoning in this case was adopted by the Supreme Court of Canada in *Descôteaux v. Mierzwinski* (1982), 1 C.R.R. 318.

freedom of the press and the fact that people other than the news media were at the demonstration. The court quashed the warrant on the basis that the Department hadn't shown that it had tried to find the information through any other reasonable channels. In other words, a search warrant against the news media, for purposes such as this, is only to be used as a last resort.

If a search warrant is invalid, any person in control of the premises is entitled to eject the peace officer using as much force as is necessary.[10] But this would be risky without legal advice. Also, any active resistance or obstruction of a valid search could theoretically result in a charge under section 129 of the Code (that is, obstructing a peace officer or public officer). The most important thing to do when presented with a search warrant is to immediately contact legal counsel.

INJUNCTIONS

An injunction is an extraordinary remedy and the power to issue an injunction is exercised carefully.[11] Among other things, an injunction can be used to prevent a defamatory or contemptuous publication. Here are some common injunctions:

1. *interlocutory*: This injunction is issued after notice of an action has been served and restrains an act or maintains the status quo until a proper hearing on the matter can be held.
2. *quia timet*: This court order is issued in anticipation or in fear of an act which the applicant for the injunction wants to stop. It may be an illegal act or a lawful act which could cause injury, for which money would not provide an adequate remedy.
3. *ex parte*: This is an injunction issued without hearing from the party it affects. It's only issued when time is of the essence and the applicant for the injunction establishes he could suffer harm if it's not granted. Such an order can be used to prevent the broadcast or publication of a contemptuous or defamatory story.
4. *perpetual*: This injunction restrains an act forever after a proper hearing has been held on the merits of the case.

---

10 In *Colet v. R.*, [1981] 1 S.C.R. 2, the Supreme Court of Canada held that a warrant that was made out only "to search" a home didn't also include the authority to seize anything (in this case, firearms) unless it was specifically stated in the warrant. The court said Colet was justified in using force to eject the police.

11 *Browning v. Ryan* (1887), 4 Man. R. 486 at 490 (Q.B.).

When is an Injunction Issued?

An injunction won't be granted unless there's a clear basis for a court action.[12] This is especially so in cases of alleged defamation. For instance, in one case the court held that an injunction shouldn't be issued for an allegedly defamatory story unless the words complained of are so manifestly defamatory that any jury verdict to the contrary would be considered perverse by a court of appeal.[13] The same court also said the injunction also shouldn't be issued if damages would constitute a sufficient remedy.

In another commonly cited case (which will be discussed more fully below), an injunction was issued to stop the broadcast of defamatory matter in a radio documentary on the CBC. On appeal, the injunction was dissolved and the appeal court said such an order should only be issued for an alleged libel in the clearest of cases.[14] The court said the story must be clearly defamatory, clearly untrue and clearly not fair comment. The court held that if the publisher of the defamatory matter is of the opinion that he can prove the truth of his statements or offer some other defence, then no injunction will be issued. The matter can then be resolved in a proper defamation action.

In other matters, such as cases alleging a breach of confidence, the law is less clear. A journalist may have to prove that there's a "public interest" at stake in allowing publication. The court will try to balance the interests of all parties and find the least "harmful" decision. This is known as the "balance of convenience" test.

For instance, an injunction may be issued to stop the publication of a story or broadcast which could endanger the fair trial of an individual. In 1985, an Alberta court judge banned the showing in Alberta of a CBC drama which was loosely based on the controversial case of James Keegstra, a schoolteacher convicted of inciting racial hatred. The judge felt the one-hour program was "a thinly-guised characterization of . . . Keegstra" and would interfere with Keegstra's appeal of his conviction.[15]

However, the CBC later challenged the injunction and the order was set aside by the appeal court.[16] That court noted that the CBC drama was to be broadcast before Keegstra's appeal took place and in the event

---

12 In *Church of Scientology of B.C. v. Radio N.W. Ltd.*, [1974] 4 W.W.R. 173 (B.C. C.A.), an interim injunction was granted to the plaintiff because the defendant was unwilling to offer any evidence of the truth of the story's defamatory allegations and, furthermore, said it would broadcast them despite the lack of solid proof.

13 *Rapp v. McClelland and Stewart Ltd.* (1981), 34 O.R. (2d) 452 at 455 (H.C.).

14 *Can. Metal v. CBC* (1974), 3 O.R. (2d) 1 at 16 (H.C.).

15 Quoted in *CBC v. Keegstra* (1986), 35 D.L.R. (4th) 76 at 77 (Alta. C.A.).

16 *Ibid.*

a new trial was ordered, it would not begin for at least two or three years. The appeal court held that there was no real or substantial risk of prejudice to any potential re-trial and hence no case for an injunction.

While the Keegstra case involved proceedings at the appeal stage, another case looked at whether any danger exists when a trial is closer at hand. In 1986, the last of seven people awaiting trial in the murder of Hanna Buxbaum applied for an injunction to delay publication of a book about the high-profile trial of co-accused Helmuth Buxbaum, husband of Hanna.[17]

The court noted that the author of the book was aware of the upcoming trial of the accused and had given an undertaking not to use the plaintiff's name in the book. Citing the freedom of the press and the need for public reporting of trials, the judge pointed out that the previous trial had been widely-reported and a fair and accurate report of it in book form should not be enjoined.

An injunction may also be issued in connection with an alleged breach of a contract or an agreement made with a journalist. In one case, a book publisher got an injunction which prevented the broadcast of an interview with a noted celebrity, Margaret Trudeau.[18] The publisher had an agreement with the CTV television network that the network would not broadcast the interview until just prior to the book's release. But disagreements arose after parts of the unreleased book were published elsewhere and the network maintained it no longer had an agreement and tried to broadcast the interview at an earlier date. The book publisher went to court and the result was that an injunction was issued until the matter of the breach of the alleged contract could be tried in court.

In 1985, a similar situation arose for the CBC's current affairs program, *The Fifth Estate*. The program was planning to broadcast a story involving a convicted serial killer. The accused was appealing some of his convictions at the time and applied for an injunction to stop the broadcast. The Alberta court judge was told by the accused that the CBC had agreed to let him see the finished product before it went to air.

In court, the CBC maintained that the agreement in question applied to an earlier interview and the story was using material from a later interview at which no such promise was made. The judge held that there was an agreement and that it had been breached. He issued a cross-country injunction against the airing of the television documentary based on the breach of the agreement.

---

17 *Foshay v. Key Porter Books Ltd.* (1986), 36 D.L.R. (4th) 106 (Ont. H.C.). An interesting aside is that this case was decided in March of 1986, yet a court order banned its publication until after the plaintiff's trial.

18 *Paddington Press Ltd. v. Champ* (1979), 43 C.P.R. (2d) 175 (Ont. H.C.).

What Happens After an Injunction is Delivered?

Obviously, anyone who is the subject of an injunction should call a lawyer. A lawyer may be able to have the injunction quashed and, at the very least, can advise a journalist on how to properly comply with the order.

Compliance can be a complex matter. It's important that the injunction be obeyed not only to the letter, but in spirit as well. This means one shouldn't try to "split hairs" when deciding how an injunction affects a story. A prominent example of this involved the CBC.[19]

In 1974, the CBC was preparing to broadcast a radio documentary on *As It Happens* involving two lead smelting companies. The documentary was entitled "Dying of Lead."

On the day of the broadcast, the smelting companies applied for an *ex parte* injunction to stop the CBC from making certain allegations about the safety of its smoke stacks. The action by the companies was prompted by a newspaper article outlining what the CBC story alleged.

The injunction was granted with this endorsement:[20]

> Ex parte injunction granted to plaintiffs restraining defendants, and each of them from alleging or implying by broadcasting on television or otherwise publicizing that the plaintiffs and/or either of them, have bought misleadingly favourable medical evidence and concealed material evidence from medical experts, and from mis-stating the amounts the plaintiffs are spending to install pollution control systems.

The CBC was notified by telephone of the injunction and shortly after, a copy of the injunction was personally delivered. By the time the notice of the injunction was delivered the program had already been heard in the Maritimes because of the earlier time zone.

The CBC producers and legal counsel sat down to edit the script for the Ontario and Western audiences to conform to the injunction. Some offending statements were removed and the program was broadcast in its revised form. But, the court was later to hold that substantial parts of the remaining story were also in contravention of the injunction. In addition, to explain the alterations to the story, the court order was read word-for-word at one point in the program. Later that same night, the CBC's national news program ran a story reporting the fact that the court injunction had been issued against the radio program. The television story also went on to quote the exact words of the injunction.

---

19 *Can. Metal v. CBC (No. 2)* (1974), 19 C.C.C. (2d) 218 (Ont. H.C.). This decision holding the CBC and some of its employees in contempt of the injunction was upheld in the Ontario Court of Appeal at (1975), 65 D.L.R. (3d) 231.

20 (1974), 19 C.C.C. (2d) 218 at 221 (Ont. H.C.).

The judge felt that very little had been edited out of the story after the injunction was received. He said the airing of the story should have been postponed to allow for more careful examination of the script. The judge felt the people responsible for the story shouldn't have tried to edit it in such a short time. Besides the fact that errors in judgment were made in editing down the story, a major complaint of the judge was that the quotation of the injunction's endorsement published the exact allegations that the court was seeking to prevent from being broadcast.

As a result of the CBC broadcasts, other news agencies carried the story, quoting the wording of the injunction and also stating what was not intended to be published. The court found the publication of the wording of the injunction by the CBC and the other news outlets to be against the spirit of the court order. The court held that anyone who knows of the substance or nature of an injunction must obey it, even if they aren't named in the injunction. Therefore, the other news agencies were also in violation of the injunction and in fact several were cited for contempt along with the CBC.

SUBPOENAS

A *subpoena* is a judicial order requiring a person to appear in a court at a certain place and time to give evidence in a criminal or civil proceeding. The subpoena may require a person to personally take the stand and testify (that is, a *subpoena ad testificandum*) and/or it may require the person to present any documents in his possession or under his or her control relating to the subject-matter of the proceedings (that is, a *subpoena duces tecum*). In criminal cases, anyone who is "likely to give material evidence in a proceeding" may be the subject of a subpoena.[21]

When is a Subpoena Issued?

A subpoena may be issued by a superior court judge, a provincial court judge, justice of the peace or even a clerk of the court. Subpoenas issued by a Superior Court are effective throughout Canada, while those issued by a provincial court have authority only within that province. Clerks can issue subpoenas for certain courts (for example, superior and appellate courts) and usually do so without questioning the lawyer who requested it.

But if a judge or justice of the peace issues a subpoena, he or she will have to be convinced that the person receiving it has "material evidence" to give at the trial. Material evidence is that which is necessary

---

21 Criminal Code, s. 698(1).

to the resolution of the dispute or has an important bearing on the issues in question.

Not all witnesses with material evidence can be subpoenaed. For example, a lawyer can't be called as a witness to testify to matters within solicitor-client privilege.[22] Although journalists may consider their relationship with sources to be similar to solicitor-client relationships, the courts have a different view in most cases and will usually require a journalist to reveal a source.[23]

What Happens After a Subpoena is Delivered?

The subpoena will usually be personally delivered to the witness. But if the witness can't be conveniently found, the subpoena can be left at his or her home with anyone who appears to be at least 16 years old.[24] Once a subpoena is received, the witness is required to attend the court as directed and cannot leave until excused by the judge.[25] If someone refuses to obey a subpoena and fails to show up, the court can issue a cross-country warrant for the arrest of the witness.[26] The witness may then be detained until the trial or released on recognizance.

The issuance of a subpoena may be challenged in a superior court. For example, a subpoenaed witness may not actually have "material evidence" or the material evidence could be gathered easily through other channels. Journalists themselves may be called upon to appear in court to testify to any number of things. The journalist may have seen a crime committed, he or she may have to bring interview notes as evidence in a defamation action or an editor may be asked to bring copies of published stories to prove that they appeared (for example, as in a change of venue hearing based on prejudicial news reports).

Some witnesses may agree to show up in court, but will refuse to testify. The court has several options. If the refusal comes during the preliminary hearing in a criminal proceeding, the presiding judge may commit the witness to jail for a period of up to eight days.[27] If the witness refuses to answer questions after the end of the eight day period, the judge may continue to issue eight day internments — theoretically forever. In a criminal trial, the judge can cite the witness with contempt and under

---

22 *R. v. Stupp* (1983), 32 C.R. (3d) 168 (Ont. H.C.).
23 See the chapter on "News Sources."
24 Criminal Code, s. 509(2).
25 *Ibid.*, s. 700.
26 *Ibid.*, ss. 698(2) and 705.
27 *Ibid.*, s. 545.

the Criminal Code the sentence is at the complete discretion of the judge, theoretically, with no limit as to the severity of the punishment.[28]

A COURT ORDERS CHECKLIST

Search Warrants

1. The Charter guarantees in section 8 "the right to be secure against unreasonable search or seizure." The minimum requirements for a warrant are that:
   - there must be a belief based on reasonable and probable grounds, established upon oath, that an offence has been committed;
   - there is a belief the evidence of the offence is to be found at the place to be searched;
   - the area to be searched must be clearly described and the search must be limited to that area;
   - the authorization for the search warrant must come from a neutral person who, if not a judge, is capable of acting judicially.
2. For a search warrant to be valid:
   - the warrant must disclose the offence in relation to which the search is being conducted and the grounds of belief upon which the request for the warrant is made;
   - the place to be searched must be accurately described; and
   - the items to be searched for and seized must be described so they can be easily identified by the person at the premises and the officer executing the search.
3. The person conducting the search is required to meet the following conditions:
   - the warrant must be in his or her possession during the search;
   - the warrant must be exhibited for inspection upon request;
   - if the premises to be searched is a residence, there should first be a demand to open before a forced entry is attempted; and
   - a peace officer can only use the force which is necessary to enter the premises.
4. If a search warrant is invalid, anyone in control of the premises is entitled to eject the peace officer with as much force as necessary. But active resistance or obstruction of a valid search could result in a criminal charge of obstruction. Always contact legal counsel when presented with a search warrant.

---

28 See *R. v. Clement*, [1981] 2 S.C.R. 468, where the Supreme Court of Canada held that the power to punish for contempt under sections 9 and 10 of the Code includes the right of the presiding judge to determine the proper punishment at his own discretion.

Injunctions

1. Among other things, an injunction can be used to prevent a defamatory or contemptuous publication. It may restrain an act for a limited period or forever.
2. Generally, an injunction will not be granted unless there's a clear need for immediate action. In defamation matters, courts have held that an injunction shouldn't be issued except in cases of obvious defamation when damages would not constitute a sufficient remedy, and even then, shouldn't be granted if the news outlet indicates it's willing to defend any action. Where there is a risk of contempt of court and endangering a fair trial, the danger of prejudicing the trial must be real and substantial.

    In other matters, such as cases alleging a breach of confidence, the law is less clear. A journalist may have to prove there is a "public interest" at stake in not granting an injunction. The court will try to balance the interests of all parties and find the least "harmful" decision.
3. Anyone who knows of the substance or nature of an injunction must obey it, even if they aren't named in the injunction.

Subpoenas

1. A subpoena is a judicial order requiring a person to appear in a court at a certain place and time to give evidence in a criminal or civil proceeding. If someone refuses to obey a subpoena and fails to show up, the court can issue a warrant for the arrest of the witness. The witness may then be detained until the trial or released on recognizance.
2. A subpoena may be issued to anyone with "material evidence" in the dispute or issues in question. A lawyer may be able to challenge a subpoena. For example, a subpoenaed witness may not actually have "material evidence" or the material evidence could be gathered easily through other channels.

12

Confidential Information and Official Secrets

At some time in their career, many journalists come to know the excitement of receiving the famous "plain brown envelope" containing some confidential or secret document. Or perhaps a disgruntled company employee walks into the newsroom with a bundle of papers suggesting his employer has committed some illegal or immoral act.

Can a journalist publish these confidential documents? The answer is not an easy one and, as with many of the news media's legal problems, a lawyer must be called in to examine the circumstances of each case. What's certain is that anytime a journalist receives secret or confidential information belonging to someone else, it must be handled carefully or the journalist could end up in civil or even criminal court.

JOURNALISTS AND THE "PLAIN BROWN ENVELOPE"

There can be many problems with publishing confidential documents. One of the first questions to be asked is, who is the source of the information?

If the source is known, a journalist must then consider whether that person is possibly breaching a confidence or trust. If so, the source and the journalist could be sued by the person or body to whom the confidence is owed. For example, a lawyer who hands a journalist incriminating documents belonging to a client may be breaching the solicitor-client privilege. The client could seek an injunction to prohibit publication and sue for damages.

If the source is unknown, other questions must then be answered. Is the information what it purports to be? For example, was that damning letter really written by the company president or is it a forgery using purloined letterhead? Without knowing the source, it's sometimes difficult to tell.

In either case, it's possible the documents may have been stolen or passed on without the owner's consent. If that's the case, publication could result in a civil lawsuit or even criminal charges.

This was amply illustrated in 1989 when a Global Television reporter was charged with possession of a stolen document after a "Deep Throat" handed him a copy of the federal government's budget brief on the day before the budget was to be brought down. While many people criticized, on a public policy basis, the RCMP's decision to charge the reporter, it's reasonable to assume such a document could have been stolen or the product of a government employee's breach of public trust. The police obviously felt that only a criminal trial could sort out the details.

If a lawyer determines that a document was stolen or a breach of confidence, the journalist may be advised to return it to its owner or hand it to the authorities. However, this doesn't mean that you can't use the information in the documents to ask questions or look for another source to corroborate what is in the documents.

JOURNALISTS AND OFFICIAL SECRETS

As one might suspect, the Official Secrets Act occasionally crops up when an agent for a foreign power is caught with military secrets or a journalist receives information involving national security. In theory, the Act could even be used to stop the publication of any non-military government information. However, there have been few prosecutions under the Act, largely because of its cumbersome and confusing language.[1]

The Act is actually an adaptation of two English statutes dating back to the early part of the century and has remained largely unchanged since then. One of its problems is that it doesn't define an "official secret." It does make several references to that which is "prejudicial to the safety or interests of the State" and information or documents that could be "directly or indirectly useful to a foreign power." The Act also makes opaque references to "official documents" and "secret official code word[s]" or "password[s]." But this mixed bag of phrasing makes a prosecution under the Act very difficult.

Still, journalists shouldn't feel too secure. The vagueness of the Act makes it a potentially dangerous instrument for censorship. This was clearly illustrated in the mid-1980s when the British government tried unsuccess-

---

1 R.S.C. 1985, c. O-5. See the *Mackenzie Royal Commission on Security*, June, 1969, where deficiencies in the Official Secrets Act are discussed.

fully to use the U.K. Official Secrets Act to prevent publication of *Spycatcher*, a book examining the world of covert agents. In Canada, the same potential for abuse exists and the Act is badly in need of revision.

Generally, it appears that an official secret could be military (for example, information on the development of a new weapon), political (for example, cabinet documents) or even administerial (for example, secret government discussion papers). The penalty for violating the Act can be up to 14 years in jail.

There are several offences under the Act which could affect journalists. They involve spying near prohibited places and the communication and possession of secret information.

Spying

Section 3(1) of the Act states:

Every person is guilty of an offence under this Act who, for any purpose prejudicial to the safety or interests of the State,
    (a) approaches, inspects, passes over, is in the neighbourhood of or enters any prohibited place;
    (b) makes any sketch, plan, model or note that is calculated to be or might be or is intended to be directly or indirectly useful to a foreign power; or
    (c) obtains, collects, records or publishes, or communicates to any other person, any secret official code word, or password, sketch, plan, model, article, note, document or information that is calculated to be or might be or is intended to be directly or indirectly useful to a foreign power.

A variety of types of spying are covered in these sections. Section 3(1)(a) is concerned with people lurking about a "prohibited place," which is further defined in section 2(1) as:

    (a) any work of defence belonging to or occupied or used by or on behalf of Her Majesty, including arsenals, armed forces establishments or stations, factories, dockyards, mines, minefields, camps, ships, aircraft, telegraph, telephone, wireless or signal stations or offices, and places used for the purpose of building, repairing, making or storing any munitions of war or any sketches, plans, models or documents relating thereto, or for the purpose of getting any metals, oil or minerals of use in time of war,
    (b) any place not belonging to Her Majesty where any munitions of war or any sketches, plans, models or documents relating thereto are being made, repaired, obtained or stored under contract with, or with any person on behalf of, Her Majesty, or otherwise on behalf of Her Majesty, and
    (c) any place that is for the time being declared by order of the Governor in Council to be a prohibited place on the ground that information with respect thereto or damage thereto would be useful to a foreign power.

Sections 3(1)(b) and 3(1)(c) are more concerned with the actual passing of secret information which might be useful to a foreign power. For definition purposes, a *sketch* "includes any mode of representing any place or thing."[2] Consequently, publishing a photograph of a top secret military project could prompt a charge under the Act if it could be directly or indirectly useful to a foreign power (for example, showing the location of the project).

The wording of these two subsections is extremely widesweeping because the information in question need only be "directly or indirectly useful to a foreign power." It would be difficult to say what information might be indirectly useful. Today's spies already glean great amounts of information from daily news reports and public documents.

The Act creates a dangerous atmosphere for journalists because many of the offences place a "reverse-onus" on the defendant to prove his or her innocence first, which could be a violation of the right to be presumed innocent under the Canadian Charter of Rights and Freedoms.[3] For instance, under section 3, to prove that an act or omission is "for any purpose prejudicial to the safety or interests of the State," the Crown must only show that a person's purpose "appears" to be prejudicial to the safety or interests of the State. The Act says a person can be convicted completely on circumstantial evidence, without any direct proof that a particular act is prejudicial to the safety or interests of Canada. Section 3(2) says a conviction can be based on the circumstances of the case, the accused's conduct or his known character and the appearance that the accused's "purpose was a purpose prejudicial to the safety or interests of the State."

Section 3(3) says an act is deemed to be for a purpose prejudicial to the safety or interests of the State if the Crown can prove that any secret information about a prohibited place or any secret official code or pass word, is communicated to another person without lawful authority. The onus again is on the defendant to prove otherwise. And sections 3(4) and 3(5) say that any communication with an agent of a foreign power, whether inside or outside of Canada, is evidence of a purpose prejudicial to the safety and interests of the State with the onus on the defendant to prove otherwise.

Wrongful Communication

Section 4 sets out the offences that journalists are most likely to be in a position to worry about. This section deals with the wrongful

---

2 S. 2(1).

3 Part 1 of the Constitution Act, 1982, being Schedule B of the Canada Act 1982 (U.K.), 1982, c. 11. Reverse onus clauses are frequently being struck down by the courts. See, for example, the Supreme Court of Canada's ruling in *R. v. Oakes*, [1986] 1 S.C.R. 103.

communication of secrets and there are several offences set out in the subsections of section 4.

Subsection 4(1) lists seven examples of confidential information coming under the ambit of the Act, namely any secret official code word or password or any sketch, plan, model, article, note, document or information:

1. relating to or used in a prohibited place or anything in such a place;
2. that has been made or obtained in contravention of this Act;
3. that has been entrusted in confidence to him by any person holding office under Her Majesty;
4. that he has obtained or to which he has had access while subject to the Code of Service Discipline within the meaning of the National Defence Act;
5. that he has obtained or to which he has had access owing to his position as a person who holds or has held office under Her Majesty;
6. that he has obtained or to which he has had access as a person who holds or held a contract made on behalf of Her Majesty or carried out in whole or in part at a prohibited place; or
7. that he has obtained or to which he has had access as a person working for someone who holds or held such a contract.

Subsection 4(1) then makes it an offence for any person who has possession or control of any secret official code word or password or any sketch, plan, model, article, note, document or information to:

1. communicate it to an unauthorized person;
2. use the information for the benefit of a foreign power;
3. use it in a manner prejudicial to the safety and interests of the State;
4. unlawfully retain it; or
5. fail to take reasonable care of the information or endanger its safety.

Section 4(2) makes it an offence to directly or indirectly communicate to a foreign power an official secret about munitions of war or communicate it in any other manner prejudicial to the safety and interests of the State.

Section 4(3) is also a potential problem for journalists. It says it's an offence to receive any official secret knowing, or having a reasonable ground to believe at the time it's received, that it's being communicated in contravention of the Official Secrets Act. To be found innocent, a person placed in this position would have to prove that he or she received the secret "contrary to his desire."

Section 4(4) makes it an offence to keep, for purposes prejudicial to the safety and interests of the State, any "official document" which a person was once authorized to have or to allow an unauthorized person to have possession of that secret. It also is an offence under this sub-section to unlawfully receive an official secret and then neglect or fail to return it to "the person or authority by whom or for whose use it was issued, or to a police constable."

Criminal Code and Official Secrets

The Criminal Code[4] also addresses the communication of official secrets under the offence of high treason. Among other offences, section 46(2)(b) states that anyone commits high treason who:

> without lawful authority, communicates or makes available to an agent of a state other than Canada, military or scientific information or any sketch, plan, model, article, note or document of a military or scientific character that he knows or ought to know may be used by that state for a purpose prejudicial to the safety or defence of Canada.

The Case of *R. v. Toronto Sun Publishing Ltd.*

There has been only one case in recent years involving journalists charged under the Official Secrets Act. In 1978, the *Toronto Sun* and two employees were charged with violating the Act by publishing information obtained from a classified RCMP document on KGB activities in Canada.[5]

The document in question was entitled "Canadian Related Activities of the Russian Intelligence Services." It was stamped "Top Secret" and "For Canadian Eyes Only." The journalists and newspaper were charged with wrongfully communicating secrets (section 4(1)) and knowingly receiving the information in contravention of the Act (section 4(3)).

The case is an excellent example of why the Official Secrets Act is a confusing and cumbersome law. At a preliminary hearing, the Crown began by calling an expert witness to testify about the potential damage the newspaper article could have to the safety and interests of Canada. But at that point, the lawyers for the journalists objected that the testimony would only be hearsay since there was no documentary proof that Canada's safety or interests were actually damaged.

The Crown then decided it had enough evidence to support the charge without the expert's testimony and withdrew the witness. The result of this little bit of courtroom jostling was that the preliminary hearing judge then did not have to decide whether the publication of the information was actually prejudicial to Canada's security.

The sole issue then became whether the report was in fact "secret." The judge examined in detail what had been previously published. Most

---

4 R.S.C. 1985, c. C-46.
5 *R. v. Toronto Sun Publishing Co.* (1979), 98 D.L.R. (3d) 524 (Ont. Prov. Ct.).

of the details in the Sun's story by Peter Worthington had in fact been published previously. There was evidence that information from the document had been broadcast on television, had been mentioned in the House of Commons and was even reported in Hansard. There were also 67 copies of the "official" document distributed throughout the government.

The court referred to two Canadian court judgments which held that information that has already been published is neither "official" nor "secret."[6] The judge said that even stamping the documents with the words "Top Secret" has no official meaning and, here, was mainly for administrative convenience. There was also no evidence from the Crown regarding how the information was obtained and whether it was obtained unlawfully.

The court discharged the accused at the preliminary hearing. The justice said the Crown had failed to prove that the document was secret and had not proven that the accused had reasonable grounds to believe at the time that the information was communicated to them in contravention of the Act.

Since the Act's inception, civil rights advocates have lobbied for its repeal. Although the *Toronto Sun* escaped prosecution, a journalist who receives information which he or she believes is an "official secret" would be wise to contact legal counsel. The Act is so vaguely worded that journalists receiving confidential government information could theoretically be thrown into lengthy and expensive legal proceedings.

A CONFIDENTIAL INFORMATION AND OFFICIAL SECRETS CHECKLIST

1. A journalist receiving confidential information should consult a lawyer. For example, the documents may have been stolen. If the source is known, a journalist must then consider whether that person is possibly breaching a confidence or trust. If the source is unknown, the documents themselves may be forgeries, incomplete or misleading.
2. While confidential documents may have to be returned, the information in them can still be used by a journalist to ask questions or to seek out a corroborating or alternative source.

---

6 The court referred to the 1962 case of *R. v. Biernacki* (unreported) in which the accused collected information on social status, employment and the character of Polish immigrants, which appeared to be for the purposes of espionage. The court felt this information was neither secret nor official, even though it may have been for the purposes of espionage. The other case was *R. v. Boyer* (1948), 94 C.C.C. 195 (Qué. K.B.) in which the court said the Official Secrets Act doesn't apply to material which has already been published or publicized or can be found in the public domain.

3. Under the cumbersome wording of the Official Secrets Act, it appears that an official secret could involve military, political (such as, cabinet documents) or even administerial information (for example, a secret policy paper).

4. Under the Official Secrets Act, a person may be charged with "spying" for lurking about a government designated "prohibited place," making a sketch, plan, model or note that "might be or is intended to be directly or indirectly useful to a foreign power," or passing on any secret official code or password.

5. Under the Official Secrets Act, a person may be charged with "wrongful communication" of confidential government information or unauthorized possession of such information. It's also an offence for any person to have possession or control of an official secret and communicate it to an unauthorized person, use the information for the benefit of a foreign power, use it in a manner prejudicial to the safety and interests of the State, unlawfully retain it, or fail to take reasonable care of it or endanger its safety.

6. Court decisions have held that information which has already been published is neither "official" nor "secret." Stamping documents with the words "Top Secret" has no official meaning.

13

Copyright

When a radio journalist broadcasts a word-for-word version of a newspaper story or an article quotes a popular song at length, there may be an infringement of someone's copyright.

Simply put, a copyright is a legal right to make public, produce or reproduce any written or artistic work, or a substantial part of it, in any material form.

Canada's copyright law has a long and tortured history. The federal Copyright Act[1] has been around in much of its present form since the 1920s and has changed little since then. While televisions, computers and photocopiers were becoming a part of our lives, the Act remained frozen in its archaic state with no amendments or mention of such devices. The Act quickly became obsolete.

In recent years, an attempt has been made to bring the Act up to date. In June 1988, the first major amendments recognized computer programs, increased penalties for infringements and strengthened the rights of both creators of works and copyright holders (often separate individuals).[2] The amendments have also boosted the importance of moral rights.

---

1 R.S.C. 1985, c. C-42.
2 S.C. 1988, c. 15.

As will be discussed below, even when creators sell their copyright to others, they continue to enjoy a moral right in their works. In the future, this "new" right could affect both journalist-creators and their editors.

The amendments also laid the groundwork for copyright "collectives" which will license the use of copyrighted material and collect royalties on behalf of copyright holders. Other amendments can be expected in the near future.

GENERAL PRINCIPLES OF COPYRIGHT LAW

What Can Be Copyrighted?

A copyright can be attached to any original writing, music, lyrics, choreography, pictures, sound recordings, art or architecture. It even applies to unpublished works.

When Does a Copyright Take Effect?

What many people may not realize is that the actual act of creating an original work immediately establishes a copyright for the creator or, sometimes, his or her employer.[3] There's no requirement that a creator register his or her work with an official body or publish it to establish a copyright.

This can have interesting consequences. For example, a book publisher wanting to publish personal letters written by a prominent person to a friend could theoretically find there are copyright problems. Neither the publisher possessing the letters nor the friend to whom they were written holds the copyright. The right to reproduce the letters rests with the creator.

Is Any Copying an Infringement?

The defence of "fair dealing" allows the reproduction of parts of copyrighted material for the purposes of comment in news reports or other publications. That being said, reproducing even a small part of an original work could still be an infringement of copyright if it could be considered to be a "substantial" part of the work. This will be discussed further below.

Can Pure Information Be Copyrighted?

Generally, there's no copyright in the ideas or information in works.[4] The law has clearly set out that copyright only protects the way in which an idea or information is expressed (that is, its format), not the idea or information itself.[5] For example, information in a copyrighted news story can still be re-published by competitors so long as subsequent stories don't

---

3 *Ibid.*, ss. 13(1) and 13(3).
4 *Deeks v. Wells*, [1931] O.R. 818 at 834 (C.A.).
5 *Stevenson v. Crook*, [1938] 4 D.L.R. 294 at 303 (Ex. Ct.).

copy the original story's wording or manner of expression. This will also be discussed further on.

THE COPYRIGHT ACT

Definitions

Parliament enacted the Copyright Act in 1921[6] and although steps are being taken to bring the Act up to date with amendments, much of it is still written in the cumbersome and awkward manner of our forefathers. For example, the present Act defines "copyright" itself as:[7]

> the sole right to produce or reproduce the work or any substantial part thereof in any material form whatever, to perform, or in the case of a lecture to deliver, the work or any substantial part thereof in public or, if the work is unpublished, to publish the work or any substantial part thereof.

The Act goes on to state, in its obsolete terminology, that copyright also includes the sole right:

(a) to produce, reproduce, perform or publish any translation of the work;
(b) in the case of a dramatic work, convert it into a novel or other non-dramatic work;
(c) in the case of a novel or other non-dramatic work, or of an artistic work, to convert it into a dramatic work, by way of performance in public or otherwise;
(d) in the case of a literary, dramatic, or musical work, to make any record, perforated roll, cinematograph film, or other contrivance by means of which the work may be mechanically performed or delivered;
(e) . . . in the case of any literary, dramatic, musical or artistic work, to reproduce, adapt and publicly present the work by cinematograph, if the author has given the work an original character [but if such original character is absent the cinematographic production shall be protected as a photograph],
(f) in the case of any literary, dramatic, musical or artistic work, to communicate such work by radio communication;

and to authorize any such acts aforesaid.

Who's Protected?

The Act protects works of Canadian citizens, British subjects or residents of "Her Majesty's Realms and Territories."[8] However, Canada has also signed several international conventions or agreements on copyright, which have provisions similar to our Act.[9] Over 90 countries have signed the conventions

---

6 S.C. 1921, c. 24.
7 S. 3(1).
8 S. 4.
9 Canada is a signatory of the *Berne Convention* (1885), *Berlin Convention* (1908), *Rome Convention* (1928) and the *Universal Copyright Convention* (Geneva, 1952), the latter of which was signed by Canada on May 10, 1962.

and we are bound by the agreements to respect copyrights existing in member countries. Consequently, copyrighted material created in one of these member countries (for example, the United States) is entitled to the same protection in Canada as "home-grown" works.[10]

But the international conventions themselves are not considered a part of the domestic law of Canada and our Copyright Act still has the final say on questions of copyright.[11]

How Long Does Copyright Last?

In Canada, the copyright for published works subsists for the life of the creator and for a period of 50 years after.[12] This is so even if the copyright has been sold to another individual. Works published after the death of the creator have copyright protection for 50 years after they are published. Works produced for Her Majesty (that is, the Crown), such as government reports or information booklets, are under copyright protection for 50 years from the date of first publication, unless some other agreement has been struck with the author.[13] The copyright on photographs and cinematographic works subsists for 50 years from the creation of the original negative.[14]

Who Owns the Copyright?

The author, as first owner of the copyright, has a right to sell or assign his or her copyright to someone else.[15] But the assignment of copyright, other than in a will, can only be held (that is, owned) by a purchaser for 25 years after the creator's death, at which time the copyright reverts back to the creator's estate for the remaining 25 years.[16]

If the creator of a work was employed by another individual and the work was made in the course of employment, then the employer will be

---

10 The Universal Copyright Convention, *ibid.*, provides for international copyright protection without any formal registration of the copyright. But the Convention does require placing a circled "c" on the work, along with the name of the copyright owner and the year it is published. This convention was spearheaded by the United States and reflected its copyright law at the time.

However, in 1988, the U.S. acceded to the Berne Convention, prompting some copyright specialists to question the relevance of the Universal Copyright Convention.

11 See Fox, *The Canadian Law of Copyright and Industrial Designs*, 2nd ed. (Toronto, Carswell, 1967), p. 548.

12 S. 6.

13 S. 12.

14 S. 10.

15 S. 13(1).

16 S. 14.

the first owner of the copyright.[17] But an author and an employer can also agree to another arrangement.[18] For example, freelance writers often sell the first serial rights to a story. After the newspaper or magazine uses the story, the copyright reverts back to the freelancer. However, this should be covered in a contract between the two parties.

There is also a statutory exception to the rule that copyright ownership rests with an employer. When the work (such as, an article or art) is for a newspaper, magazine or similar periodical, the creator is deemed to have a right, subject to a contract stating otherwise, to restrain the publication of the work in any form other than as a part of a newspaper, magazine or similar periodical.[19] For example, a consumer magazine couldn't publish an article you wrote for it on car care in a subsequent book unless there was some agreement to the contrary.

Similar rules apply to other works. When someone pays for an engraving, photograph or portrait, that person becomes the first owner of the copyright unless there's some other agreement.[20]

The 1988 amendments to the Act established the authority of copyright "collectives" to license the use of copyrighted material and collect any royalties generated. Previously, only the music industry had such collectives and fees were collected from radio stations, theatres and other commercial operations on behalf of the copyright holders. Now, collectives can be formed for most any type of work. At the time of this publication, collectives were still in the process of forming and it appears they won't have any direct effect on news gathering operations.

What are Moral Rights?

Moral rights for creators are nothing new. The Copyright Act has always asserted that moral rights exist in a work and that they are separate from copyright.[21] But amendments to the Act in 1988 have raised the moral rights provisions to a new level of significance.

The moral rights sections protect works against distortion, mutilation or major changes that are serious enough to damage or lessen the reputation or honour of a creator.[22] The new sections, however, go into even more

---

17 S. 13(3).

18 *Ibid.*

19 *Ibid.*

20 S. 13(2).

21 S. 14(4) states that, "Independently of the author's copyright, and even after the assignment, either wholly or partially, of the copyright, the author has the right to claim authorship of the work, as well as the right to restrain any distortion, mutilation or other modification of the work that would be prejudicial to the honour or reputation of the author."

22 Ss. 18.1 and 18.2 (enacted by S.C. 1988, c. 15, s. 6).

detail and make it clear that violations of moral rights carry the same remedies and penalties as for copyright infringements.

The bolstered moral rights sections allow a creator to protect the integrity and original form of a work even when the copyright has been sold or assigned to another individual. In fact, the moral rights of a creator can't be sold or assigned to anyone else. They can only be waived in writing by the creator.

The amendment was driven by a prominent court case in the early 1980s involving a well-known sculpture in The Eaton Centre in Toronto.[23] A flock of 60 Canadian geese had been fashioned by artist Michael Snow and sold to the shopping centre to be hung permanently from the ceiling. During one Christmas season, the mall's management decided to festively decorate the geese with red ribbons. Snow objected, saying it was an insult to his work and hurt his reputation. The dispute ended up in court where a judge sided with Snow and ordered the ribbons removed. Snow's moral rights came to his rescue, even though the copyright in the geese had been sold to the mall.

Given the Snow case, it's expected that a creator's own opinion regarding whether his or her reputation is harmed will carry much weight in the interpretation of these new sections. For most works, minor changes and modifications probably wouldn't be considered serious enough to harm the reputation or honour of a creator. However, for art works, any unauthorized change whatsoever to a work is deemed to be an infringement (such as cropping a picture or somehow altering it without permission).[24]

What does this mean for journalists? It could be a double-edged sword when it comes to editing material. On the one hand, it allows journalists, whether employed or freelance, to assert a right over how their work is edited or re-written. If a journalist wished, a battle over editing a book or article could theoretically end up in court.

The other side of this is that it presents a potential hurdle for editors who know only too well that some journalists can be pig-headed about changes to stories. The solution to all this is an easy one. Any employment or freelance contract should state that the creator agrees to waive moral rights or, at least, that it is understood that final editing decisions rest with the editor.

It should be noted that under the Act's new sections, a moral right can also be infringed if a work is used in association with a product, service, cause or institution to the prejudice of the honour or reputation of the creator.[25] For example, using a piece of magazine art in a promotion

---

23 *Snow v. The Eaton Centre Ltd.* (1982), 70 C.P.R. (2d) 105 (Ont. H.C.).
24 S. 18.2(2).
25 S. 18.2(1)(b).

campaign without the artist's approval could be considered an infringement, even if the copyright was purchased.

The moral rights in a work exist for the same period as the copyright and upon the creator's death, the rights pass on to the estate or to anyone to whom they are bequeathed.[26]

The moral rights sections also ensure that a creator has the right to be associated with a work in whatever manner he or she wants, whether by pseudonym or real name.[27]

What are the Penalties for Copyright Infringement?

Copyrighted works, such as the ones mentioned above, can only be reproduced in their original form with the written permission of the owner of the copyright and possibly the payment of a fee. If you infringe upon someone's copyright you can be sued in civil courts for damages and, under the copyright legislation, you may be subject to a hefty fine and/or a jail term. In most cases, the copyright holder will ask a civil court for an injunction to prevent publication of the copies and sue for damages suffered (such as lost profits).

A summary conviction under the Copyright Act could bring a maximum fine of $25,000 and/or up to six months in jail, while a conviction on indictment could lead to a maximum fine of $1 million and/or up to five years in jail.[28]

COPYRIGHT AND JOURNALISTS

Can News be Copyrighted?

Just as there's no copyright in ideas, there is no copyright in the "news."[29] As mentioned above, the copyright exists in the manner in which the news is expressed, not the news itself. Generally, a journalist who reprints a story from another news outlet will infringe the copyright only if the exact mode of expression, or a substantial part of it, is repeated. An exception is when the journalist's employer has a contract with the other news outlet allowing use of the stories (for example, wire services).

A complete or "substantial" re-write of the news story will not infringe a copyright. For example, an "exclusive" story in a newspaper can still be reported by other news outlets if the story is re-written in a different way. But this means changing more than just a few words or paragraphs

---

26 S. 12.2 (enacted by S.C. 1988, c. 15, s. 4).

27 S. 12.1(1) (enacted by S.C. 1988, s. 15, s. 4).

28 S. 42, amended S.C. 1988, c. 15, s. 10.

29 *Gribble v. Manitoba Free Press Co.*, [1931] 3 W.W.R. 570 (Man. C.A.).

around. The story should be completely re-written.

It's difficult to say what constitutes copying a substantial part of a work such as to amount to a copyright infringement. The courts have generally taken a quantitative approach to deciding whether a work has been "substantially" copied. Courts may try to determine if one-half, one-third or just one-sixteenth of a copyrighted work was used and then decide if it could be considered "substantial."

To determine what's "substantial," a court wouldn't have to look for any particular percentage of the original work to have been copied (for example, 50 percent or more). For instance, taking only a few paragraphs from some works can be an infringement of the copyright if the paragraphs are among the best and most detailed in the work. It depends on the length of the work and the degree of individual character involved in the manner of expression.

There's no requirement to give credit for a story to another news agency if the story is rewritten. But simply giving credit to the originator of the story isn't enough to escape liability for copyright infringement. If the story is to be used in its original form, a journalist must get written permission to use it.

Does the Copyright Act Say Anything about Journalists?

There are a few provisions of the Act which recognize, to some degree, the needs of journalists. Section 27(2) states that the following can be defences to alleged copyright infringements:

> (a) any fair dealing with any work for the purposes of private study, research, criticism, review, or newspaper summary;
>
> . . .
>
> (e) the publication in a newspaper of a report of a lecture delivered in public, unless the report is prohibited by conspicuous written or printed notice affixed before and maintained during the lecture at or about the main entrance of the building in which the lecture is given, and, except while the building is being used for public worship, in a position near the lecturer; but nothing in this paragraph affects the provisions in paragraph (a), as to newspaper summaries;
> (f) the reading or recitation in public by one person of any reasonable extract from any published work.

Subsections (a) and (f) allow a journalist to use extracts of a work without infringing on the copyright. The reference to newspapers, and not radio, television or other print media, is the result of the age of the Act. At some future point, it's expected that the definition of news media in the Act will be expanded.

Although there have been few cases of news media being accused of copyright infringement, the defence that most likely would come into play is subsection (a), which states that "fair dealing" with the work for the purposes of comment or review in the news media is acceptable.

Fair dealing is generally accepted to mean that copying of parts should be kept brief and for a clear purpose, such as to demonstrate the copied author's viewpoint. For example, in most cases, you could not quote large portions of an author's work to form the body of your report.

There are also points to note about photographing works of art or architecture. Section 27(2)(c) states that taking photographs of sculpture or art permanently displayed in a public place or building does not infringe on the copyright. Photographs of architectural works of art are also not infringements. But, strangely, this only applies to photographs, drawings, paintings and engravings. "Cinematographs" (that is, film or video) weren't included in this section. This is another example of the problems the old Act creates.

Another provision of the Act, section 28, allows the reproduction in a newspaper of an address of a political nature delivered at a public meeting. Parliament is thought to have added this section to ensure its members' speeches were covered by the press.

FUTURE REVISIONS OF THE COPYRIGHT ACT

The federal government is working on further changes to the Act and someday there may even be a completely new law. A federal White Paper was commissioned in 1984 to review the Act and a Parliamentary sub-committee report analysing the paper's recommendations was tabled in the fall of 1985.[30]

The following recommendations are of interest to journalists and may eventually make it into the form of new amendments or a new Act.

Broadcasts

The White Paper recommended that it shouldn't be a copyright infringement to incidentally use an artistic work without authorization in a broadcast. This would allow broadcasters to use small portions of literary, dramatic, musical or artistic works in a broadcast and would clear up any uncertainty about whether broadcasts are included in the "fair dealing" section.

---

30 See the White Paper, *From Gutenberg to Telidon: A Guide To Canada's Copyright Revision Proposals,* and the sub-committee's report, *A Charter of Rights for Creators.*

Fair Dealing

The White Paper recommended a new provision to replace the "fair dealing" section. This concept would have been renamed "fair use," which is the phrasing used in the United States. It would allow exemptions from copyright laws for any use which doesn't conflict with the "normal exploitation of a work" or unreasonably prejudice the interests of the copyright owner. For instance, a commercial use of the work would not qualify as a "fair use."

The White Paper recommended that sections 28 and 27(2)(a) and (e) be deleted because they are restrictive. Instead, the new law would contain an explicit exemption from copyright for the press in the course of "necessary reporting and analysis functions."

The Parliamentary sub-committee did not disagree with the idea that section 27(2)(e) (that is, publishing lectures) and section 28 (that is, political speeches) should be repealed. But it rejected the idea of substituting "fair use" (an American concept) for the present fair dealing section. The sub-committee says the American fair use doctrine has increased the number of legal claims of copyright infringements, while our fair dealing provision has prompted few law suits.

The sub-committee therefore recommended no change to the fair dealing section other than to specify in the new Act that copying done for research must be for private research and the provision dealing with "newspaper summary" should be expanded to include all methods of news reporting.

A COPYRIGHT CHECKLIST

1. Copyright applies to any published or unpublished original writing, music, lyrics, choreography, cinematography, sound recording, photograph, computer program, art or architecture.
2. Copyright does not apply to:
    • News, ideas or pure information
    • Quotations of short parts of original works for the purposes of comment or review
    • Complete or substantial rewrites of another's work
    • Copying for the purposes of private study or research
    • Speeches, lectures or public recitations of works
    • Photographs of sculpture or art that is permanently displayed in a public place or building, and photographs of architectural works of art
3. When done without permission, copyright infringement occurs with:
    • Substantial or wholesale reproduction of an original work

- Copying of the form of expression of an idea or information (for instance, reprinting information in a directory)
- Translation and substantial reproduction of another's original work
- Converting a non-dramatic work or novel into a dramatic work, or vice versa
- Visual or audio recording of a literary, dramatic or musical work, except in small portions for the purposes of review or comment

4. Copyright subsists for the life of the creator plus 50 years. If a work is published after the creator's death, copyright subsists for 50 years after publication. Photographs and cinematographic works are protected for 50 years from the creation of the original negative.

5. Moral rights may be infringed by distortion, mutilation or major modifications to a work that are serious enough to damage or lessen the reputation or honour of a creator (for example, substantial edits of writing or physical alteration of artwork). A moral right can also be infringed if a work is used in association with a product, service, cause or institution to the prejudice of the honour or reputation of the creator.

14

Reporting on Elections
and Political Broadcasts

The federal and provincial election laws are applied strangely and unevenly to the news media. While the print media have almost no restrictions on their activities, broadcasters are over-regulated.

For example, during national and local referenda and provincial and municipal elections, there are restraints on what the broadcast news media can report on the day of, and the day before, vote-taking. But the same restrictions don't apply during federal elections nor are there any such restrictions on print media. And even at times when there is no election campaign, there are regulations governing partisan or political broadcasts.

PUBLISHING ELECTION RESULTS

One of the few laws affecting both broadcast and print media involves the timing of the publication of any election results (albeit print media are less likely to be affected). The federal, as well as most provincial and territorial, Elections Acts prohibit the premature publication of election results.[1]

Publication of results or purported results cannot take place in any electoral district before the hour fixed by election officials for the closing of polls in that district. This applies to by-elections, as well as general elections.

This prohibition will be of particular concern to any media outlets having the opportunity to publish results in two time zones. Although it applies to all news media, it's largely a concern of broadcasters and the

---

1 For example, see Canada Elections Act, R.S.C. 1985, c. E-2, s. 328.

Canadian Radio-television and Telecommunications Commission (C.R.T.C.) has set out some guidelines. As a rule, polling stations close at 8:00 p.m. and for broadcasters who may beam results into an earlier time zone, the C.R.T.C. recommends that broadcasts of election results not happen before 9:00 p.m.[2]

PUBLISHING FALSE STATEMENTS

It should be noted that the federal and many provincial Elections Acts state that anyone who, before or during an election, makes or publishes a "false statement of fact" in relation to the personal character or conduct of a candidate is guilty of an offence under the Act.[3] Penalties vary from fines to jail terms, depending on the particular Act.

Suffice it to say that care should be exercised, as always, when asserting "facts" about a candidate's personal life or actions.

RESTRAINTS ON BROADCASTERS

Election Black-out Periods

For television and radio stations, the broadcast of "partisan" programming is heavily regulated as voting day approaches. While the primary aim is to restrict commercials and paid political messages in the final days of the election, it also applies to news programming, particularly editorials.

Section 19(1) of the Broadcasting Act proscribes the following rule for federal, provincial and municipal referenda and provincial and municipal elections:[4]

> No broadcaster shall broadcast, and no licensee of a broadcasting receiving undertaking shall receive a broadcast of, a program, advertisement or announcement of a partisan character in relation to
> > (a) a referendum, or
> > (b) except as provided by any law in force in a province, an election of a member of the legislature of that province or the council of a municipal-corporation in that province
>
> that is being held or is to be held within the area normally served by the broadcasting undertaking of the broadcaster or licensee, on the day of any such referendum or election or on the day immediately preceding the day of any such referendum or election.

Note that this section does not apply to federal elections. At one time, it did. But an amendment in 1973 changed the law such that it only applies

---

2 See CRTC Circular no. 251, May 15, 1979.
3 See s. 264 of the federal Elections Act, above, note 1.
4 R.S.C. 1985, c. B-9.

to referenda and provincial and municipal elections. Violations of this section are liable to summary conviction and a fine not exceeding $5000.

The Act states that the black-out period applying to provincial and municipal elections may be changed or entirely eliminated by provincial legislation. However, most provinces haven't enacted any law to deal with black-out periods, so the effect of the Broadcasting Act stands unchanged in most jurisdictions.

Two provinces and one territory do have provisions dealing specifically with black-outs. But the Elections Acts in the Northwest Territories[5] and Alberta[6] only reiterate that there shall be no programming or advertising of a partisan nature on the polling day or on the day immediately preceding polling day.

New Brunswick is the only province which has a different black-out period. Partisan political broadcasts are not permitted on polling day or on the two days preceding it. This includes broadcasts of speeches, entertainment or advertising in favour of, or on behalf of, a political party or any candidate. It also applies to any broadcasts emanating from outside of New Brunswick.[7]

The CFRB Case and "Partisan Programming"

The constitutionality of the Broadcast Act's black-outs was challenged in 1973.[8] In that case, a Toronto radio station was charged under section 19 after it broadcast an editorial that supported the incumbent Premier, within the black-out period of a provincial election.

The court heard how veteran reporter Gordon Sinclair broadcast an editorial on the day before the provincial election advocating the re-election of then-Premier William Davis as a "man of decision" who had qualities which would be "an asset in any leader." Not only did the broadcaster express an opinion on the election, but the late Mr. Sinclair also spoke to the "stupid rule" which prevents the electronic media from making political comments during the black-out period.

The Ontario Court of Appeal held that Parliament had a right not only to control the physical use of the airwaves, but also the intellectual content of programs. The court said this wasn't an unreasonable infringement on the freedom of the press:[9]

It is to be noted that the section applies only to a comparatively short period

---

5 S.N.W.T. 1986(2), c. 2, s. 223.

6 R.S.A. 1980, Chap. E-2, s. 129.

7 R.S.N.B. 1973, c. E-3, s. 117(3) and (4).

8 *CFRB v. A.G. Canada* (1973), 38 D.L.R. (3d) 335 (Ont. C.A.).

9 *Ibid.*, pp. 342-343.

before the election, the period during which an effective rejoinder would be difficult to make. This indicates to me a clearly defined intention not to put restrictions on the use of radio at times when statements made could be denied or discredited before they had an effect on the election.

So, then, what is partisan programming? After unsuccessfully arguing against the constitutionality of the black-out periods, the radio station's lawyers then turned to arguing against the actual offence and whether the broadcast was partisan.[10]

The trial judge found the radio station guilty and fined it $5000. In his decision, the judge rejected the argument that "partisan" denotes a particular affiliation with one party or candidate. The court held that a partisan broadcast need not have any political sponsor. The judge felt the words "partisan character" implied that there need only be some sort of bias, prejudice or favouring of one view. The judge noted that Mr. Sinclair wasn't reporting news and was expressing his own political views.

The radio station appealed the conviction to the Ontario Court of Appeal. But that court upheld the trial judge's ruling and agreed that a partisan broadcast is one which is intended to favour one candidate over the others or, in a referendum, to favour one point of view over another.

Is "News" Partisan?

So, what can a reporter broadcast during a black-out period? The intention of the legislation is not to restrict the reporting of political news, only the broadcast of opinion which is of a partisan nature.

For example, it's not partisan to broadcast a review of the events of the election campaign, the details of the candidates' activities or any last-minute political announcements as long as the reporting is balanced.

However, stories to watch are man-on-the-street interviews and surveys. "Streeters" are often inaccurate guides to public opinion and since the selection of interview clips would have to consist of opinions favouring all parties to avoid being called partisan, their news value is worthless during the black-out.

Surveys may be even more dangerous. Polls are gauges of opinion at one moment in time and the results may be released several days or weeks after the survey actually took place. They obviously give the impression that one party is doing better or worse than the others. Consequently, a poll would probably be considered partisan if broadcast during the black-out period.

While the purpose of the restrictions is obviously to allow the electorate to come to its decision without partisan prodding by political parties or

---

10 *R. v. CFRB Ltd.* (1976), 30 C.C.C. (2d) 386 (Ont. C.A.).

anyone else, it seems unfair that newspapers and other print media aren't restricted in the same way. More to the point, some people believe there shouldn't be any restrictions at all on political news reporting or commentary.

The case involving the late Mr. Sinclair unsuccessfully argued that the black-out period is an inequality in the law. But that was before the introduction of section 15 of the Canadian Charter of Rights and Freedoms,[11] which guarantees equality before the law in much stronger wording than the provision in the Bill of Rights.[12] It may well be in the future that black-out periods will be found to be a form of unreasonable discrimination against broadcasters.

ALLOCATION OF POLITICAL BROADCAST TIME

As noted above, broadcasters must also be aware of regulations governing political broadcasts at all times during the period of their licence, not just during elections. While the average journalist won't have any need to be concerned about these regulations, they do apply to news broadcasts.

The federal Elections Act deals with some aspects of the allocation of free broadcast time in sections 303 to 322. The Canadian Radio-television and Telecommunications Commission's regulations require each station or network operator which allocates time for the broadcast of partisan programs, advertisements or announcements to do so on "an equitable basis to all parties and rival candidates" during elections and throughout the licence period.[13]

The question of what is "an equitable basis" for allocating time is difficult to define. It usually becomes an issue during election campaigns. The CRTC regulations say the political parties, candidates and broadcasters are all supposed to come to an agreement on what is an equitable distribution of time. If they can't agree, the matter may be referred to the Commission.

In 1983, an independent candidate in the federal election was not invited to speak at a national free-time political broadcast and took his case to the Federal Court, saying the allocation of time wasn't "equitable."[14]

However, the court said "equitable" time doesn't mean equal time. It held that determining an equitable allocation isn't a purely mathematical

---

11 Part 1 of the Constitution Act, 1982, being Schedule B of the Canada Act 1982 (U.K.), 1982, c. 11.

12 R.S.C. 1985, App. III.

13 See Radio Regulations, 1986, SOR/86-982, s. 6 and Television Broadcasting Regulations, SOR/87-49, s. 8.

14 *Turmel v. CRTC* (1985), 16 C.R.R. 9 (Fed. T.D.).

equation devoid of discretion. With the wide variety and large number of candidates attracted to elections, the logistics of having them all speaking in a broadcast debate would be unconstructive. The Federal Court also said there was no duty on the CRTC to set out what an equitable allocation is, even though the Commission has the authority to do so.

In another 1983 decision, the Ontario Supreme Court held that "equitable" referred not only to the political parties, but also to the viewing public.[15] The court said common sense must prevail and organizers of a debate are expected to use some discretion in deciding which parties should be represented. The court felt the tolerance level of the audience must be considered and a limited-time broadcast could not be expected to include every possible candidate.

Although, CRTC regulations speak primarily to the equitable use of airtime for political commercials and free-time political broadcasts between and during elections, they also apply to news editorials and any other program where a partisan opinion is expressed. For example, CRTC guidelines suggest the regulations apply to news stories which use partisan audio and audio-visual material produced by a party (for example, using a sound or visual bite from a candidate's commercial).[16]

While broadcast journalists should be aware of the CRTC requirements regarding equitable use of broadcast time, particularly during elections, the regulations aren't meant to change the way news is reported and the regulations don't apply to objective news reports. A journalist shouldn't be concerned about whether one party has been "making the news" more often than another.

Journalists are also not compelled by the regulations to include comments from all the parties in every report that's done. Nor does each newscast have to have a story about all the parties in the running.

AN ELECTIONS CHECKLIST

1. According to federal and provincial Elections Acts, the publication of election results or purported results cannot take place in any electoral district before the hour fixed by election officials for the closing of polls in that district. This applies to by-elections, as well as general elections.
2. The Broadcasting Act prohibits the broadcast of any partisan programming on the day of, or day before, any federal, provincial or municipal referenda and any provincial or municipal elections. Note that this restriction doesn't apply to federal elections.

---

15 *Gauvin v. CBC* (1984), 5 C.R.R. 2-50.
16 For example, see CRTC Circular No. 249, s. 9.

3. The prohibition against partisan broadcasts on the day of and before a vote does not apply to objective news reports. The intention of the law is not to restrict the reporting of political news, only the broadcast of opinions or editorials which are of a partisan nature.

15

Access to Public Information

Information is the stock and trade of a journalist and getting it calls for thorough research, asking the right questions and knowing "just where to look." Although the latter often involves tapping private sources, a surprising amount of valuable information is available from public or government bodies.

Knowing how to gain access to this information can yield fascinating data on public spending, the results of environmental or health studies, business trends, crime statistics and most any topic imaginable. This chapter outlines how to get access to a variety of sources of public information.

USING ACCESS TO INFORMATION LAWS

The federal government is arguably the largest storehouse of information in Canada. In many cases, the reports and studies it generates are readily available through its departments and agencies, such as Statistics Canada or the Law Reform Commission of Canada. Provincial governments also churn out mountains of data of potential interest to the news media.

Sometimes, though, journalists and other individuals want information beyond what's available in canned reports and studies. For a long time, that wasn't possible and federal and provincial governments jealously guarded their information vaults. However, some enlightened politicians recognized that such secrecy often does a government more harm than good.

Since the early 1980s, Ottawa and five provinces have enacted laws which recognize a general right of citizens to have access to public information in government files. Each of the laws sets out how requests for information are to be handled and identifies certain sensitive information which may or may not be released, depending on a number of exemptions set out in the laws.

It is important to note that the access laws were not meant to change the way the public normally gets information. For instance, it is not necessary to apply under access legislation for a government publication which is intended for public consumption. The purpose of the laws is to help individuals get unusual or unique information, even if it is ultimately embarrassing to the government.

The Pitfalls of Access Laws

Off the top, it should be said that most government officials charged with handling access requests are extremely helpful and efficient. Many are quite willing to help a journalist identify the proper government sources or routes for information. Sometimes, a simple telephone call to a department's access to information officer will be all that is needed to find a source or even secure the information.

As noted above, however, the legislation does not guarantee access to all information and the numerous exemptions are often loosely worded, giving government officials maximum freedom to deny access.

There are two main categories of exemptions within most access laws. One is the mandatory denial of access to specific information, such as personal records about a third person. The other category allows a government minister or bureaucrat to exercise a discretionary power of release over the records.

Journalists who frequently use the various provincial and federal access laws have noted certain delaying tactics by government officials looking to wriggle out of releasing information, such as inconsistent policies on access amongst departments, unfair extensions of time limits and exorbitant search and photocopy fees. Another tactic allowed by the legislation is to allow access to a document, but "sever" or black-out sections (for example, names) which officials feel are exempt from the law. Some journalists have received documents with almost every word blacked-out by a marker or physically cut out from the document.

There have been roughly over a dozen court challenges of denials of access and exorbitant search fees. To date, there have been no landmark decisions setting the tone for interpreting access laws and most cases have dealt with particular statute sections, such as denying access to personal information. In about half the cases involving the federal access law, the government's decision was supported by the courts because the Act clearly supported the denial or action. For example, the court told a reporter seeking access to cabinet documents that it couldn't interfere with the government's decision to require deposits to cover search time since the fees were authorized by the Act.[1]

However, there have been some victories. In a decision involving the Immigration Appeal Board, a court held that a person's right of access to their own personal information overrides immigration legislation allowing the Board to seal refugee records, even from the refugee himself.[2]

Tips for Access Requests

1. Apply to more than one government department for access. Information is sometimes gathered on the same topic by several departments and if it is censored prior to release, it may not be censored the same way by each department.
2. Try to identify the exact nature and name of the document you are requesting. Government officials may tell you over the telephone what documents you should apply for.
3. Indicate a willingness to negotiate your request. Sometimes, the information you want may be too costly to gather or impossible to obtain in the detail you requested. By suggesting your request is negotiable, you may still end up with the information you want and perhaps more.
4. If appropriate, identify that you are a journalist and that the information is for public consumption. You don't have to explain why the information is needed, but requests sometimes receive less scrutiny when the end

---

1 *Rubin and Minister of Finance, Re* (1987), 35 D.L.R. (4th) 517 (Fed. T.D.).
2 *Re Information Commissioner and Immigration Appeal Board* (1988), 51 D.L.R. (4th) 79 (Fed. T.D.). For cases in which the courts have supported a federal government decision to deny access, see: *Re Montana Band of Indians and Minister of Indian and Northern Affairs* (1988), 51 D.L.R. (4th) 306 (Fed. T.D.); *Re Robertson and Minister of Employment & Immigration* (1987), 42 D.L.R. (4th) 552 (Fed. T.D.); *Re Twinn and McKnight* (1987), 37 D.L.R. (4th) 270 (Fed. T.D.); *Re Rubin and President of CMHC* (1987), 36 D.L.R. (4th) 22 (Fed. T.D.); and *Minister of EMR v. Auditor General* (1987), 35 D.L.R. (4th) 693 (Fed. C.A.). For cases in which a court ordered disclosure or access, see: *Re Information Commissioner and Minister of Fisheries & Oceans* (1988), 50 D.L.R. (4th) 662 (Fed. T.D.); *Re Noel and Great Lakes Pilotage Authority; Dominion Marine Association* (1987), 45 D.L.R. (4th) 127 (Fed. T.D.); and *Davidson v. Solicitor General of Can.* (1987), 41 D.L.R. (4th) 533 (Fed. T.D.).

use of the data is explained.

5. Always make a request in writing, even if the law allows a request for access orally. At the very least, it gives you a physical record of the initial request date and other particulars.

6. Ask for reviews of excessive fees, delays or refusals. For instance, if you are told you will have to pay for a search, ask for an estimate of costs and details on the qualifications of people serving you. In some cases, fees may be waived altogether for journalists who are gathering information for the "public benefit."

THE FEDERAL ACCESS TO INFORMATION LAW

Generally

The stated purpose of the Access to Information Act is to extend the present laws of Canada to provide a right of access to information held in records under the control of a government institution.[3] It also says any necessary exemptions to the right of access should be limited and specific.

Any person who is a Canadian citizen or a permanent resident (that is, a landed immigrant) has a right of access to records under the control of a government institution. It is a good practice to identify yourself as a citizen or landed immigrant in your application for access. It should be noted that corporations do not have a right of access, but their employees do as citizens. For instance, a request in the name of CXYZ Broadcasting might be rejected, while a request by CXYZ reporter Jane Doe will be handled normally.

There are some general definitions to note. A *government institution* is defined as any department, ministry of state, body or office of the Government of Canada listed in a schedule of the Act. The list includes over 140 government departments and institutions. A *record* includes "any correspondence, memorandum, book, plan, map, drawing, diagram, pictorial or graphic work, photograph, film, microform, sound recording, videotape, machine readable record, and any other documentary material, regardless of physical form or characteristics, and any copy thereof." An *Information Commissioner*, provided by the Act and situated in Ottawa, acts as an ombudsman between government departments and applicants.

There is a small administrative fee for each request (at present, $5) and the cost of any photocopies may have to be borne by the applicant. If a request involves substantial search time or research, the applicant may have to pay for the costs of the search, including wages of personnel. Note however, that search and copy fees may be waived at the discretion of the access official or upon appeal to the Information Commissioner.

---

3 R.S.C. 1985, c. A-1, s. 3.

If no waiver is obtained, there is a charge of 25 cents for each photo-copy, 40 cents for microfiches and $12 per 30.5 metre microfilm roll. For search time over 5 hours, the government can charge $2.50 per quarter hour per person. If computer usage is involved, the charge for the computer time is $16.50 per minute and $5.00 per quarter hour per person.

While the Information Commissioner can handle appeals of access refusals, the ultimate decision to release any information under this Act is with the Federal Court. A minister designated by the federal cabinet oversees the administration of the Act (usually, the minister for the Treasury Board). But, heads of individual government institutions often deal with specific requests.

Not less than once a year, the minister who oversees the Act must publish a directory, called the *Access Register*, containing descriptions of:

1. The organization and responsibilities of the government institutions;
2. The classes of records under the control of each institution;
3. The manuals of employees used to administer the programs and activities of each government institution; and
4. The title and address of the appropriate officer for each government institution to whom requests for access to records should be sent.

Unfortunately, the register is not as helpful as might be hoped. For instance, the discussion of classes of records available in each department generally involves only an identification number, a brief title, a brief idea as to the subject matter and a list of key topics covered by the class. None of this may actually tell you what to expect or whether it is the information needed.

The Access Register and formal request forms are located in public libraries and government information offices in major population centres. The publications may also be available at postal stations in most areas. At least twice a year, the designated minister must publish a bulletin updating the main publication.

How to Make a Request

The request The request must be made in writing by filling out a formal access to information request form (found in the Access Register or through government offices) or writing a detailed letter setting out the information needed. Send the request directly to the government institution that has control of the record along with the $5 application fee. Some institutions may refuse requests which are not on official forms. The request must contain enough detail to allow an experienced employee to find the record with a reasonable effort.

The time limits Once received, the head of the government institution (or access to information officer) must reply in writing to the request within

30 days. However, there are two circumstances in which the 30 day limit may be extended.

First, if the head of the government institution feels another government institution has a *greater interest* in the record, he may transfer the request within 15 days of receiving it. (A *greater interest* occurs where the record was originally produced for the other institution, or the other institution was the first to receive the record). If this happens, the department that originally received the application must notify the applicant in writing of the transfer. The head of the other government institution must reply in writing within the remaining 15 days.

Second, the Act permits the head of a department to extend the time limit for a reply where the request is for a large number of records, where consultations are necessary to comply with the request or where it is necessary by law to give notice of the request to a third party (such as another government or a corporation). In the latter case, the notice of extension must be sent within the original 30 day limit. However, the extension itself can then be as long as 80 days. There is a right to appeal the extension.

Where a third party must be notified, such as a corporation which supplied confidential information to the government, it must be notified within the first 30 days of the application. Upon notice, the corporation or third party has 20 days to decide whether it will allow access to its information. Upon receiving the third party's reply, the government has 10 days to decide whether it agrees with the third party.

If the government decides to grant access to the information against the third party's wishes, the third party has another 20 days to decide whether to appeal to the Federal Court. If an appeal is launched, the applicant must then wait for the court process to run its course.

The appeal process   If an access request is not granted, the head of the institution must give written reasons and cite the provisions of the Act supporting the refusal. An appeal can be launched first to the Information Commissioner and then the Federal Courts. An appeal to the Commissioner can be made within one year of the request. Unfortunately, the Commissioner has no time limit in dealing with the appeal and can not be forced to hurry an investigation.

If the Commissioner also rejects the access request or the government institution fails to comply with the Commissioner's recommendation of disclosure, an appeal can be launched to the Federal Court within 45 days of receiving the Commissioner's report.

Statutory Exemptions to the Right of Access

Under the Act, government officials may exercise discretion in granting access to certain records or may have a mandatory duty to refuse access to some records. However, there are exceptions within the exemptions and the loosely-defined parameters of the Act suggest journalists should still apply for records that may fall under the mandatory or discretionary categories.

The Eight Discretionary Categories

1. *Federal-provincial affairs*   Under section 14, the government may use its discretion to refuse information which could reasonably be expected to be injurious to the conduct of the Federal government in federal-provincial affairs, including information on federal-provincial consultations, deliberations, and information on Federal strategy relating to the conduct of federal-provincial affairs.

2. *International affairs and defence*   Under section 15, the government may use its discretion to refuse information which could reasonably be expected to be injurious to the conduct of international affairs, the defence of Canada or any state allied or associated with this country. The section also protects information dealing with the detection, prevention or suppression of subversive or hostile activities. This includes information:

(a) relating to military tactics or activities;
(b) relating to defence weapons;
(c) relating to defence forces;
(d) obtained or prepared for the purpose of intelligence for the defence of Canada, its allies and associates;
(e) obtained or prepared for the purpose of intelligence respecting foreign states, international organizations of states or citizens of foreign states used by the Government in the process of deliberation and consultation or in the conduct of international affairs;
(f) on methods or scientific equipment involved in the information gathering process referred to in (d) and (e) or on sources of such information;
(g) on the positions of the Government, foreign states or international organizations of states for the purpose of negotiations;
(h) that constitutes diplomatic correspondence;
(i) relating to the communications or cryptographic systems of Canada or foreign states used for the conduct of international affairs, the defence of Canada, its allies and associated states or in relation to the detection, prevention or suppression of subversive or hostile activities.

3. *Law enforcement and investigations*   Under section 16, the head of a government institution may use its discretion to refuse:

(a) information obtained or prepared by any government investigative body in the course of lawful investigations of crime or the enforcement of any law of Canada or a province if the record came into existence less than 20 years prior to the request;

(b) information relating to investigative techniques or plans for specific lawful investigations;

(c) information which could reasonably be expected to be injurious to the enforcement of any law in Canada or a province or the conduct of lawful investigations, including information relating to the existence or nature of a particular investigation, the identity of the confidential source of the information, or any record obtained or prepared in the course of an investigation;

(d) information which could reasonably be expected to be injurious to the security of penal institutions.

Section 16 also allows the government to refuse access to a record that could reasonably be expected to facilitate the commission of a criminal offence (including information on criminal techniques, technical information relating to weapons or potential weapons or any record on the vulnerability of particular buildings, structures or systems, including computer or communication systems).

The section also protects information obtained or prepared by the RCMP while performing policing services for a province or a municipality, where the Federal government has agreed not to disclose the information.

4. *Safety of individuals*   Section 17 allows an official the discretion to refuse any record which could reasonably be expected to threaten the safety of individuals.

5. *Economic interests of Canada*   The following information may be refused by the head of an institution under section 18:

(a) valuable trade secrets or financial, commercial, scientific or technical information that belongs to the Federal government or a government institution;

(b) information which could reasonably be expected to prejudice the competitive position of a government institution;

(c) scientific or technical information obtained through research by an officer or employee of a government institution;

(d) information which could reasonably be expected to be materially injurious to the financial interests of the federal government or the economy of the country. This includes information which could reasonably be expected to result in an undue benefit to any person in relation to:

  i) the currency of Canada;

  ii) contemplated changes in the rate of bank interest or in government borrowing;

iii) a contemplated change in tariff rates, taxes, duties or any other revenue source;
iv) a contemplated change in the conditions of operation of financial institutions;
v) a contemplated sale or purchase of securities or of foreign or Canadian currency;
vi) a contemplated sale or acquisition of land or property.

6. *Operations of government* Section 21 states the head of an institution may refuse to disclose any record which came into existence less than 20 years prior to the request if it contains:

(a) advice or recommendations developed by or for the government;
(b) an account of consultations or deliberations involving government officials or employees;
(c) positions or plans developed for the purpose of government negotiations;
(d) plans relating to the management of personnel or the administration of a government institution that have not yet been put into operation.

This section does not apply to a record that contains an account of or a statement of reasons for a decision that is made in the exercise' of a discretionary power or an adjudicative function and that affects the rights of a person. It also does not apply to a report prepared by a consultant or advisor who was not, at the time the report was prepared, an officer or employee of a government institution or a member of the staff of a minister of the Crown.

7. *Testing procedures* Under section 22, the government may refuse information relating to the testing, auditing procedures, techniques or details of specific tests to be conducted where such disclosure would prejudice the use or results of particular tests or audits.

8. *Solicitor-client privilege* Under section 23, any information which pertains to lawyer-client privilege may be refused.

The Three Mandatory Categories

1. *Personal information* Section 19 states that the head of a government institution must refuse access to any *personal information* as defined in the federal Privacy Act, about an identifiable individual. Personal information includes:

(a) information relating to the race, national or ethnic origin, colour, religion, age or marital status of the individual;
(b) information relating to the education or the medical, criminal or employment history of the individual or information relating to financial transactions in which the individual has been involved;

(c) any identifying number, symbol or other particular assigned to the individual;

(d) the personal opinions or views of the individual except where they are about another individual or about a proposal for a grant, an award or a prize to be made to another individual by a government institution;

(e) correspondence sent to a government institution by the individual that is implicitly or explicitly of a private or confidential nature, and replies to such correspondence that would reveal the contents of the original correspondence;

(f) the views or opinions of another individual about the individual;

(g) the views or opinions of another individual about a proposal for a grant, an award or a prize to be made to the individual by an institution or a part of an institution or a part of an institution referred to in (e), but excluding the name of the other individual where it appears with the views or opinions of the other individual, and

(h) the name of the individual where it appears with other personal information relating to the individual or where the disclosure of the name itself would reveal information about the individual.

For the purposes of the Access to Information Act, personal information does not include:

(a) information about a past or present officer or employee of a government institution that relates to the position or functions of the individual, including the fact of employment, the title, business address and telephone number of the individual, the classification, salary range and responsibilities of the position held by the individual, the name of the individual on a document prepared by the individual in the course of employment, the personal opinions or views of the individual given in the course of employment;

(b) information about an individual who is or was performing services under contract for a government institution that relates to the services under contract, including the terms of the contract, the name of the individual and the opinions or views of the individual given in the course of the performance of such services;

(c) information relating to any discretionary benefit of a financial nature, including the granting of a licence or permit, conferred on an individual, including the name of the individual and the exact nature of the benefit, and

(d) information about an individual who has been dead for more than 20 years.

Personal information about an individual may be released where the individual consents to the disclosure, where the information is publicly available or in these instances:

(a) where the information was intended to be made publicly available;
(b) where Federal law authorizes disclosure;
(c) where there is a subpoena or warrant;
(d) where the Attorney General of Canada wants it for legal proceedings involving the Crown or the Federal government;
(e) where an investigative body specified in the Act's regulations requests it for the purpose of enforcing any law or carrying out a lawful investigation;
(f) under an agreement or arrangement between the Federal government, a province, or foreign state for the purpose of enforcing any law or carrying out a lawful investigation;
(g) to a Member of Parliament for the purpose of assisting the individual to whom the information relates in resolving a problem;
(h) for internal audit purposes;
(i) for the Public Archives for archival purposes;
(j) to any person or body for research or statistical purposes if the head of the government institution is satisfied that the purpose for which the information is disclosed cannot reasonably be accomplished unless the information is provided in a form that would identify the individual to whom it relates, and the person or body gives a written undertaking that no subsequent disclosure of the information will be made in a form that could reasonably be expected to identify the individual to whom it relates;
(k) to any aboriginal group or government body for the purpose of researching or validating the claims, disputes or grievances of any of the aboriginal peoples of Canada;
(l) to any government institution for the purpose of locating an individual in order to collect a debt owed to the Crown or to make a payment to the individual, and
(m) for any purpose where, in the opinion of the head of the institution, the public interest in disclosure clearly outweighs any invasion of privacy or the individual in question would clearly benefit.

2. *Information obtained in confidence*   Section 13 states that the head of a government institution must refuse to disclose any record requested that contains information that was obtained in confidence from:

(a) a foreign government or one of its institutions;
(b) an international organization of states or one of its institutions;
(c) a provincial government or one of its institutions; or
(d) a municipal or regional government.

Subsection (2) states that the head of a government institution may use its discretion to disclose the record if he or she gets the consent of the affected body or the information is made public by that body.

3. *Third party information*   Section 20 states that a head of an institution must refuse access to a record that contains:

(a) trade secrets of a third party;
(b) financial, commercial, scientific or technical information that is confidential information supplied to a government institution by a third party and is treated consistently in a confidential manner by the third party;
(c) information which could reasonably be expected to result in material financial loss or gain to, or could reasonably be expected to prejudice the competitive position of, a third party, or
(d) information which could reasonably be expected to interfere with contractual or other negotiations of a third party.

In cases of product or environmental testing, the head of a government institution is not allowed to refuse to disclose the results of a test carried out by or on behalf of a government institution unless the testing was done as a service to a person, group or organization, other than a government institution, for a fee.

The head of a government institution also has a discretionary right to release any record that contains information described in this section where the third party consents to the disclosure or it would be in the public interest. The public interest is defined as a situation relating to public health, public safety or the protection of the environment.

Some General Exemptions

The government may refuse to disclose information in a record where there is reasonable ground to believe the information will be published by the government within 90 days from receiving the request or within the period of time necessary for translation and printing.

The Act also does not apply to federal Cabinet documents, memoranda of recommendations or proposals, discussion papers, agendas, minutes or records of Cabinet decisions, briefs, draft legislation and policy documents. However, this exemption does not include cabinet documents in existence for more than 20 years.

In addition, where discussion papers have been prepared upon which decisions were made, a person may request immediate access to the discussion paper if the decisions have been made public. If the decision is not made public, access may still be requested, but not until four years after the time of the decision.

Note that other statutes also have provisions restricting public access to information. For example, there are privacy provisions in the Income Tax Act and the Bank Act protecting personal information.

Provincial Access to Information Laws

MANITOBA'S ACCESS TO INFORMATION LAW

Generally

Manitoba's Act gives any person, including non-residents, the right to apply for access to examine or copy any record in the custody or control of the government.[4] It provides access to documents in the control of government departments and Crown agencies. A Crown agency includes boards, commissions and associations (whether incorporated or not) in which all directors are appointed by the government. It also includes corporations which have boards of directors controlled by the Crown or a government board, commission or association.

An *Access Guide* is published by the provincial government, outlining the types of documents held by the various departments. It must be updated every two years or less.

The Act has created several exemptions to the right to access. However, the head of a department must release any portions of a record which do not qualify under the exemptions. The exempted material may be severed, where possible, from the record and the rest shall be released to the applicant.

This is a relatively new piece of legislation in Manitoba. Early indications are that it is being supported by the bureaucracy as concerted effort is being made to fulfil requests.

How to Make a Request

The request An application must be made in writing to the head of the government department (or an access to information officer) believed to possess the record. The request must supply sufficient detail to allow an experienced member of the department to locate the record. There is no fee charged to review a request.

The time limits The head of the department must send a written notice

---

4 Freedom of Information Act, R.S.M. 1985-86, c. 6.

of the decision on the application within 30 days. If the application should have been made to the head of another department, it must be forwarded to that department by the "original" department. An application may also be forwarded to another department if it has a "greater interest" in the record. A "greater interest" exists where a record that was originally prepared for another department or where another department received the record first. Despite the transfer to another department, the 30 day limit continues to run from the day the original department received the application.

If an application requires a lengthy search or if the department has an unusually heavy workload, it may issue itself an extension of another 30 days. However, in addition to supplying written notice of the extension to the applicant, the applicant must be told of his or her right to appeal the extension.

The appeal process   If an application is unanswered within 30 days, it is deemed to have been refused and the applicant is free to appeal to the ombudsman. The ombudsman has the authority to hold a full investigation with no time limit. If an appeal to the ombudsman results in a further denial of access, the applicant may file an appeal with a court within 30 days after receiving notice of the ombudsman's denial. There is no appeal from the court's judgment.

Statutory Exemptions to the Right of Access

The Six Discretionary Categories

1. *Policy opinions, advice or recommendations*   Access may be refused to any record which discloses opinions, advice or a recommendation submitted by an officer or employee of the government or a minister, to the government or the minister. Records may also be denied which disclose the formulation of a policy, the making of a decision or development of a negotiating position of the government. This includes plans relating to the administration of a department and the contents of draft enactments.

However, the exemption does not apply to environmental impact statements, consumer test reports, government equipment test reports, scientific or technical research done in connection with policy formulation, instructions or guidelines to government officers or employees on programs affecting the public, reasons for a discretionary or adjudicative decision affecting the applicant or reports by consultants who are not employees or officers of the government or a minister.

Despite this category of exemption, access must be given to such records if they are more than 30 years old.

2. *Law enforcement and legal proceedings* Access may be denied to records that would harm an investigation, facilitate the commission of a crime, threaten security of a prison or other building, threaten the security of a computer or communications system, violate solicitor-client privilege or harm an existing or anticipated legal proceeding.

This does not apply to records which disclose investigative or law enforcement techniques which are contrary to the law or discloses the structure or programs of a law enforcement agency or reports on the degree of success of a law enforcement program.

3. *Economic interests of Manitoba* Access may be refused if the record discloses a trade secret of a department, innovative scientific or technical research done by a department, harms the government's competitive position, harms contractual negotiations or any government information which could result in an undue financial gain for a third party (for example, proposed tax changes).

4. *Federal-provincial relations* Access may be denied if the record would harm the conduct of the government of federal-provincial relations.

5. *Testing or auditing procedures* Information may be denied which could be used to prejudice the use or results of particular tests or audits.

6. *Materials to be made public* If the head of a department believes on reasonable grounds that the information will be released in 90 days, access may be denied.

The Four Mandatory Categories

1. *Protection of personal privacy* Access must be denied, in most cases, to a record which constitutes an unreasonable invasion of a third party's privacy. This can include details of education, health, criminal activities, employment or family history, personal details of tax matters, financial transactions or information which discloses the identity of a law enforcement informant.

This category does not apply to job-related information about government and ministerial officers or employees, details of personal-service contracts between third parties and the government or where a third party has received a licence, permit or other discretionary financial benefit (providing the third party represents 1% or more of the people in the province receiving the same benefit).

Access must also be allowed where the third party consents to the release of the information, the record is publicly available or the third party has been dead for more than ten years. Access may also be granted for *bona fide* research or statistical purposes.

2. *Cabinet confidences*   An application for any record which discloses a confidence of cabinet (for example, an agenda of a Cabinet meeting, policy analysis, proposals, recommendations) must be denied. But the Act says access shall be allowed, subject to other exemptions, if the cabinet record is more than 30 years old or the Cabinet which originally received the record consents.

3. *Information obtained in confidence*   Access must be denied, in most cases, if the record was obtained in confidence from the federal government, another province or a municipal or regional government. The information must be released if it is publicly available or the government affected consents.

4. *Commercial information belonging to a third party*   Access must be refused for records which disclose trade secrets of a third party, commercial information supplied to a department in confidence and treated consistently as confidential or information which could reasonably be expected to result in significant financial loss or gain to a third party or interfere with the competitive position or contractual negotiations of a third party.

Access must be allowed where the record discloses the final result of a product or environmental test conducted for a government department, the third party consents or the record is publicly available.

Access may also be given if the public interest outweighs the private interest of the third party in areas of health, safety, environmental protection, or improved competition in government regulation of undesirable trade practices. A third party can go to court to object to such a release.

NEW BRUNSWICK'S ACCESS TO INFORMATION LAW

Generally

Any person, including non-residents, may request information by applying to the minister of the department where the information is most likely to be kept or filed.[5]

A *department* is defined in section 1 as:

(a) any department of the Government of the Province;
(b) any Crown Agency or Crown Corporation;
(c) any other branch of the public service;
(d) any body or office, not being part of the public service, the operation

---

5 Right to Information Act, S.N.B. 1978, c. R-10.3.

of which is effected through money appropriated for the purpose and paid out of the Consolidated Fund.

The departments and agencies that fall under the Act are listed in the regulations (almost all are included).

Once a request is approved, a fee will be charged for inspection of the document and a charge may be levied for copies at the discretion of the minister.

This was among the first access to information laws in Canada, but it has a reputation for being cumbersome and erratically interpreted.

How to Make a Request

The request   The request must be made in writing and specify the records believed to contain the information or specify the subject-matter of the information with sufficient particulars as to time, place and event so as to enable a person familiar with the subject-matter to identify the document. No fee is charged for the initial review of a request.

The time limits   The appropriate minister of the department or an access to information officer must answer the request within 30 days of the receipt of the application. If a document cannot be found, the minister must tell the applicant and allow the applicant to supply additional details on the request. If a document is likely to be found in another department, the minister must tell the applicant.

The appeal process   If an applicant is not satisfied with the decision of the minister or the minister has failed to reply, the matter can be referred to a Supreme Court judge or to the ombudsman. There are some important considerations in choosing between the two appeal routes. The ombudsman can only make a recommendation to the appropriate minister. The judge, however, can order the information to be released. But if a matter is referred to a judge and the request is denied, it cannot then be referred to the ombudsman. As well, if a matter is referred to the ombudsman, it can only be appealed to a judge if the minister ignored a recommendation from the ombudsman to disclose the record.

In an appeal to a judge, the onus is on the minister to show why the document must remain secret. There is no further appeal allowed, such as to the court of appeal.

The Ten Statutory Exemptions to the Right of Access

The exceptions to the right to information are listed in section 6 of the Act. It states that there is no right to information (mandatory) where its release:

(a) would disclose information the confidentiality of which is protected by law;
(b) would reveal personal information, given on a confidential basis, concerning another person;
(c) would cause financial loss or gain to a person or department, or would jeopardize negotiations leading to an agreement or contract;
(d) would reveal financial, commercial, technical or scientific information:
　　(i) given by an individual or a corporation that is a going concern in connection with financial assistance applied for or given under the authority of a statute or regulation of the Province, or
　　(ii) given in or pursuant to an agreement entered into under the authority of a statute or regulation, if the information relates to the internal management or operation of a corporation that is a going concern;
(e) would violate the confidentiality of information obtained from another government;
(f) would be detrimental to the proper custody, control or supervision of persons under sentence;
(g) would disclose legal opinions or advice provided to a person or department by a law officer of the Crown, or privileged communications as between solicitor and client in a matter of departmental business;
(h) would disclose opinions or recommendations by public servants for a minister or the Executive Council;
(i) would disclose the substance of proposed legislation or regulations, or
(j) would impede an investigation, inquiry or the administration of justice.

In this Act, *personal information* is defined as information respecting a person's identity, residence, dependents, marital status, employment, borrowing and repayment history, income, assets and liabilities, credit worthiness, education, character, reputation, health, physical or personal characteristics or mode of living.

NOVA SCOTIA'S ACCESS TO INFORMATION LAW

Generally

The Nova Scotia legislation begins with the statement that the government should operate openly and be accountable for its actions.[6] It states that these principles can be maintained by providing public access to all information, except that which would impede the operation of

---

6 S.N.S. 1977, c. 10.

government or disclose personal information pertaining to people or certain other matters.

Unlike in other Acts, *access* is defined as the opportunity to either examine an original record or to be provided with a copy. Charges may be levied for requests and copies of documents. *Department* is defined as any department, board, commission, foundation, agency, association, or other body of persons, whether incorporated or unincorporated, all the members of which, or all the members of the board of management or board of directors of which, are appointed by the government. If a member is not appointed by the government, the definition includes those who are public officers or servants of the Crown in the discharge of their duties and those who are directly or indirectly responsible to the Crown in the proper discharge of their duties.

Personal information means information respecting a person's identity, residence, dependents, marital status, employment, borrowing and repayment history, income, assets and liabilities, credit worthiness, education, character, reputation, health, physical or personal characteristics or mode of living.

Any person, including non-residents, may apply for access to information respecting:

(a) organization of a department;
(b) administrative staff manuals and instructions to staff that affect a member of the public;
(c) rules of procedure;
(d) descriptions of forms available or places at which forms may be obtained;
(e) statements of general policy or interpretations of general applicability formulated and adopted by a department;
(f) final decisions of administrative tribunals;
(g) personal information contained in files pertaining to the person making the request;
(h) the annual report and regulations of a department;
(i) programs and policies of a department; and
(j) each amendment, revision or repeal of the foregoing.

If a department record contains some information which cannot be released, that portion will be deleted or severed and the remainder will be released.

The Nova Scotia access law is awkwardly constructed, limited in scope and easily lends itself to abuse in interpretation.

How to Make a Request

The request   An application for access is made by contacting the department where the information is kept, either by telephone or in writing. The request must identify the information precisely. No initial fee is charged for reviewing a request.

The time limits   The application must be answered within 15 working days. If no answer is received within 15 working days, the request is deemed to be denied.

The Appeal Process   If access is not granted, a written application must then be made to the deputy head of the department where the information is kept. Within 15 days after that request is denied, the applicant may appeal in writing to the minister of the department. The minister has 30 days in which to affirm, vary or overrule the decision.

The final and only stage of the appeal process is before the Nova Scotia House of Assembly. The appeal must be presented by a member in the form of a motion.

The Statutory Exemptions to the Right of Access

Access must be denied (mandatory) for information which:

(a) might reveal personal information concerning another person;
(b) might result in financial gain or loss to a person or a department, or which might influence negotiations in progress leading to an agreement or contract;
(c) would jeopardize the ability of a department to function on a competitive commercial basis;
(d) might be injurious to relations with another government;
(e) would be likely to disclose information obtained or prepared during the conduct of an investigation concerning alleged violations of any enactment or the administration of justice;
(f) would be detrimental to the proper custody, control or supervision of persons under sentence;
(g) would be likely to disclose legal opinions or advice provided to a department by a law officer of the Crown, or privileged communications between barrister and client in a matter of department business;
(h) would be likely to disclose opinions or recommendations by public servants in matters for decision by a minister or the Executive Council;
(i) would be likely to disclose draft legislation or regulations;
(j) would be likely to disclose information the confidentiality of which is protected by an enactment.

ONTARIO'S ACCESS TO INFORMATION LAW

Generally

The stated purpose of the Ontario legislation is to provide a right of access to information under the control of a provincial government ministry, agency, board, commission, corporation or other designated body.[7] One of the principles of the Act is that decisions on the disclosure of government information should be reviewed independently of government through an ombudsman, as in the federal law. Every person, including non-residents, has a right of access to records, unless the information falls within one of the exemptions.

An access guide, listing all of the institutions and general details on their records, is published annually. In addition, each institution must make available any documents produced to aid employees in handling access requests.

The Act allows an institution to demand fees for searches lasting longer than two hours, the cost of preparing the record, computer and other costs of retrieving, processing and copying a record and shipping costs. The head of the department in question must give the applicant a reasonable estimate of the costs if they total more than $25. The Act gives the head discretion to waive the fees in certain circumstances, such as financial hardship, or public health or safety. The applicant may also ask Ontario's information commissioner to review the decision regarding fees.

One unique aspect of the Act is the requirement that the head of a government institution or ministry must disclose, as soon as possible, to the public or any people affected, any record which the head has reasonable and probable grounds to believe is in the public interest and reveals a grave environmental, health or safety hazard to the public.

Although the legislation is relatively new, it has already been criticized for being too restrictive in its wording. The province's ombudsman or information commissioner has also been criticized for tending to side with government decisions to deny requests. However, the law has greater scope than most provinces and has yielded some valuable information.

How to Make a Request

The request An application for access must be made in writing to the institution which is believed to have custody or control of the record. The letter must provide "sufficient detail to enable an experienced employee of the institution, upon a reasonable effort, to identify the record."

---

7 Freedom of Information and Protection of Individual Privacy Act, 1987, S.O. 1987, c. 25.

If the request does not give sufficient detail, the institution must notify the applicant and must offer assistance to allow the request to conform to the requirements. There is no initial fee to review requests.

If the request should have been made to another institution, the head of the institution that received the request must make "all necessary inquiries" to find the appropriate institution. An application may also be transferred to another institution if it has a "greater interest." A greater interest exists where the record was originally produced for another institution or the other institution was the first to receive the record.

The time limits   If a request is re-directed, the head of the "original" institution must forward the application to the other institution and notify the applicant within 15 days after the request was received.

Upon the appropriate institution receiving the request, a decision must be made within 30 days after the request was first made. The time limit may be extended for a time that is "reasonable in the circumstances" if the request is for a large number of records or if consultations on whether to grant the request will not be completed within the 30 day limit or to notify a party affected by the disclosure of the government's intention to release the information.

The applicant must be notified of the length of the extension, the reason for the extension and told that the Act's Information Commissioner may be asked by the applicant to review the extension.

If notice is given to a third party, that party has 20 days upon receiving the notice to reply. The head of an institution must make a decision within thirty days of notifying the third party, but not before either the day the third party replies to the notice or 21 days after notice is given, whichever is earliest.

The appeal process   If the request is refused, the head of an institution must state whether the record exists and the reason under the Act for the refusal. The applicant must also be told that he or she may appeal to the Information Commissioner. Under certain provisions of the Act, the head may refuse to confirm or deny the existence of the record, but must notify the applicant that he or she can appeal to the Information Commissioner.

The appeal process is then distinctly different from any other jurisdiction. An appeal may be made to the Information Commissioner on any decision, with the exception of those decisions involving the exercise of discretion in all of the exempt categories. Of course, apart from appealing a mandatory denial, it is hard to imagine what one has left to appeal from. The only exception to that rule is if the request involves a question of personal privacy.

A written notice of appeal must be made within 30 days of receiving notice of the decision. The Commissioner will appoint a mediator to investigate the request, and if that fails to resolve the issue, an inquiry may be conducted in public or in private.

Statutory Exemptions to the Right of Access

The Eight Discretionary Categories

1. *Advice to government*   Access may be denied to the records of advice or recommendations of public servants or any other person employed by an institution (including consultants).

But, access cannot be refused to advice or recommendations which disclose factual material, statistics, environmental impact statements, product tests, reports by valuators, efficiency studies of government institutions, feasibility studies of government policies or projects, results of field research performed for formulating a policy proposal, details of reorganization plans for institutions or programs, reports of interdepartmental committees or task forces, reports of committees, councils or bodies making inquiries or recommendations for institutions and final decisions by officers of institutions involving an exercise of discretionary power.

Access must also be given to records more than 20 years old.

2. *Law enforcement*   Access may be denied if the record could be reasonably expected to: interfere with law enforcement matters or investigations, reveal investigative techniques or procedures, disclose the identity of informants, endanger a life, interfere with judicial proceedings, interfere with intelligence operations, endanger security, facilitate the escape of someone from custody or help in the commission of an offence. It also includes investigative reports and certain law enforcement records.

Under this category, the head of an institution may even refuse to confirm or deny the existence of a record.

3. *Relations with other governments*   Access may be denied to records that could prejudice the conduct of intergovernmental relations, information received in confidence from another government or its agency or information received in confidence from an international organization of states. In addition, the provincial Cabinet must approve the disclosure.

4. *Defence*   Access may be refused where the record could reasonably be expected to prejudice the defence of Canada or its allies or information which would be injurious to efforts against espionage, sabotage or terrorism. In addition, the provincial Cabinet must approve the disclosure.

5. *Third party information*   Access may be denied if the record discloses a trade, scientific, technical, commercial or financial secret supplied in confidence. The release of the information must be reasonably

expected to: prejudice the competitive or contractual position of the third party, result in a loss of future information to the institution which is supplied in confidence and necessary in the public interest or result in an undue loss or gain to anyone.

The record must be disclosed if the public interest outweighs the private interest.

6. *Economic and other interests of Ontario*   Access may be refused if the record discloses a trade secret of a department, discloses innovative scientific or technical research done by a department, harms the government's competitive position, harms contractual negotiations or any government information which could result in an undue financial gain for a third party (for example, proposed tax changes).

This does not include results of product or environmental tests carried out by an institution unless someone paid for the tests or the tests were conducted to help develop testing methods. The record must be disclosed if the public interest outweighs the government interest.

7. *Solicitor-client privilege*   These are documents such as correspondence between a lawyer and his client.

8. *Danger to safety or health*   Access may be denied where it is reasonably expected the information could seriously threaten the safety or health of an individual.

The Two Mandatory Categories

1. *Personal privacy*   Access to personal information must be refused except where the individual consents in writing to disclosure of a record to which the person has access, compelling circumstances of health or safety dictate disclosure, for the purpose of creating a public record, or where an Act of Ontario or Canada authorizes the disclosure and for research purposes.

2. *Cabinet records*   Access to cabinet records must be refused if the information would reveal the substance of deliberations of the Executive Council. This can include agendas, minutes of meetings, recommendations and briefs.

But, a head of an institution cannot refuse to disclose a record which is more than 20 years old or to which the Cabinet it was originally prepared for, consents to its disclosure.

QUÉBEC'S ACCESS TO INFORMATION LAW

Generally

The Québec Act recognizes that every person, including corporations and other artificial "people," has a right of access to the documents held by public bodies, subject to certain restrictions.[8] Non-residents may also apply.

The public bodies encompassed by the Act are the Conseil exécutif, the Conseil du trésor, the Lieutenant-Governor, the National Assembly, government departments, government agencies, municipal bodies, school bodies, and health and social services establishments (including universities and other public institutions).

Under the legislation, a *document* can be recorded in writing or print, on sound tape or film, in computerized form or otherwise. The Act does not apply to acts and registers of civil status, documents registered in a registry office or the central register of matrimonial regimes or notices. It also does not apply to sketches, drafts, outlines, preliminary notes or similar documents.

The person with the highest authority in a public body is in charge of access to documents. But, that power can be delegated to any other member of the organization. The Ministry of Communications publishes a list each year of the names, addresses and telephone numbers of the people responsible for access to documents.

This Act has a good reputation for fulfilling access requests.

How to Make a Request

The request   The request can be made orally or in a written form to the appropriate person. It must provide enough detail to allow the appropriate official to find it. No initial fee is charged to review a request.

The time limits   The person in charge of access has 20 days to reply to a request. If access to a document is granted, there will be no charge if the document is viewed on the spot where it is kept. If that is not possible, there may be charges for transcription, reproduction or transmission of the document.

The appeal process   Any refusals must be accompanied by reasons. If a written request is refused, a person may then appeal to the Commission d'accès à l'information. Any decisions based on points of law or competence can be further appealed to the Provincial Court.

---

8 Access to Documents Held by Public Bodies, R.S.Q., c. A-2.1.

Statutory Exemptions to the Right of Access

The Five Discretionary Categories

1. *Information respecting intergovernmental relations*   There is a discretionary power to refuse any information received from another government, agency of another government or international organization.

2. *Information affecting negotiations between public bodies*   A public body may use its discretion to refuse to disclose information which would likely hamper negotiations in progress with another public body.

3. *Information affecting the economy*   There is a discretionary power to refuse economic information which could:

(a) unduly benefit or seriously harm a person;
(b) have a serious adverse effect on the economic interests of the public body or group of persons under its jurisdiction;
(c) constitute an industrial secret owned by a public body;
(d) hamper negotiations for a contract, or result in a loss for the public body or a considerable profit for another person.

In addition, the industrial secrets of a third party or confidential industrial, financial, commercial, scientific, technical or union information which is supplied by a third party, and considered confidential by that party, cannot be released without consent.

Consent is also needed to release information supplied by a third party which might hamper negotiations in a contract, result in losses for the third party or considerable profit for another person or substantially reduce the third party's competitive margin. Also any information which would reveal the strategy concerning the negotiation of a collective agreement or a contract, may be refused for a period of eight years from the opening of negotiations. A study prepared for the purposes of taxation, tariffing or the imposition of dues may be refused for a period of ten years from its date.

No public body can refuse to disclose industrial, financial, commercial, scientific, technical or union information which reveals or confirms the existence of an immediate hazard to the health or safety of persons, or a serious or irreparable impediment to their right to a healthy environment.

4. *Information affecting administrative or political decisions*   The Conseil exécutif may refuse to disclose or confirm the existence of a decision resulting from its deliberations or orders. The same applies to the Conseil du trésor.

A public body may refuse to disclose a legal opinion concerning the application of the law to a particular case, or the constitutionality or validity of legislative or regulatory provisions, or a preliminary or final draft of a bill or regulations. Information may also be refused if it would affect the outcome of judicial proceedings.

5. *Information affecting auditing* The Auditor General or a person carrying out an auditing function in or for a public body may refuse to release or confirm information which would hamper an audit, reveal an auditing program or operation plan, reveal a confidential source of information regarding an audit, or seriously impair the power of appraisal granted to the Auditor General.

The Three Mandatory Categories

1. *Information affecting the administration of justice and public security* A public body must refuse to release or confirm the existence of information received by a person responsible under the law for the prevention, detection or repression of crime or statutory offences, if its disclosure would likely:

(a) impede the progress of proceedings before a person or body carrying on judicial or quasi-judicial proceedings;
(b) hamper an investigation;
(c) reveal a method of investigation, a confidential source of information, or a program or plan of action designed to prevent, detect or repress crime or statutory offences;
(d) endanger the safety of a person;
(e) cause prejudice to the person who is the source or the subject of the information;
(f) reveal the components of a communications system intended for the use of a person responsible for law enforcement;
(g) reveal information transmitted in confidence by a police force having jurisdiction outside Québec;
(h) facilitate the escape of a prisoner; or
(i) prejudice the fair hearing of a person's case.

A public body must also refuse information concerning a method or a weapon likely to be used to commit a crime or statutory offence, or the efficiency of a security system.

2. *Information affecting administrative or political decisions* The preliminary draft of a bill or regulation must remain secret for ten years following its date. A communication between the Conseil exécutif and certain other bodies or persons must remain secret for 25 years. For example, this includes recommendations to the Conseil, unless the author

or the person receiving them decides otherwise. The same rule applies to an executive committee of a municipal body, to the recommendations made to it by its members, and to communications among its members.

Access to a document of a member of the National Assembly of Québec, or a document produced for that member by the Assembly's services must be refused unless the member deems it expedient. The same applies to documents from the office of the President of the Assembly or documents from staff of a member of a municipal or school body.

A public body must refuse to disclose the records of a meeting of its board of directors, or of its members in the performance of their duties until 15 years from its date. Recommendations to a public body must remain undisclosed for up to ten years. Certain studies of recommendations have a five year restriction.

3. *Personal information*   Any information which allows a person to be identified is "personal information" under this Act and must be refused to everyone other than the person the information is about. This does not apply to information about a person which is public. Public information includes:

(a) names, addresses, duties, and other job-related facts of public body officials and employees (not including those involved in the prevention, detection or repression of crime),
(b) information about a person as a party of a service contract entered into with a public body (including the terms and conditions of the contract),
(c) the name of a person who is getting an economic benefit from a public body by virtue of a discretionary power and any information on the nature of the benefit.

The information may be released if the person concerned consents. Certain government agencies and officials can have access to the personal information.

UNITED STATES ACCESS TO INFORMATION LAW

Generally

The benefits of the United States' Freedom of Information Act are available to non-citizens, as well as to the American public.[9] It applies only to documents held by the administrative agencies of the "executive" branch of the U.S. government. This includes the military, government corporations and independent regulatory agencies, but it does not include

---

9 5 U.S.C.A. (1970).

agencies in legislative and judicial branches. The *United States Government Manual* and *The Congressional Directory* list all of the agencies that come under the Act and their functions. It is available from the U.S. Government Printing Office or at some Canadian libraries.

In addition, the Act grants public access to manuals, handbooks and policy statements of any of the particular agencies. A person can gain access to records in any form (for example, computer records, paper or tape). The request can be made to the agency headquarters in Washington or to branch offices in the state that is believed to have the information. A request can also be addressed to the Freedom of Information Act officer with most agencies.

Each agency is required to publish a schedule of fees and the fee cannot exceed the actual cost of the search and obtaining copies. Rather than asking for copies, a person may request to simply inspect records. It is possible to have the fee waived or reduced if the information will benefit the public. Journalists frequently have their fees waived.

For more information, an excellent source is *A Citizen's Guide on How to Use the Freedom of Information Act and the Privacy Act in Requesting Documents*, obtainable for a fee from the U.S. Government Printing Office, Washington or at some Canadian libraries.

How to Make a Request

The request   A request must be made in writing to the head of the agency or a person directly responsible for the documents. The letter should state that the request is being made under the provisions of the Act. The request must "reasonably describe" the documents, which allows "a professional employee of the agency who was familiar with the subject area of the request to locate the record with a reasonable amount of effort." There is no requirement to express a reason for making the request. But, it is suggested that where an agency head has a discretion in releasing the information, an explanation may facilitate disclosure.

The time limits   The targeted federal agency is required to reply to a request within ten working days. In certain cases, an agency may be unable to respond within the time limit and must then notify the person making the request that an extension is needed. However, the extension cannot be for more than ten working days.

If a request is denied (that is, it falls within one of the exemptions), the person making the request must be notified in writing with reasons for the refusal.

The appeal process   Once a request has been refused, an appeal should be made to the head of the agency involved stating a case for being allowed access to the information. In most cases, appeals must be made within 30 days. A reply to the appeal must be made within 20 working days or 30 working days if the initial request was answered within the ten day limit. If there is no answer after 20 working days from when the agency received the appeal, a court action may be launched. The burden will be on the agency in question to justify its decision to withhold the information.

The Nine Statutory Exemptions to the Right of Access

The federal government allows agency heads to reject requests for the following information on a discretionary basis:

1. *Classified documents concerning national defence and foreign policy*   Documents which are classified as "Top Secret" may still be requested. The Act requires the agency head to review whether a document should continue to be classified. On appeal of a rejected request, a judge is given authority to review the documents and the agency decision.

2. *Internal personnel rules and practices of an agency*   This applies to information such as rules on internal employment practices and policies and use of agency facilities, such as parking spaces.

3. *Information exempt under other laws*   The statute barring public access must leave no room for discretion or provide a set of criteria to be met before information is released. This can include income tax returns and records on nuclear testing.

4. *Confidential business information*   This includes trade secrets and commercial or financial information obtained from a person confidentially. Confidential information is that which could harm the government or the competitive position of the company.

5. *Internal communications*   This includes memos and letters within and between agencies which would not normally be available unless a party needed it for litigation. This exemption does not apply to documents written after a policy or decision has been made. It only applies to documents involved in free-for-all discussions prior to a policy being developed.

6. *Protection of privacy*   This includes medical and personnel files, the disclosure of which would constitute a clear invasion of privacy.

7. *Investigatory files*   This refers to files prepared for law enforcement purposes, but applies only to records that would interfere with enforcement proceedings, deprive someone of a fair trial, constitute an unwarranted invasion of personal privacy, disclose the identity of a confidential source

of information, disclose investigative techniques or endanger the lives of law enforcement personnel.

8. *Information concerning financial institutions*   This includes documents or reports concerning banks, stock companies or similar institutions.

9. *Information concerning wells*   This includes geological wells and geophysical information, including maps.

ACCESS TO MUNICIPAL RECORDS AND INFORMATION

Municipalities are only bound to provide public access to certain documents as set out in provincial legislation. Beyond that, the inspection of any other municipal documents is entirely at the discretion of the local municipal authorities.[10]

Most provinces specifically allow public inspection of minutes of open council meetings, council agendas, minutes of open committee meetings, audit statements, voting lists, assessment rolls, consultant's reports submitted to open council, contracts, budgets, and by-laws.[11] Some provinces may only allow some of the above to be inspected. In some cases, only residents of the municipality or ratepayers enjoy the right of public inspection.[12] Usually, confidential, internal or "in-house" reports are not required to be produced.[13] For example, legal opinions submitted to municipal councils are usually considered privileged or confidential.

ACCESS TO CORPORATE INFORMATION

Corporate bodies operating in Canada are required by legislation to publicly disclose certain information, some of which could be useful to a reporter. There is one cautionary note about using such information. While corporations may be required by law to disclose information, it may not be up-to-date. In many cases, information must only be filed once a year and some corporations may not even bother to file on time or for several years. This affects the accuracy of information about company directors, officers, share allocations or financial information.

---

10 *Journal Printing Co. v. McVeity* (1915), 33 O.L.R. 166 (C.A.).

11 Only Alberta and Prince Edward Island have no mention of the public's right to municipal documents. Some of the provinces (for example, Manitoba, Saskatchewan and Newfoundland) are very explicit in what documents may be examined and copied. Other provinces may only refer to the public's right of access to "records" of a municipality, which is a vague term subject to the discretion of municipal officials.

12 This is the case in New Brunswick, Newfoundland and Québec.

13 *Charbonneau v. London and Reynolds* (1958), 15 D.L.R. (2d) 74 (Ont. H.C.).

Corporations and Labour Unions Returns Act

Under this legislation, corporations and labour unions are required to file specific information with the government each year.[14] The Act applies to public, private and holding corporations, with the exception of Crown corporations. It should be noted that this Act's days may be numbered. In 1985, Parliament considered the repeal of this Act because it was said to place a financial strain on corporations and labour unions. The proposed repeal died on the order paper.

As it now stands, the corporation must file the following information with the chief statistician of Canada:

1. The corporate name of the corporation;
2. The address of the head office of the corporation, and in the case of a corporation not resident in Canada, the address of its principal place of business in Canada or place to which communications may be directed;
3. The manner in which the corporation was incorporated, and the date and place of its incorporation;
4. The amount of authorized share capital, the number of shares of each class, and a description of the voting rights;
5. The number of issued shares of each class, and the numbers of shares owned by residents and non-residents of Canada;
6. The number of shares held by other corporations (where the shareholding is 10% or more);
7. The name and address of each person, other than a body corporate, holding 10% or more of the issued shares;
8. The details of any body corporate holding 10% or more of the issued shares;
9. The total face value of issued and outstanding debentures of the corporation;
10. For public corporations, the total number of shares and debentures offered in Canada during the past five years;
11. The name, address, nationality, and citizenship of each corporate director;
12. The name, address, nationality, and citizenship of each officer of the corporation; and
13. The number of shares of each class owned by each director and officer and a description of the voting rights attached to such shares.

A *holding corporation* is entitled to file the above information on behalf of its subsidiaries. A labour union operating in Canada must file similar

---

14 R.S.C. 1985, c. C-43.

information in regard to its membership, executive and organization.

The Act states the above information must be made available for inspection to any person for a nominal fee. The information on corporations is to be made available by the Minister of Consumer and Corporate Affairs. The information on labour unions is to be made available by the Minister of Labour.

Canada Business Corporations Act

This Act applies to every federally incorporated company.[15] It does not apply to banks, insurance companies, trust companies or loan companies or companies incorporated only under provincial statutes (provincial or federal incorporation is often a matter of choice). The public rights of access are very limited in regard to the records of private companies (those that do not sell shares to the public). But the public does have a right of access to certain corporate records of *distributing corporations* under section 21(1). A distributing corporation is defined in section 126(1) as meaning:

> a corporation, any of the issued securities of which are or were part of a distribution to the public and remain outstanding and are held by more than one person.

The corporate records of distributing corporations which can be examined for a fee at the corporation's registered office are:

(a) the articles and the by-laws, and all amendments thereto, and a copy of any unanimous shareholder agreement;
(b) minutes of meetings and resolutions of shareholders;
(c) copies of all notices of directors or changes of directors;
(d) a securities register of all securities issued and the names and addresses of the security holders.

Private corporations are also required to keep these records in their registered office, but only shareholders, creditors and their legal representatives can demand access.

Under section 160, financial statements for publicly traded (that is, distributing) corporations must be filed with the director (administrator) of the Act and according to section 266, these and most any other documents required to be submitted to the director are available to anyone through the director upon payment of the prescribed fee. Financial statements must include comparative financial statements from the first year to the present, the report of the auditor and any other information

---

15 R.S.C. 1985, c. C-44.

respecting the financial position of the corporation.

Non-distributing corporations falling under this Act are generally not required to disclose corporate records to the public. But, section 160 states that any non-distributing corporation which, together with its affiliates, has annual gross revenues exceeding $10 million or assets exceeding $5 million must send copies of the above financial statements to the director of the Act. Affiliates include parent and subsidiary companies, whether or not they are incorporated in Canada. In certain cases, a corporation may apply to the director for an exemption from the requirement of financial disclosure. The exemption will generally be granted where the disclosure would be detrimental to a corporation's financial well-being.

Section 129 requires the director to regularly publish a periodical, available to the public, consisting of information about any insider trading of shares in a distributing corporation. Regulatory exemptions which are granted under the take-over provisions of the Act are also to be included in this periodical.

Provincial Corporations Acts

All provincial and territorial jurisdictions have Companies Acts or Business Corporations Acts which require private and publicly-traded corporations to file basic declarations with a provincial government department overseeing corporations, such as a ministry of consumer and corporate affairs. Once deposited with the government, the documents can be viewed by anyone, usually for a small fee. In some provinces, the government department may give out general information about a company over the phone.

Even private companies are required to file information such as the address of the corporation, names and addresses of company directors and notices of changes in directors or corporate structure. Publicly-traded corporations (also called distributing corporations, in some provinces) file the same documents and may also have to file the names and addresses of shareholders, the number of shares held by each shareholder and names and addresses of individuals holding options to purchase shares.

Depending on the province, the information supplied to the government and available for public scrutiny may be scanty. Alberta, the Northwest Territories, Manitoba and Saskatchewan have fairly detailed filing requirements.[16] But most other jurisdictions only require information such as the latest address of the corporation and changes in its directors.[17]

---

16 For example, see Alberta, Business Corporations Act, S.A. 1981, c. B-15, s. 21(4) and (5).

17 For example, see British Columbia, Company Act, R.S.B.C. 1979, c: 59, s. 359.

Public and private corporations may also be required to make minutes of shareholder or director meetings and financial records available at their registered office or head office of the corporation. But access is restricted according to the type of company. In most provinces and both territories, such information is available on publicly-traded corporations to anyone during normal business hours, sometimes for a small fee. Private corporations, however, do not have to make this information available in their offices to anyone other than shareholders and directors. In the latter case, a journalist must rely on information available through government corporate records offices or a corporate registry. In New Brunswick, Prince Edward Island and Québec, both private and public companies are required to allow access to records to shareholders, creditors and their legal representatives and directors of the corporation.

Business Organizations Other Than Corporations

Sole Proprietorships

There is no general requirement for a sole proprietor (unincorporated) to make information about his or her business available to the public. But, if a sole proprietor plans to operate under a name other than his or her own, the law in all jurisdictions requires that that name be registered with the provincial corporate affairs department. The registration process usually requires a declaration setting out the name and address of the sole proprietor and this then is available to the public.

Partnerships

If a partnership is required by provincial law to be registered, the public may gain access to a declaration consisting of the names of the partners, addresses, the name of the partnership and other general details.

Non-Profit Corporations

A non-profit corporation may also by required by provincial law to register its address, directors and other general information and this information is also available to the public.

Securities Legislation

Journalists may want to keep provincial securities bodies in mind when researching information about a particular company. Any public offering of securities (such as shares, debentures, bonds, private placements) requires disclosure of financial information such as earnings, income projections, expenses and other important information for prospective shareholders. Securities bodies also compile regular bulletins noting insider trades by directors, company executives and shareholders. The information and reports are filed with the provincial securities commission and are generally available to the public.

USING STATISTICAL INFORMATION

The Statistics Act[18] gives Statistics Canada the authority to demand and gather information on many aspects of Canadian life: social and cultural, economic, manufacturing, trade and commerce, agricultural, education and employment. The information is published on a regular basis, sometimes even weekly or monthly. Since Statistics Canada is an agency of the government, most of the information collected is for public consumption. In fact, "Stats Can" actively encourages people to use their services.

Statistics Canada publishes an annual catalogue containing an index of the publications available through the department. The catalogue also contains a brief abstract or summary of each publication along with the date of publication and the price. A copy of this catalogue is available to anyone, free of charge, from any Statistics Canada User Advisory Service (listed below). The publications in the catalogue may be ordered from:

Statistics Canada
Publications Sales and Services
Ottawa, Ontario
K1A 0T6

There are also over 45 libraries throughout the country which are "depositories" for Statistics Canada material. Compiled information may be found in university libraries, public libraries and legislative libraries.

Statistics Canada also provides toll free numbers to allow researchers to quickly find facts and figures (contact local directory assistance or 1-800-555-1212 for the 800 number nearest you). This service is free of charge where the information is readily accessible. If the request requires extensive research, you may be charged on a cost-recovery basis. The staff can quickly, often within a day, find figures on almost anything or offer advice on other potential sources of information.

---

18 R.S.C. 1985, c. S-19.

Interpreting Statistical Information

Be sure that you check the introduction, footnotes, explanatory notes and definitions published with statistical reports. In accordance with the Statistics Act, certain information gathered by the department may have to be kept secret. Some tables, for instance, may contain an "x" in place of a statistic. This is because the Statistics Act forbids the publication of statistics which might identify a company or individual.

For example, when dealing with industrial statistics the *rule of three* is followed. That is, no figure made up of data from fewer than three industries can be published. If only two companies were in one industry, one company would obviously know about the figures from the other.

Another method of protecting the information obtained by Statistics Canada is random rounding. The final digit in every number in a table is rounded up or down to a 0 or a 5. This technique is used in the Census of Population tables where there is a danger of an individual being identified. Statistics Canada points out that its survey areas sometimes cover only a few city blocks and the possibility of identifying a source of information is possible.

CANSIM

CANSIM is a Statistics Canada database which provides time series and cross-classified data on Canadian social and economic issues. The time series data shows changes over a certain period (for example, consumer price index) and cross-classified data shows the relationship between different social and/or economic issues at a given point in time (for example, how and if unemployment rates affect vacancy rates).

This database is an excellent source for custom-made statistics. It is operated on a cost-recovery basis for the public and the minimum charge starts at about $50.00. Quotes are available upon request and CANSIM staff members can offer you help in determining what the database has to offer. CANSIM can be accessed through any of the User Advisory Regional Reference Centres located in St. John's, Halifax, Montreal, Ottawa, Toronto, Winnipeg, Regina, Edmonton and Vancouver.

Sample Publications

Here is a brief list of Stats Can publications of interest to reporters.

Canada Yearbook A reference book giving textual and graphic information on physical and natural resources, social and economic conditions, government organizations, industry, finance and the legal system.

Canada Handbook   This biennial book offers text and statistical tables with current information on aspects of Canadian life, such as economic development, history, education, farming, recreation, communications, technology and government services.

Bibliography of Federal Data Sources, Excluding Statistics Canada   This has gathered other sources of social and economic data which are produced on a regular basis by other federal departments and agencies. It covers almost all departments, a cross-section of agencies, commissions and boards and some Crown corporations.

Juristat   This has statistical information on a variety of justice related programs, including areas of law enforcement, legal aid, adult and young offender courts, and corrections. It is prepared by the Canadian Centre for Justice Statistics.

16

Miscellaneous Laws

The Criminal Code[1] and other statutes contain sections which journalists should note. While the provisions may not always be directed at the news media, it's best to be forewarned.

PUBLISHING OBSCENE MATERIAL

The publication of obscene pictures and words is the subject of both the Criminal Code and broadcasting regulations. Determining what is obscene is difficult because the level of tolerance in a community changes over time. The laws we have enacted don't provide any clear guidelines regarding what's obscene so each case must be judged individually.

For example, obscene material presented as a form of art may be allowed on a television broadcast, but the same material presented in an exploitative manner in a magazine may be obscene. These inequities, often based on a judge's assessment of community standards, result in an uncertain legal climate for the news media.

In recent years, pressure has been building on the federal government to come up with a more comprehensive definition of obscene matter. The following are the relevant provisions in current law.

---

1 R.S.C. 1985, c. C-46.

Criminal Code

Section 163(1)(a) of the Criminal Code makes it an offence to publish any

> obscene written matter, picture, model, phonograph record or other thing whatsoever.

A complex issue is precisely what is a "publication" of obscene matter. A 1985 Supreme Court of Canada decision suggests that almost anything can be a publication. A Montreal store selling sex aids (for example, vibrators and inflatable dolls) was charged and convicted under the Code's obscenity section. The court dismissed an appeal by the store and the majority ruling was that the sex aids were "publications." The court said a publication is "an article, the character of which is made public."[2]

The motive for publishing the obscene material is irrelevant[3] and ignorance of the obscenity law is no excuse.[4] Section 163(8) also offers this general definition of what is "obscene":

> any publication a dominant characteristic of which is the undue exploitation of sex, or of sex and any one of more of the following subjects, namely, crime, horror, cruelty and violence, shall be deemed to be obscene.

Generally, in deciding whether a publication is obscene, the courts will look to see what is the "dominant characteristic" of the publication.[5] If the dominant characteristic is one of "undue exploitation of sex," or of sex combined with acts of violence, then the publication will probably be held to be obscene.[6]

To decide whether the use of sex in a publication is "undue exploitation," the courts will look to the overall standards of tolerance in Canadian society. An undue exploitation of sex is one which has no redeeming purpose in the eyes of the community and is in bad taste.[7]

However, just because a publication has objectionable or sex-related material doesn't make it obscene. The courts will look at why the author published the material.[8] As well, the material may be included for "a frank and sincere depiction of a non-sexual subject."[9] The objectionable material may also be part of the "internal necessities of the work" in question. For example, an expert may be able to testify about the artistic or literary merit of the work.[10]

---

2 *Germain v. R.*, [1985] 2 S.C.R. 241.

3 Section 163(5).

4 Section 163(6).

5 *R. v. Brodie* (1962), 132 C.C.C. 161 (S.C.C.).

6 *R. v. Ariadne Devs. Ltd.* (1974), 19 C.C.C. (2d) 49 (N.S. C.A.).

7 *R. v. Standard News Distributors Inc.* (1960), 34 C.R. 54 (Que. Mun. Ct.).

8 Note 5, above.

9 Note 6, above.

10 *Ibid.*

As mentioned above, deciding whether something is obscene involves a court's interpretation of the standards of acceptance in a community and this is how one judge viewed his task:[11]

> Those standards are not set by those of lowest taste or interest. Nor are they set exclusively by those of rigid, austere, conservative or puritan taste and habit of mind. Something approaching a general average of community thinking and feeling has to be discovered.

Determining the community's standards can involve evidence of public opinion polls and testimony from experts. But the courts are likely to give little weight to these "opinions" and, in the end, a judge will decide whether the publication is obscene.[12] The courts have maintained that they must consider contemporary community standards of all of Canada and that all segments of the community must be considered, not just one faction (for example, a college campus or a church group).[13]

This was stressed by the Supreme Court of Canada in 1978 when considering whether a restricted movie was obscene if consenting adults were the only ones viewing it.[14] The court said the standards of tolerance are not what Canadians think is right for themselves to see, but what Canadians would not "abide" others to see.

Courts also don't judge all publications in the same way. For example, newspapers are handled differently from magazines. In a case involving a gay newspaper, the court looked at the entire newspaper to determine if the publication of some of the articles was obscene. There were only three articles judged to be obscene and the charge was dismissed.[15]

But, in a case involving a men's magazine, the court felt it could look at the publication page-by-page because there was no overriding theme.[16]

Finally, the Code recognizes that a publication of obscene material may be in the public interest and this defence is set out in section 163(3):

> No person shall be convicted of an offence under this section if he establishes that the public good was served by the acts that are alleged to constitute the offence and that the acts alleged did not extend beyond what served the public good.

---

11 See, *Dominion News and Gifts v. R.*, [1964] S.C.R. 251, which adopted this statement from the dissenting judgment in the lower court ruling (that is, (1963), 42 W.W.R. 65 at 80).

12 *R. v. Pink Triangle Press* (1980), 51 C.C.C. (2d) 485 at 496 (Ont. Co. Ct.).

13 *Towne Cinema Theatres Ltd. v. R.*, [1985] 1 S.C.R. 494.

14 *R. v. Sudbury News Serv. Ltd.* (1978), 39 C.C.C. (2d) 1 (Ont. C.A.).

15 *R. v. McLeod* (1970), 10 C.R.N.S. 229 (B.C. Co. Ct.).

16 *R. v. Penthouse International Ltd.* (1979), 23 O.R. (2d) 786 (C.A.), leave to S.C.C. refused (1979), 23 O.R. (2d) 786n (S.C.C.).

Broadcasting Regulations

The Canadian Radio-television and Telecommunications Commission (CRTC) has regulations on the broadcasting of obscene, indecent or profane matter via radio or television.[17] For example, the television regulations (which mirror the radio regulations except for the words "or pictorial representation") say:

> 5. (1) A licensee shall not broadcast
>   (a) anything in contravention of the law;
>   (b) any abusive comment or abusive pictorial representation that, when taken in context, tends or is likely to expose an individual or a group or class of individuals to hatred or contempt on the basis of race, national or ethnic origin, colour, religion, sex, age or mental or physical disability;
>   (c) any obscene or profane language or pictorial representation; or
>   (d) any false or misleading news.

These regulations are meant to prevent a broadcaster from using obscene material for shock value or without an appropriate or artistic reason. Many broadcasters make it a point to warn their audience of potentially objectionable material.

Proposed Changes to the Criminal Code

In 1984, the Federal government considered this change to the "definition" section of the Criminal Code. Section 163(8) would be replaced with the following:[18]

> For the purposes of this Act, any matter or thing is obscene where a dominant characteristic of the matter or thing is the undue exploitation of any one or more of the following subjects, namely, sex, violence, crime, horror or cruelty, through degrading representations of a male or female person or in any other manner.

This amendment would have removed the necessity for a link between sex and crime, horror, cruelty or violence in order to constitute "obscenity." It also includes "degrading representations" as a means of undue exploitation. In addition, this amendment would have made it clear that the test for obscenity applies to any "matter or thing" and isn't limited to publications. The amendments weren't enacted and soon after, the Fraser Committee Report[19] outlined more extensive proposals for the revision of obscenity law.

---

17 See *Radio Regulations, 1986*, SOR/86-982, s. 5(1) and *Television Broadcasting Regulations*, SOR/87-49, s. 5(1).

18 Set out in s. 36 of Bill C-19, introduced by the Liberal government in the 1983-84 session of Parliament. First reading given in February, 1984, but it did not reach second and third reading.

19 "Pornography and Prostitution in Canada," Report of the Special Committee on Pornography and Prostitution, Minister of Supply and Services (Ottawa), 1985 (2 vol.).

The Fraser Committee recommended first that the term "obscene" be done away with in the Criminal Code because it doesn't adequately describe all the material which the committee felt should be controlled. The report suggests a three-tiered system for dealing with pornographic material.

The Committee recommends the repeal of section 163 of the Code and suggests three major offences which would make it a crime to make, print, publish, distribute or possess for the purposes of publication or distribution the following:[20]

1. The first tier is reserved for the most serious offences, such as those showing a person under 18 years old participating in explicit sexual conduct. *Sexual conduct* is "any conduct in which vaginal, oral or anal intercourse, masturbation, sexually violent behaviour, bestiality, incest, necrophilia, lewd touching of the breasts or the genital parts of the body, or the lewd exhibition of the genitals is depicted." The first tier also includes material which advocates, encourages, condones, or presents as normal the abuse of children or material which actually involved physical harm to a person in its making.

   This is an indictable offence with a maximum sentence of five years in jail. Anyone who sells or rents these materials can be charged with an indictable offence with a maximum sentence of up to two years or a summary conviction offence liable to up to six months in jail, a fine between $500 and $2000 or both.

2. The second tier is less onerous and involves any material which depicts or describes sexually violent behaviour, bestiality, incest or necrophilia. *Sexually violent behaviour* involves sexual assault and any physical harm depicted for the purpose of causing sexual gratification or stimulation to the viewer.

   This is an indictable offence punishable with a maximum sentence of five years. Anyone who sells, rents or displays these materials can be charged with an indictable offence with a maximum sentence of up to two years or a summary conviction offence liable to up to six months in jail, a fine between $500 and $1000 or both.

3. The third tier of offences involve the display of visual pornographic materials in public. *Visual pornographic material* "includes any matter or thing in or on which is depicted vaginal, oral or anal intercourse, masturbation, lewd touching of the breasts or the genital parts of the body, or the lewd exhibition of the genitals," but does not involve a depicted person under 18 years of age or sexually violent behaviour.

   This offence is punishable on summary conviction.

---

20 Recommendations 5 and 7 of the Fraser Report.

Among the recommended defences is that the pornographic material is a part of a work of artistic merit. The recommended provisions would require a court to look at the impugned material in the whole context of the work when it's presented in a book, film, video recording or "broadcast which presents a discrete story." It says "in the case of a magazine or any other composite or segmented work" the court should look at the material in the context of "the specific feature of which it is a part."

Other defences involve the use of these materials for a genuine educational or scientific purpose. The display of pornographic materials can be excused where the public would encounter a "prominent warning notice advising of the nature of the display therein." There is also a "due diligence" defence for anybody who sells or rents the material who can prove that they did everything which could reasonably be expected to be done to ensure the pornographic material wasn't in violation of the Code.

Another attempt by Ottawa in 1988 to introduce a new obscenity law was also unsuccessful.

HATE PROPAGANDA

Criminal Code

Sections 318 and 319 establish indictable and summary conviction offences involving the promotion of hatred. A provincial or federal Attorney General must give permission to prosecute these offences. There have been few prosecutions or convictions under these sections. The most notable case in recent times has been the conviction of Alberta school teacher James Keegstra, who taught his students that the Jewish Holocaust may not have happened.

Section 318(1) states:

> Every one who advocates or promotes genocide is guilty of an indictable offence and is liable to imprisonment for a term not exceeding five years.

The offending statements can be spoken or in a written form. According to section 318(2), "genocide" means:

> any of the following acts committed with intent to destroy in whole or in part any identifiable group, namely,
> (a) killing members of the group; or
> (b) deliberately inflicting on the group conditions of life calculated to bring about its physical destruction.

The Code defines an "identifiable group" as any section of the public distinguished by colour, race, religion or ethnic origin. A "public place" is defined as including any place to which the public has access as of right or by invitation, express or implied. The actual offences are outlined in the following sections:

Section 319(1):

> Every one who, by communicating statements in any public place, incites hatred against any identifiable group where such incitement is likely to lead to a breach of peace, is guilty of
> > (a) an indictable offence and is liable to imprisonment for a term not exceeding two years; or
> > (b) an offence punishable on summary conviction.

Section 319(2):

> Every one who, by communicating statements, other than in private conversation, wilfully promotes hatred against any identifiable group is guilty of
> > (a) an indictable offence and is liable to imprisonment for a term not exceeding two years; or
> > (b) an offence punishable on summary conviction.

The defence to a charge under section 319(2) is set out in section 319(3):

> No person shall be convicted of an offence under subsection (2)
> > (a) if he establishes that the statements communicated were true;
> > (b) if, in good faith, he expressed or attempted to establish by argument an opinion upon a religious subject;
> > (c) if the statements were relevant to any subject of public interest, the discussion of which was for the public benefit, and if on reasonable grounds he believed them to be true; or
> > (d) if, in good faith, he intended to point out, for the purpose of removal, matters producing or tending to produce feelings of hatred towards an identifiable group in Canada.

The Fraser Committee Report, mentioned above, recommends that the definition of "identifiable group" in section 318(4) be broadened to include sex, age and mental or physical disability. The Report also recommends the word "wilful" be removed to do away with the requirement that there must be a specific intent to promote hatred against an identifiable group. The word "statement" was also considered to be too narrow by the Committee and it was suggested that it should be expanded to include graphic images of pornography. Finally, the Report suggests that the section calling for the Attorney General's consent for a prosecution be repealed.[21]

Broadcasting Regulations

The CRTC also seeks to prevent the spread of hate propaganda. For

---

21 See recommendations 38 to 41 of the Fraser Committee Report.

example, the television regulations (which mirror the radio regulations except for the words "pictorial representation"), in part, say:[22]

> 5. (1) A licensee shall not broadcast
>   (a) anything in contravention of the law;
>   (b) any abusive comment or abusive pictorial representation that, when taken in context, tends or is likely to expose an individual or a group or class of individuals to hatred or contempt on the basis of race, national or ethnic origin, colour, religion, sex, age or mental or physical disability.

MISCELLANEOUS CRIMINAL CODE SECTIONS

Advertising Rewards

Section 143 prohibits any public advertisement of a reward for the return of any stolen or lost item, in which words are used to indicate that no questions will be asked if it is returned. The offence also extends to anyone who prints or publishes such an advertisement.

Counselling Offences

Section 22 forbids anyone from counselling or getting another person to be a party to an offence, such that a crime is committed. It doesn't matter that the offence may have been committed in a different way from what was counselled. The Code will hold the counsellor responsible for any foreseeable consequence of the counselling. In addition, section 464 will hold you responsible for counselling or procuring another person to be a party to an offence, even though an offence may not be committed as a result. In one case involving a British Columbia newspaper, readers were told how to grow marijuana and the newspaper was charged under this section.[23] The newspaper tried to argue that the person who complained about the "advice" to the authorities did not even try to grow the illicit plant. The paper was convicted and the court held the recipient of the counselling doesn't have to be influenced by it to sustain a conviction.

Ignorance of the Law

You can't get away from a conviction by simply saying you didn't know you were committing a crime. Section 19 states that ignorance of the law is not an excuse for committing an offence.

---

22 Note 17, above.
23 *R. v. McLeod* (1970), 1 C.C.C. (2d) 5 (B.C. C.A.).

Counselling Mutiny or Desertion

Section 62 prohibits the publication of anything which counsels or urges insubordination, disloyalty, mutiny or refusal of duty by a member of a military force (Canadian or any other military force lawfully in the country).

Disturbing an Assemblage

Section 176 creates a summary conviction offence for anyone who willfully disturbs an assemblage of persons meeting for religious worship or for a moral, social or benevolent purpose.

False News

Section 181 makes it an offence to knowingly publish false news which causes or is likely to cause injury or mischief to a public interest. Even the publication of false news in the form of humour must be done carefully. It must be obvious to the average person that the false news is satire. (It should also be noted that broadcasting regulations make it an offence under the Broadcasting Act to spread false or misleading news.)[24]

Harassment

Journalists shouldn't become pests while chasing down a story such that a person feels he or she is relentlessly being hounded. Section 372 prohibits harassing or threatening telephone calls.

Photographing Money

Section 457(2) makes it a summary conviction offence to print or publish anything *in the likeness or appearance of* a current bank note, paper money or government or bank security or obligation. But, section 457(3) states no conviction will result if the reproduction does not:

1) display a complete word, letter or numeral (except the word Canada),
2) display more than general details in a human face or figure,
3) display more than one colour, and
4) nothing in the appearance or likeness of the back of a bank note or paper money is printed or published.

---

24 Note 17, above.

PROVINCIAL HUMAN RIGHTS CODES

All provinces and both territories have human rights laws that bar the publication of any "notice, sign, symbol, emblem or other representation" discriminating against any person or class of persons for any purpose because of race, religion, religious creed, political opinion, colour or ethnic, national or social origin.[25] But, the legislation also states nothing in this provision shall be deemed to interfere with the free expression of opinions on any subject.[26]

One Manitoba case has held a newspaper report doesn't fit into the category of a "notice, sign, symbol, emblem or other representation."[27] The article in question made allegedly racist remarks about Indians while discussing the topic of native leaders attending an Ottawa conference. In turning down the appeal, the Court of Appeal turned to one of the principles of statutory interpretation which states that the meaning of a word in a statute is "coloured" by the words surrounding it. The Court said a notice or a sign isn't the same as a complicated newspaper article and found the newspaper not guilty of violating the human rights legislation.

WAR MEASURES ACT

In the event of a war, invasion or insurrection, the War Measures Act empowers the Governor in Council (that is, the cabinet) to do or authorize among other things, the censorship, control and suppression of publications, writings and photographs.[28] There has been some discussion in legal circles that this Act may violate our rights under the Canadian Charter of Rights and Freedoms.[29]

---

25 *Newfoundland Human Rights Code*, R.S.N. 1970, c. 262, s. 11(1), as amended S.N. 1974, No. 114, s. 7; S.N. 1981, c. 29, s. 5; S.N. 1984, c. 31, s. 2.
26 *Ibid.*, s. 11(2).
27 *Warren v. Chapman* (1985), 31 Man. R. (2d) 231 (C.A.).
28 R.S.C. 1985, c. W-2, s. 3(1).
29 Part 1 of the Constitution Act, 1982, being Schedule B of the Canada Act 1982 (U.K.), 1982, c. 11.

Appendix 1

The Legal System

Simply speaking, Parliament and the provincial legislatures make the laws and the courts interpret and enforce them. But that is "simply speaking." In actual fact, our courts sometimes end up making the law by virtue of the way legislation is interpreted. This chapter is a primer on the court system, leaving the explanation of the legislative process to political scientists.

Generally, there are two main bodies of law administered by the courts. The *civil law* is concerned with private rights and remedies, such as in contracts or defamation. The *criminal law* punishes behaviour which is an offence against the State or society.

SOURCES OF THE LAW

The courts look to many sources to interpret our laws and decide issues: Constitution Acts, statutes, previous cases and even the writings of learned authors. In some instances, Canadian courts will consider the court decisions of other countries, particularly those in the United Kingdom and the United States.

The Constitution

The documents and unwritten conventions (that is, traditions or customs) that form our Constitution date from early English history to Confederation to the present. Because of our parliamentary system of government, we share many of the constitutional traditions of England and the courts often reach back to early times to help interpret a point of constitutional law. There are also numerous constitutional documents, the most important of which are the Constitution Acts (including the former

British North America Act and the Canadian Charter of Rights and Freedoms). The Constitution is sometimes referred to as the "Supreme Law of the Land" because it forms the basis upon which the courts determine the individual powers and limits of the federal and provincial legislatures.

Statutes

Statutes are the tools of governments. They may create completely new laws to govern behaviour or they may just codify existing practices. Statutes are passed by the federal Parliament or provincial legislatures according to the powers and limits set out by the constitutional law. For example, the Constitution Act, 1867 (that is, British North America Act) states that the federal Parliament has exclusive jurisdiction to create criminal offences, but the provincial governments have the right to administer the operations of the criminal courts. Sometimes, a legislature will over-step its boundaries and the courts will declare a statute *ultra vires* or beyond the legislature's power and thus having no effect.

Case Law

All of the provinces, with the exception of Québec, have a system of law which gives great authority to previously-decided cases on various topics of law. The legal system which relies heavily on case precedents is known as the *common law*. Although no two cases are ever the same, certain general principles can be extracted from similar cases. The legal principle of *stare decisis* gives precedents great authority and, in most cases, case precedents are binding on lower courts.

All of the provinces and territories use case precedents in the criminal law. Precedents are also used in civil cases, except in Québec, where there is a European-based *civil law* system as opposed to the English-based *common law* system followed in the rest of Canada. In Québec, a precedent is authoritative in civil law only because of the soundness of its reasoning, rather than the fact other judges have followed it. Québec courts are not bound to follow the previous decisions of other judges and theoretically decide cases according to civil law principles codified in a text known as the Civil Code. These basic statements or principles attempt to fit every possible legal problem. If the Code does not speak directly to the problem, then the judge may use the general provisions of the Code to come to a decision. However, in practice, Québec judges generally do follow precedents.

OUR COURT SYSTEM

As stated earlier, the purpose of the courts is to interpret the law, not to make the law. But as times change, so do the attitudes of the courts and new principles can evolve to interpret the law. When a court makes a decision which is unique, it is important to consider the court's decision in the context of the judicial hierarchy or pecking order. This basic point is made because some members of the news media overreact when a lower court makes an unusual ruling. It should be remembered that such a decision could be quickly overturned by an appeal court if it is appealed.

The Court Hierarchy

The Supreme Court of Canada is the ultimate court of appeal and has the final word on the interpretation of the law of the country. For example, if a Supreme Court of Canada decision states that a certain statute is invalid, only an act of Parliament or a legislature can change the resulting effect of the interpretation. Until that happens, the decision of the Supreme Court of Canada is binding on all other courts.

The next level down is the Court of Appeal of each province. The decisions of the Court of Appeal are binding on all of the lower courts in that province. Other courts of appeal will note decisions of the appeal court in other provinces, but, while the other court's decision is persuasive, there is no express requirement to follow the decision.

Lower courts in other provinces are also obliged to take note of the decisions of other courts of appeal, but the decisions are not expressly binding, as is the case when their own court of appeal makes a decision.

Below the appeal courts, are the trial courts and, below the trial courts, are specialized courts which deal with minor criminal offences and/or small civil actions. Throughout the hierarchy, the principle is that a lower court must follow the precedents set by higher courts in that province. Decisions by courts of equal or higher ranking in other provinces must be noted and may be persuasive, but are not binding.

Canadian courts also consider decisions in other common law countries such as Australia, England or the United States. Often where there is no precedent in a certain area of the law, the courts will look to other jurisdictions for guidance.

Court Jurisdictions

The structure of our courts is rooted in the Constitution Act, 1867. Under the Constitution, the individual provinces establish the actual framework of their court system. There are two major categories of courts which are found in each province's judicial system: Superior Courts and Inferior Courts.

Superior Courts are the high level trial and appeal courts. The judges to these courts are appointed by the federal government (even though the province enacts legislation establishing the particular levels of Superior Courts). Below the Superior Courts are the so-called Inferior Courts or provincial courts with judges appointed by the province.

The number of court levels can vary from province to province. Some provinces have county and district courts. Some have special courts to handle wills and estates. Most trial and appeal courts in each province and territory have authority to deal with matters in both criminal and civil law, but some, particularly low level provincial courts, may be restricted to either criminal or civil law. The following charts set out the general structure of our criminal and civil courts:

The Civil Court System

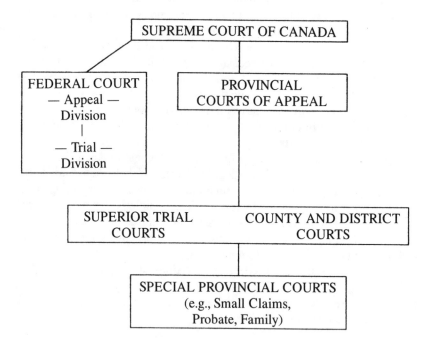

Supreme Court of Canada   The ultimate court of appeal. Only cases of national, constitutional or legal importance are given permission to be heard in this court. The court can confirm or overturn a decision or order a new trial.

Federal Court   Formerly known as the Exchequer Court, the two divisions of this body have exclusive jurisdiction over patents, copyrights, trademarks, disputes over shipping and navigation, inter-governmental disputes and certain actions against the federal government.

Provincial Courts of Appeal   The highest court in each province. It can confirm or overturn a decision or order a new trial.

Superior Trial Courts   These courts are generally the first level for a civil law case. They are known variously in the provinces as the Court of Queen's Bench, Superior Court, Supreme Court, and Supreme Court, Trial Division.

County and District Courts   Both county and district courts presently exist in Nova Scotia, Newfoundland and British Columbia. Ontario has combined its County and District Courts to become simply District Courts. In Québec, so-called Québec Courts fulfil similar duties to county courts and hear small civil matters. These courts usually have jurisdiction over civil actions involving claims with a ceiling of small to medium amounts (for example, $50,000). This level of courts may soon be extinct. At the time of writing, Ontario and British Columbia governments had announced plans to merge this level with the superior trial courts.

Special Courts   These courts have limited jurisdiction over such matters as small claims, wills, estates and family law matters.

The Criminal Court System

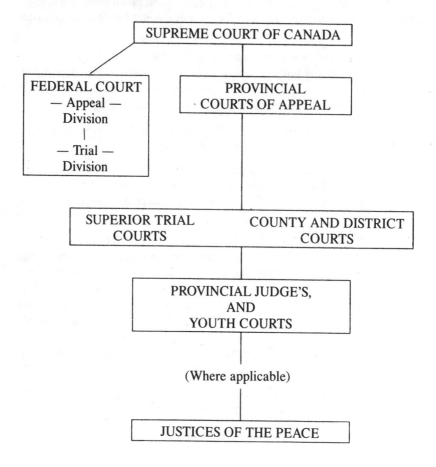

Supreme Court of Canada   This is the ultimate court of appeal. Only cases of national, constitutional or legal importance are given permission to be heard in this court. The court can confirm or overturn a decision or order a new trial.

Federal Court   Formerly known as the Exchequer Court, the two divisions of this body hear some criminal matters (for example, income tax prosecutions).

Provincial Courts of Appeal   The highest court in each province. The court can confirm or overturn a decision, or order a new trial. For criminal cases, these courts are defined as "superior courts of criminal jurisdiction."

Superior Trial Courts   These courts handle any offences that are not within the jurisdiction of a provincial court judge or when an accused has elected this trial level. These courts are known variously in the provinces as the Court of Queen's Bench, Superior Court, Supreme Court, and Supreme Court, Trial Division. These courts are also considered "superior courts of criminal jurisdiction" for the purposes of jurisdiction in the criminal justice system. In Québec, the Court of Queen's Bench is both a court of appeal and court of original jurisdiction for criminal matters.

County and District Courts   County and District Courts exist in Nova Scotia, Newfoundland and British Columbia. Ontario has combined its County and District Courts to become simply District Courts. In Québec, the Court of the Sessions of the Peace hears criminal cases without a jury and is similar to a County Court. This level of the court system has jurisdiction over most criminal matters, except those within the jurisdiction of the "superior courts" (for example, murder). This level of the court system is known simply as a "court of criminal jurisdiction." This level of courts may soon be extinct. At the time of writing, Ontario and British Columbia governments had announced plans to merge this level with the superior trial courts.

Provincial and Youth Courts   These are often the courts of first appearance in a criminal case. The power of the Youth Court may be vested in provincial court or family court judges depending on the province.

Justices of the Peace   The justice of the peace is the court of first appearance in a few provinces, such as Ontario and Québec. Justices adjudicate a few minor criminal offences or violations of provincial and municipal laws. But for serious offences they have no jurisdiction other than to process the accused for a higher court (for example, justices of the peace cannot take an accused's plea for offences which they have no authority to adjudicate).

ADMINISTRATIVE TRIBUNALS

There is another decision-making process within the legal system which can affect the rights of individuals and can involve the courts. Although most official bodies in government exercise purely administrative or "rubber-stamping" powers, statutes can create tribunals or bodies which exercise a quasi-judicial or judicial function. Many of these tribunals are not courts *per se*, but do make decisions in a judicial or quasi-judicial manner after considering presentations or evidence (for example, public utility boards, public inquiries, municipal boards, disciplinary committees). Some administrative tribunals even have the same authority as superior courts to enforce their rulings.

Many of these bodies, such as labour boards, have exclusive jurisdiction to make decisions under the legislation. For example, a dispute over whether a company has used unfair bargaining practices will be settled by a labour board and not by the courts. However, in most cases, the courts have the power to review the decisions for procedural defects (rather than the correctness of the decision) which are not in accordance with the principles of natural justice or fairness. If the tribunal is found to have made its decision improperly, the court may be able to order a new hearing or other suitable remedy.

UNDERSTANDING COURT JUDGMENTS

To understand the legal system, it is helpful to understand how court decisions are structured. As formidable as court judgments may sometimes seem, they are generally understandable to the layman who takes the time to follow them. Some are poorly written and thought out, and even a lawyer may not be able to fully understand the judge's points.

But there is a pattern to look for when reading a court judgment. The decisions usually begin with a recital of the facts presented at trial. The judge will outline the events leading up to trial and what each party wants. The judge will then discuss the arguments presented at trial. This will include a review of the case law and the statutes which the lawyers feel supports an argument. This is often the most difficult part of a judgment to follow. But it is among the most important because the judge will begin to indicate which argument is best supported and why.

Eventually, the judge will select one or several points which he or she feels will win the case for one of the parties. The winning point or points of the case are known as the *ratio decidendi*. This is the "bottom line" which determines the final decision. During the discussion of the case law or arguments, the judge may also offer an opinion which is not directly concerned with the matter at hand or crucial to the *ratio decidendi*. This opinion is known as *obiter dictum*. It is an opinion which is totally unnecessary for the resolution of the case. The comments do not form a binding precedent to be followed by other courts. Sometimes, it is difficult for lawyers to figure out if a comment is the *ratio* of a case, or merely *obiter*.

As the judgment nears the end, many judges will summarize the reasons for the decision in the last few paragraphs.

CITATIONS

Cases

When the courts first started issuing judgments with reasons, a system was designed to note and catalogue significant judgments. Lawyers refer to this unique series of numbers and words as *citations* (for example, *Smith v. Smith* (1980), 7 D.L.R. (3d) 354 (Ont. H.C.)). Citations are used to identify cases and statutes throughout this book, in legal texts and in the court judgments you may read.

If you want to know more about a particular case or law, the citations will help you find it in local law libraries. The structure of the citation for cases is very simple:

Name of Case	Year	Volume	Reporting Series	Page	Court
A v. B et al.,	[1971]	3	O.R.	222	(C.A.)
C v. D	(1985),	5	O.R. (2d)	123	(C.A.)

The first thing to notice is the name of the case (style of cause). The plaintiffs or initiators of the action are the first name or names encountered and the defendants are the name or names after the *v.* (*versus*). Sometimes, an "et al." will be in the case name. This is Latin for "and others" and is used as an abbreviation for listing other parties.

Next is the year. The year of the judgment is always included, in "(   )" (round brackets), except where a particular reporting series uses the year of publication to identify a volume, in "[   ]" (square brackets). In that case, if the judgment year and publication year are the same, only the publication (square bracketed) year is included; if the judgment year and publication year are different, then the judgment (round bracketed) year is included first, followed by the publication year.

The next number, if there is one, is the volume of the reporting series. "Reporting series" are publications containing full texts of the decisions rendered by the court. By knowing the reporting series, it is easy to identify the province. In the above examples, the case will be found in the Ontario Reports. Sometimes, in old cases or cases from other countries, the letters of the reporting series will not indicate the jurisdiction (for example, (1883), B. & R. 234). In a case such as this, a law librarian will help you find the case.

The letters of the reporting series will sometimes be followed with a "(2d)" or "(3d)," to denote the second or third series. A new series of reports is started when the number of volumes of cases becomes unwieldy. The page at which the case can be found is next. Finally, the level of the court is indicated in brackets (and is usually abbreviated) after the citation (for example, Court of Appeal would be abbreviated as (C.A.)).

Statutes

For statutes, the citations are somewhat different:

Statute Name	Statute Series	Year	Chapter
X Act	R.S.C.	1985	c. X-100
Y Act	S.C.	1989	c. 100

The system of cataloging statutes is simpler than for cases. The name of the Act comes first, followed by the statute series. In the above example, R.S.C. stands for Revised Statutes of Canada. In 1985 (the year indicated), the government revised and reassembled its legislation. This placed all of the statutes in one series for one year. All of the provinces have revised their statutes at one time or another. In the second example, only the letters S.C. are used, meaning Statutes of Canada for 1989 (the year indicated). Since laws are amended and new ones have been passed in the years since 1985, the citation is making reference to a law passed in 1989. The same practice is followed in the provinces. Finally, the chapter of the relevant legislation is indicated and, in some cases, the section number at issue.

Figuring out which province the citation for a statute series is referring to is fairly easy (for example, R.S.A. is Revised Statutes of Alberta). Here is a guide to some of the abbreviations used for case reporting series, which can be more difficult to decode:

REPORTING SERIES

A.C.W.S.	— All Canada Weekly Summaries
A.P.R.	— Atlantic Provinces Reports
All E.R.	— All England Reports
Alta. L.R.	— Alberta Law Reports
A.R.	— Alberta Reports
B.C.L.R.	— British Columbia Law Reports
C.A.	— Recuils de jurisprudence de Québec, Cour d'appel
C.C.C.	— Canadian Criminal Cases
C.P.R.	— Canadian Patent Reporter
C.R.	— Criminal Reports
C.R.D.	— Charter of Rights Decisions
C.S.	— Recuils de jurisprudence de Québec, Cour supérieure
D.L.R.	— Dominion Law Reports
M.P.R.	— Maritime Provinces Reports
Man. R.	— Manitoba Law Reports
N.B.R.	— New Brunswick Reports
N.S.R.	— Nova Scotia Reports
Nfld. & P.E.I.R.	— Newfoundland and P.E.I. Reports
Nfld. R.	— Newfoundland Reports
O.A.R.	— Ontario Appeal Reports

O.L.R.	— Ontario Law Reports
O.R.	— Ontario Reports
O.W.N.	— Ontario Weekly Notes
Qué. C.A.	— Quebéc Official Reports, Court of Appeal
R.F.L.	— Reports of Family Law
S.C.R.	— Supreme Court of Canada Reports
Sask. L.R.	— Saskatchewan Law Reports
W.W.R.	— Western Weekly Reports

Appendix 2

Court Procedure

As mentioned in Appendix 1, the two bodies of law administered by the courts are civil law and criminal law. Journalists should have a general understanding of the different procedures involved with each body of law, as well as the stages at which the law places restrictions on what can be reported about the court proceeding.

Once a case is within the formal jurisdiction of the courts, or *sub judice*, comments concerning the merits of the case or the law involved must be carefully considered. Further detail on the *sub judice* rule is given in the chapter on contempt.

CIVIL COURT PROCEDURES

A civil legal action may involve people, corporations or other legally recognized groups. The party starting the lawsuit is known as the *plaintiff.* The plaintiff is seeking a remedy, such as money or the enforcement of a civil right. The *defendant* is the party denying the plaintiff's claim. An important point to remember in a civil case is that no one is charged with anything. The parties usually go to court because they cannot agree on a matter which has arisen between themselves. A civil lawsuit does not involve any crimes against society and the defendant will not be found guilty or not guilty in the end. The court will instead find for or against the defendant or plaintiff. These are the steps in a civil action:

Notice of Intention to Sue

In many cases, this is the first step in the civil process. The government and certain Crown corporations may have to be given notice by the plaintiff within a set time period of a potential lawsuit. A failure to give such notice may mean a plaintiff cannot include the government as a party in an action. Notices may also be required for parties in certain other actions. For example, defamation legislation requires the plaintiff to serve notice on newspapers or broadcasting outlets within set time limits of an intention to sue.

Notice of Action

In all provinces a special document is used to signal the formal start of a lawsuit. It may be called a writ or notice of action. Once the plaintiff is prepared to sue, this formal notice is filed with the court and all of the parties named in the action.

Filing of Pleadings

At the same time the notice of action is filed, or within a specified time afterwards, a statement of allegations and claims is filed with the court and the other parties by the plaintiff. The defendant replies to the claims of the plaintiff, by filing a statement of his defences with the court and other parties, within another specified time period. These *pleadings* are the allegations and defences which may be presented during the trial. The idea is to make all of the parties aware of the issues.

A journalist should be aware that pleadings are one-sided and can distort claims, facts and allegations. Reports of pleadings are not privileged under defamation law, as are reports of some other court documents, and can be contemptuous. In a case of alleged defamation, the only defence to the wholesale publication of pleadings would be to prove the statements are true. In Alberta, the publication of civil pleadings filed in that province are partly-restricted by the Judicature Act.[1] Only the names and addresses of the parties and their solicitors and the general nature of the claim can be reported until the trial ends, or if no trial, the proper determination of the proceedings in Alberta. None of the other provinces restrict the publication of pleadings, but a journalist should still be wary of assertions in pleadings.

Examination for Discovery

Prior to a trial, one side in a dispute will usually want to question the other side and examine their documents prior to trial. This allows the parties to *discover* the various facets of the case. The discovery process, involving witnesses or parties, can be by oral or written questions which are answered under oath.

---

1 R.S.A. 1980, c. J-1, s. 30(2).

Reporters are not allowed to attend discoveries and they are not open to any other members of the public. The publication of transcripts from the discovery, before being entered into evidence in open court, could be defamatory or contemptuous. The evidence or statements at discoveries may ultimately be inadmissible or inaccurate.

Pre-Trial Conference

Many jurisdictions allow a judge to call a pre-trial conference to settle points about the trial procedure and the dispute itself. Usually, the judge will attempt to find out if the parties can come to an out-of-court settlement before starting the expensive trial process. The pre-trial conference is usually held in chambers and is not open to the public.

The Trial

The trial is the forum for the arguments and evidence. The trial may be by judge alone or judge and jury. The plaintiff must prove his case *on a balance of probabilities* which means that the allegations are in all likelihood true. The plaintiff does not have to meet the high standard of proof set for criminal cases in which the Crown must prove the allegations *beyond a reasonable doubt*. The public is permitted to attend, except in exceptional circumstances.

The reporting of open judicial proceedings is privileged in most provinces. But, there are conditions on this privilege, such as the requirement that the report be fair and accurate, that there is no comment by the journalist in his or her story, that the report is contemporaneous with the proceedings and there is no publication of any seditious, blasphemous or indecent matter.

The Appeal

After the trial of an issue and the decision of the court is handed down, an appeal may be taken to a higher court. An appeal must be launched within a specified time period (usually 30 days in most provinces). Depending on a province's rules of court, an appeal may be based on a question of pure law, a disputed fact or both. In most civil cases, the losing party has the right to appeal, but it may be necessary in some provinces to apply for permission, or *leave*, to appeal depending on whether the appeal is based on disputed points of law or simply disputed facts. The party appealing the case is called the *appellant* and the opposing party is called the *respondent*. In Canada, the courts of appeal have the power to reverse or uphold the decision or order a new trial.

The news media should not attempt to influence the decision of the appeal judges through editorial comments. In practice, the courts have been relatively tolerant of comments during the appeal process. If a new trial is ordered by the appeal court, any reports comparing aspects of the original trial with the new hearing while it is in progress, could be contemptuous.

CRIMINAL COURT PROCEDURES

The criminal court system is very complex because of the potential severity of its results. The criminal system is used to prosecute offences under a number of Federal and provincial statutes and can be of a criminal or non-criminal nature.[2]

The provinces cannot constitutionally create criminal offences. But, a province can still punish violations of laws within provincial jurisdiction[3] and all provinces use the summary conviction jurisdiction of the criminal courts for enforcing these laws.[4] Some provinces, such as Ontario, have comprehensive statutes which outline their own procedure to be followed by the criminal courts when handling provincial offences.[5]

There are three classifications of offences in the criminal court system:

1. *Indictable*   These are serious offences which are punishable by jail terms of two, five, ten or fourteen years or a life sentence (for example, murder).

2. *Summary conviction*   These offences are punishable by a maximum of a $2000 fine and/or six months in jail, unless otherwise provided by statute (for example, trespassing at night).

3. *Dual procedure*   Also known as hybrid or mixed offences, these

---

2 An offence does not have to be "criminal" in nature to be prosecuted in the criminal courts. S. 34(2) of the Interpretation Act, R.S.C. 1985, c. I-21, says that federal statutes creating offences are to use the procedure set out in the Criminal Code.

There is no exhaustive definition of what is a "criminal" offence. The Supreme Court of Canada said in *Canadian Federation of Agriculture v. A.G. Saskatchewan* (*sub nom. Reference as to the Validity of Section 5(a) of the Dairy Industry Act*), [1949] S.C.R. 1 at 49, that a crime is an act which the law forbids with penal sanctions. At p. 50, the Court went on to say a criminal law serves "a public purpose," such as in the protection of public peace, morality, health, order and security. Parliament can create a non-criminal or regulatory offence, which has as its object economic or trade control.

3 The provincial power is derived from s. 92(15) of the Constitution Act, 1867 (U.K.), 30 & 31 Vict., c. 3.

4 Part XXVII of the Criminal Code.

5 For example, see Provincial Offences Act, R.S.O. 1980, c. 400 and Offence Act, R.S.B.C. 1979, c. 305.

offences can be prosecuted either as indictable or summary conviction offences at the discretion of the Crown. With this type of offence, the accused is presumed to be charged with an indictable offence until the Crown indicates to the court that it plans to proceed under summary conviction procedures (for example, common assault).

There also are some important definitions to note regarding the judiciary in the criminal court process. The Criminal Code[6] makes reference to justices, provincial court judges and superior court judges. Essentially, a superior court judge is more powerful than a justice or a provincial court judge, and has the jurisdiction to deal with all offences. A judge serves in a "superior court of criminal jurisdiction."

A justice is defined by section 2 as "a justice of the peace or a provincial court judge." Justices of the peace have limited powers and deal only with minor offences, such as violations of provincial or municipal laws. In some provinces, the justice of the peace is the first person an accused is brought before. He or she begins the process of determining the proper court to deal with the charges. In other provinces, provincial court judges are the first people the accused appears before. Provincial court judges have more authority than justices of the peace and can try certain indictable offences.

To confuse matters, judges at the Superior Court level are referred to as "Madame Justice" or "Mr. Justice" when they are addressed. This is not to be confused with the Criminal Code's definition of a justice. To add to the confusion, justices are often referred to as judges when they are addressed.

Below are the steps involved in a criminal proceeding:

The Investigation

The court may become involved in the investigative process (that is, issuing search warrants or authorizing wiretaps). At this stage, no formal charges have been laid.

A journalist's access to court orders issued during the investigative process is usually restricted. But, some documents, such as executed search warrants, may be available for public inspection.

The Arrest or Charge

There are three ways in which an accused can be brought before a court:

1. A person may be arrested without a warrant having been issued (usually

---

6 R.S.C. 1985, c. C-46.

after being found committing an offence).[7] A number of events will then occur:[8]

(a) the accused may be detained until a first appearance before the courts, or

(b) may be released after the peace officer or officer-in-charge issues an appearance notice which sets out a time and place for the accused to appear.

As soon as possible after an appearance notice is issued or the person is detained, the peace officer must lay an *information* before a justice.[9] An information is a document sworn under oath, which outlines one or more allegations against a person or persons. The justice of the peace or a provincial court judge will then decide whether the officer has a case and confirm or quash the appearance notice or the detention of the accused.[10]

2. Anyone, who on reasonable and probable grounds believes that a person has committed an offence, may *lay an information* before a justice of the peace or a provincial court judge.[11] The justice will decide whether a case has been made out and may then issue a summons or a warrant for the arrest of the accused.[12]

3. An appearance notice or document requiring the accused to show up at court at a certain time and place, may be issued by a peace officer without actually arresting the accused.[13] As set out in section 495(2), a person will not be arrested for summary conviction offences, dual procedure offences or section 553 offences in any case:

(i) where the officer is able to identify the accused,

(ii) where there is no chance of evidence being destroyed,

(iii) where there is no chance of a repetition or continuation of the offence or another offence, and

(iv) the officer has reasonable and probable grounds to believe that the person will attend court.

As soon as possible after the appearance notice is issued, an information must be laid before a justice, who will decide if a case has been made out.

---

7 S. 494.

8 See ss. 496, 497 and 498.

9 Ss. 503 and 505.

10 Ss. 507 and 508.

11 See s. 504 for indictable offences and s. 788 for summary conviction offences.

12 See ss. 507 and 508 for indictable offences and s. 788(2) for summary conviction offences.

13 S. 496.

The First Appearance

The accused's first appearance in court usually determines the type of procedure which will be followed (that is, summary conviction or indictment procedures) and the appropriate level of court to adjudicate the matter (that is, justice of the peace, provincial court, superior court). Section 503 states that if someone has been arrested and detained, he or she must be brought before a justice within 24 hours, or if a justice is not available, as soon as possible. If a person is arrested and released, the accused must show up in court in accordance with the appearance notice ordering him or her to appear.

In some cases, the court of first appearance may not be a court which has the jurisdiction to conduct a trial of the charge.[14] For example, a justice of the peace may not have the authority to deal with an offence which is under the absolute jurisdiction of a provincial court judge.[15] In this case, the accused will not be asked to plead guilty or not guilty until an appropriate court can deal with the charges. But, some offences do allow the accused at the court of first appearance (including a justice of the peace) to *elect*, or choose, a mode of trial.[16] The accused will be asked to elect to be tried by a provincial court judge without a jury, a judge without a jury or a judge with a jury. It should be remembered that the election of the mode of trial still does not constitute a plea of guilty or not guilty. It merely establishes which court the accused wants to appear before to adjudicate the matter.[17]

The Bail Hearing

At the court of first appearance, the justice is obligated in most circumstances to grant the accused temporary release, unless the offence is one which is outlined in section 522 (for example, murder) or the accused pleaded guilty or the Crown wishes to *show cause* as to why the accused should not be released or released without conditions.[18]

If a show cause hearing is held, the court may grant the Crown or the accused a *remand* of three days in custody before proceeding with the interim release hearing.[19] The justice will eventually decide if the accused can be released and he may place restrictions or conditions on

---

14 For example, a justice of the peace would have no jurisdiction to try a case of murder. But, he or she may be able to deal with a minor provincial traffic offence.

15 S. 536.

16 Ss. 536 and 554 establish the offences offering election.

17 See s. 536(3).

18 S. 515.

19 S. 516.

the release.[20] Only Superior Courts can decide on interim release for the offences listed in section 522.

At some point, the justice or judge may make an order banning the publication of evidence taken during the bail hearing, the information given, the representations made and the reasons, if any, given by the justice. You may still report the outcome of the bail hearing and any conditions imposed on the accused. The ban on the other details is in effect until the trial ends or until the accused is discharged after a preliminary hearing.[21]

Subsequent Appearances and Mode of Trial

After the first appearance or the election of the mode of trial, the procedure to be followed will depend on the type of offence involved:

Summary conviction offences   In most provinces, the first appearance will be before a provincial court judge with the jurisdiction to deal with a summary conviction offence. Part XXVII of the Code (that is, the Summary Convictions Part) refers to the person charged as the *defendant* rather than the accused. After the charge is read to the defendant, he will be asked to plead guilty or not guilty, providing the court has the power to handle summary conviction offences.[22] Sometimes, the Crown or the defendant's lawyer will question the mental fitness of the defendant and will request a remand for a medical examination for no more than 30 days.[23] Under extenuating circumstances, the defendant may be remanded for 60 days total.[24] If the defendant does not plead guilty, the trial is conducted using the same procedure followed for preliminary hearings of indictable offences outlined in Part XVIII of the Code.

Indictable offences   There are three categories of indictable offences, two of which allow the accused to select the mode of trial:

1. Section 553 offences are within the exclusive jurisdiction of a provincial court judge. These offences include theft, fraud and keeping a common bawdy house.
2. Section 469 offences may be tried only by a superior court of criminal jurisdiction (that is, a Supreme Court, a Superior Court or a Court of Queen's Bench). These offences include high treason, inciting mutiny, sedition and murder).
3. Section 554 governs all other indictable offences. The accused has a

---

20 S. 515(2) and (4).
21 S. 517.
22 S. 801.
23 S. 803(5).
24 S. 803(6).

right to elect to be tried by a provincial court judge without a jury, a judge without a jury, or a judge and a jury.

If a justice of the peace is presented with an information outlining an indictable offence, the accused will be remanded to later appear before a court which is empowered to deal with the matter.[25] A guilty or not guilty plea will not be requested until the accused is before a court with the jurisdiction to handle the information, despite the fact the justice may ask the accused to elect a mode of trial.

The Preliminary Hearing

A preliminary hearing is held in cases involving indictable offences to determine if there is sufficient evidence to hold a trial. The deciding factor as to whether an accused will be committed for trial is whether there is sufficient evidence which, if it were believed, would result in a conviction.[26] The preliminary hearing can be held by a justice of the peace or a provincial court judge.

At the end of the preliminary hearing, the accused will either be *discharged* or ordered to stand trial. It should be noted that a discharge does not mean the accused is innocent. It means there was not enough evidence to proceed to trial.

The preliminary inquiry can be by-passed in two ways:[27]

1. The accused may waive his right to a preliminary hearing.
2. The Crown may bring an accused back to court after he has been discharged after a preliminary hearing by *preferring a direct-line indictment*. This permits the Crown to try the accused before a superior court judge without another preliminary hearing.

During the preliminary hearing, the court may impose a ban on the publication of evidence.[28] The ban is in effect until after the trial or until the accused is discharged. There is also a Criminal Code provision prohibiting the publication of admissions or confessions of the accused tendered in evidence during the preliminary hearing until it is brought out in an open trial or the accused is discharged.[29] This prohibition exists even when there is no ban on the publication of other evidence. For more information, see the chapter on restraints on court reporting.

---

25 S. 536.
26 *United States of America v. Shephard* (1976), [1977] 2 S.C.R. 1067 at 1080.
27 Respectively, s. 549 and Part XX.
28 S. 539.
29 S. 542(2).

The Trial

If the accused is committed for trial or an indictment has been preferred,[30] a trial date will be set. It may be before a provincial court judge, a judge and jury or a judge alone. The trial will begin with the Crown presenting evidence which must eventually prove the guilt of the accused *beyond a reasonable doubt*. The defence will usually respond to the Crown's evidence, but there is no requirement for the accused to testify or even present a defence.

After the two sides have presented their evidence and given their final arguments, the judge or provincial court judge will prepare for the verdict. If there is a jury, the judge will give his *charge* to the jury in which he states the law as he interprets it. The judge will also outline the responsibilities of the jury members. The jury will then retire to consider its verdict.

At some point during the trial, it may be necessary for the judge to determine if certain evidence is admissible or acceptable. If it is a jury trial, the judge will send the jury out and hold a trial within a trial, known as a *voir dire*. The Criminal Code prohibits the publication of details of any of the court proceedings conducted while the jury is out of the courtroom, until after the jury retires to consider its verdict.[31] For more details, see the chapter on contempt.

The Appeal

Both summary conviction and indictable decisions can be appealed. An appeal may be on a question of pure law, a question of fact or both. The nature of the appeal (question of fact or law) will determine whether the appellant (party seeking the appeal) must apply for permission or *leave* to go to the higher court.[32] Generally, formal notice of an appeal must be given within 30 days of the decision or the sentence.

In theory, comments by reporters during the appeal process which could be interpreted as attempting to influence the court of appeal are contemptuous. But, in practice, the courts have been tolerant of comments during the appeal period. For more information, see the chapter on contempt.

---

30 The indictment is essentially the *information* rewritten and presented as a "new" document to the higher court. See Part XX of the Code.

31 S. 648.

32 Ss. 675, 676, 813 and 839.

ADMINISTRATIVE TRIBUNAL PROCEDURES

The administration of government regulations, statutes and rules sometimes falls on the shoulders of administrative tribunals (that is, boards and commissions). These public bodies handle formal applications or investigate complaints and infractions of statutes or regulations. Each of the bodies may develop their own rules of procedure, but certain degrees of procedural standards are expected from certain administrative tribunals. These tribunals can be categorized as administrative, quasi-judicial or judicial, depending on the importance of the body's function or purpose. The minimum requirement for all tribunals in administrative law is *fairness* in the procedures. For example, a higher standard of procedural fairness is expected of public utilities boards than taxi licensing commissions.

A tribunal which handles purely administrative tasks, or "rubber-stamps" matters without any exercise of discretion, only has a duty to act fairly. There is no compulsion on these bodies to follow any judicial procedures (for example, hear evidence or allow cross-examination). A quasi-judicial or judicial tribunal has a greater duty to make its procedure follow the *principles of natural justice*. These principles can include the right to a fair hearing, the right to be represented by counsel, the right to call witnesses, the right to cross-examine witnesses or the right to examine all evidence. The civil courts can become involved with an administrative tribunal when an aggrieved individual feels there has been a defect in the procedural fairness of the body or where the decision-making process is contrary to the basic principles of natural justice. The court is usually restricted to examining the procedure followed and cannot change the decision, other than to order a new hearing. In some statutes, the courts are expressly prohibited from reviewing the decisions of certain bodies.

Appendix 3

Mini-Law Course

The purpose of this chapter is to acquaint you with some of the major branches of law. The law is constantly changing and these summaries are very general and are not meant to implant "instant legal knowledge" into a journalist. In most cases, there are exceptions to the general rule.

CONTRACTS

This is known as private law. It involves an agreement between individuals promising to do or not do something. It can be written or oral.

A legally binding promise or contract has several elements. There must be an offer by one party and an acceptance communicated back by the other party. It is important that each party have the capacity to form the contract (for example, an insane person could not sign a contract).

Along with the offer and acceptance, the parties must have an intention to form a contract. There must also be something of value exchanged for the contract, known as the "consideration." The consideration is an inducement to enter into the contract. It can be money or even an act.

The courts will only enforce a contract with a legal purpose or object. There are also various grounds which destroy or breach a contract. A misrepresentation, a mistake, the presence of duress or undue influence, and the failure to perform that which is required by the contract, can all be grounds for a lawsuit.

TORTS

A "tort" is a civil wrong by one individual against another (apart from criminal offences or contractual breaches). Tort law provides a remedy for someone who has been harmed through the fault of another (for example, defamation, personal injury and negligence). It is essentially, a violation of a duty which is imposed by statute or common law.

There are several elements to a tort action. The plaintiff must prove that the defendant owed him a duty. Then the plaintiff must prove that the duty was violated. And finally, the plaintiff must prove that the defendant was at fault for the injury.

In negligence actions, the plaintiff must also prove that the damage was foreseeable by the defendant. The court will also consider the standard of care expected of the reasonable man in the circumstances. A tort can range from simple trespass of property to medical negligence, with each "wrong" having its own complexities.

CRIMINAL LAW

This is public law. It aims to punish behaviour that is an offence against the state or society, even though only one person may have suffered.

There are usually two elements to a criminal offence. There must be a *mens rea* or a "guilty mind" or intention. There must also be an *actus reus* or "guilty act." Together, the two form the elements of a criminal offence. In a few circumstances, the law provides for "strict liability" offences in which the Crown must only prove that an illegal act has been committed.

The Criminal Code and other federal statutes spell out what constitutes the various criminal offences. Only the federal government can constitutionally enact criminal offences. The provincial governments must establish non-penal laws to enforce provincial statutes.

PROPERTY

There are two types of property. Real property is land, including everything attached, below and above (within normal use). Personal property is any tangible or intangible thing other than land, which has a right of ownership attached to it.

Real property law involves the rights and obligations attached to land. A person can own land outright (a freehold estate) or may lease or rent (a leasehold estate). A person may hold almost limitless rights to deal with land or his or her rights may be restricted by the terms of the conveyance (that is, sale or transfer) that brought the property into his or her possession. Ultimately, the Crown owns all land and local laws often add further restrictions to conveyance terms (for example, public zoning requirements).

Personal property law involves the ownership of anything from a car to stocks and bonds. An item of personal property is called a "chattel" in law and this area deals with the rights of ownership and possession. This branch of the law also concerns itself with who is responsible for the safety of chattels when the owner delivers them to another individual for safekeeping. This is known as bailment.

CORPORATE LAW

This complex body of law deals with the legislation and common law that has evolved in the business world. There are basically three types of business entities.

A "sole proprietorship" is a one-person operation (for example, a corner store) in which all profits and liabilities flow directly and personally to one individual. There is no obligation to register a proprietorship (with some exceptions where licences are needed). If someone sues a proprietorship and wins, they are entitled to both business and personal assets of the owner.

The "partnership" is an entity with two or more individuals carrying on a business "with a view to profit." It also doesn't have to be registered in most cases. Partners generally share in profits and losses, at both the business and personal level.

The "corporation" is a legally-registered entity with most of the same rights of a person. This is the most complex form of business operation. The corporation is owned by "shareholders" who elect "directors." Company "officers" (for instance, the president) run the day-to-day operations and "directors" determine policy and long-range plans. One of the chief advantages of a corporation is that generally none of the people involved or investing in a corporation are personally liable for its losses. The corporation survives apart from its owners. It can sue and be sued. But, there may be some occasions in which directors, officers or shareholders could be found by the courts to be liable for their actions (for example, a director approving of toxic wastes being dumped in a river).

A "public" corporation is one which "distributes" or sells shares in the company to the public in a stock market. A "private" corporation is held by one or more individuals who do not trade shares publicly. Other aspects of corporate law involve financial transactions and the legal responsibilities of those who run and own businesses.

LABOUR AND EMPLOYMENT LAW

This branch of the law is relatively new. Prior to unions and minimum employment standards laws, the workplace functioned with a "master-servant" relationship. An employee could be fired at any time for any reason and there were practically no limits on the conditions or terms of employment.

The principle of "collective bargaining" and unionized labour has changed the workplace significantly. All provinces have laws which regulate the relationship between unions and employers. A union must be "certified" as the official agent of the employees in a bargaining unit (usually after a vote by the employees).

The union and employer then negotiate a collective agreement within time limits established by the law. If an agreement isn't reached, the union or management may apply for government mediation or conciliation to help settle disputed issues. In some cases, the parties may agree to submit the issues to binding arbitration by an impartial third party.

The ultimate tactics are strikes (a union action) or lock-outs (a management action). In each case, all other avenues of settling the dispute must have been attempted. A strike can continue forever or until there is a voluntary or compulsory (that is, back-to-work legislation) settlement.

The contract provides the ground rules for the workplace. It tells the employer what the employees can and cannot do, and tells the employees what to expect of the employer. Any strikes or lock-outs during the period of a collective agreement are illegal and subject to punishment by law. Disputes involving the agreement are usually settled through a grievance process administered by the government or union-management committees.

There is also an area of case law dealing with those who are not governed by a collective agreement. Most of these cases involve "wrongful dismissal" actions. An employer must have "just cause" or proper reason to fire someone. If the employer cannot prove there is just cause, then the employer must have given the employee sufficient notice of dismissal. Depending on the age, position, experience and other factors concerning the employee, proper notice may range from as little as a week to a year.

CONSUMER AND COMMERCIAL LAW

This branch of law deals with the purchase and sale of goods. A "good" is generally any chattel. All provinces have laws which deal with the sale of commercial goods. Some provinces have laws that specifically protect consumers.

Under the common law, the rule was usually "buyer beware." All Acts now spell out the ground rules for selling or buying goods. For commercial transactions, the Acts determine when and how the title to goods is transferred from the seller to the buyer and what remedies are available when disputes arise. The consumer legislation seeks to protect the unsuspecting consumer who buys a good for personal use. The Acts also protect the seller in many cases.

This is really another type of contract law. Where the statutes don't help, the rights of individuals hinge on the "conditions" (that is, essential terms) of the contract. A condition should be distinguished from a "warranty" which is a promise or representation (for example, about the quality of a product). A breach of a condition is a serious infringement of a contract and may result in it being declared null or void by the courts. A breach of a warranty must be remedied, but does not necessarily destroy the contract.

ADMINISTRATIVE LAW

Government functions on rules and regulations which are often enforced and administered by administrative bodies or tribunals (for example, a labour relations board).

Administrative law deals with the principles of fairness and natural justice which should be followed by tribunals. In most cases, courts can review tribunal decisions to ensure the procedure is, at the very least, fair. A tribunal may exercise an administrative, quasi-judicial or judicial function. The type of function determines the level or standard of procedural fairness which is expected or required.

Tribunals that perform strictly administrative functions are required to be "fair," but don't usually have to abide by the principles of natural justice expected in a court (for example, the right to a hearing).

A quasi-judicial or judicial function is more easily reviewed and monitored by the courts. A judge usually can't decide an issue for a tribunal, but he or she can review the procedures of the tribunal for fairness and adherence to the principles of "natural justice." These principles could include the right to a hearing, the right to be represented by counsel, or other basic requirements of our legal system. If an administrative tribunal is found to be in the wrong, procedurally, the court may order a re-hearing of the matter or some other remedy.

INSURANCE LAW

This is an offshoot of contract law. An insurance policy is a contract where one party agrees to compensate another party for any losses suffered in certain circumstances, in return for a price (that is, a premium). The basic principle is that the risk of loss is passed on to another party (that is, the insurance company) which, in turn, shares the loss among other customers who have paid premiums.

The "insured" is the person who takes out the insurance policy. The "insurer" is the party who must pay for any loss and underwrites the policy. (The only exception is in life insurance, where the person whose life is covered by the policy is called the insurer). The party buying the insurance must have an "insurable interest." This can only occur when the party derives a benefit of some sort from the continued existence of the subject-matter of the insurance or would suffer a loss if the subject-matter were destroyed.

CONFLICT OF LAWS

This is a complex area dealing with the interaction of laws in different countries or jurisdictions. For example, a court action in a province involving a car accident in another country involves the law of several jurisdictions. The study of "conflicts" aims to determine which jurisdiction's laws should be applied to a particular case, which jurisdiction is the best forum for a case and the enforceability of laws and judgments from other jurisdictions.

INTERNATIONAL LAW

This is the law between nations. Just as individuals make contracts or follow rules of behaviour, so do countries. Treaties are a common form of international agreement. This body of law also deals with the accepted customs followed by nations in times of peace and war. For example, it is generally accepted in international law that an independent nation does not send its troops into another nation without permission or declaring war. This is an area of the law that relies on co-operation. An offending state cannot be punished as readily as an individual and violations of international law often go unpunished.

REMEDIES

This is the study of the remedies which a court can offer to a party in a civil court action. A remedy can be in the form of a court award of money or an order to do or not do something. Damages are generally compensatory and/or punitive awards of money. Depending on the dispute, the way in which damages will be awarded can vary significantly. In contract law, the court compensates a person for the loss of any benefits which were expected under the agreement. In tort law, the court will only return the victim to the point where he was before the damage occurred and does not try to compensate the victim for anything extra. Punitive damages are awarded where the judge wants to show the displeasure of the court in the behaviour of the offending party. A court can also issue an order restraining behaviour or requiring an act to be done (for example, an injunction).

TRUSTS

A trust is a right to real or personal property which is held by one person for the benefit of another individual. The creator of the trust (that is, the settlor) transfers the property to the trustee to hold for a beneficiary (*cestui que trust*). The trustee has the legal title to the property, but the beneficiary has an equitable (moral) right to it. The intention to create a trust must be clear. Sometimes, the courts will recognize a trust which is implied by law or circumstance (for example, in a divorce, business assets owned by one spouse may be split if the other spouse contributed to the firm). A trust can be invalid if the court cannot determine the subject-matter of the trust (that is, the property in question) or the object of the trust (that is, the beneficiary). A trust with an illegal purpose will also not be enforced.

Glossary

This glossary of legal terms is intended to give a journalist a general definition of some words and phrases commonly used by the courts and lawyers. As with any "point-form" glossary, the definitions are approximate and, in many cases, there are other definitions for a word.

abet: To encourage someone to do a wrongful act, usually without actually participating in the crime itself.

ab initio: Latin meaning "from the beginning" (for example, an invalid contract may be void *ab initio*).

abstract of title: A history of the chain of ownership of land with details on all restrictions and rights associated with the property.

action in personam: A civil court action against a person or involving the rights of a person.

action in rem: A civil court action directly against a "thing" without regard to ownership of it (for example, the arrest of a ship).

actus reus: Latin meaning "the wrongful act." To commit a crime, in most cases, there must be an *actus reus* along with a *mens rea* (that is, guilty mind).

affidavit: A written statement of facts sworn under oath. The "deponent" (that is, person stating the facts) must have personal knowledge of the facts and cannot base remarks on hearsay.

agent: One who acts on behalf of an employer or any other person who expressly or impliedly consents to be represented.

aid: To participate in the commission of a crime.

amicus curiae: Latin meaning "a friend of the court." This refers to a situation in which the court allows an outside party with an interest in the subject-matter of a case to present their views on the issue.

animus: Latin meaning "an intention."

appellant: The party appealing a decision. The other party is the "respondent."

arbitration: A method of settling a dispute using an impartial third party. By their own agreement, the decision of the arbitrator is usually binding on the parties.

assault: A threat or attempt to harm an individual is an assault. The victim does not have to be touched, but there must be a reasonable fear the accused was capable of causing the harm.

assign: To transfer or shift ownership of something to another individual (for example, assigning the remainder of a lease to another individual).

assumpsit: A reference to an undertaking to do something.

attempt: In criminal law, there is an "attempt" when a series of acts are performed which fall short of committing an actual crime, yet, are beyond mere preparation.

audi alteram partem: Latin meaning "hear the other side." One of the basic principles of natural justice.

automatism: A defence in criminal law referring to an uncontrollable act by the accused.

autrefois plea: Where an accused has previously been found guilty or acquitted on the same charge and circumstances, he will enter an autrefois plea.

bailment: To give something to a person, other than the owner, for delivery or safekeeping. The bailor is the one who hands the goods over and the bailee receives them (for example, giving your car keys to a parking attendant).

balance of probabilities: A standard of proof in civil cases requiring evidence that the claim is, in all probability, true. The probability must be more than fifty percent, but the standard is not as stringent as requiring proof "beyond a reasonable doubt" as in criminal cases.

battery: The use of physical force against a person.

beyond a reasonable doubt: A standard of proof in criminal cases requiring evidence that the guilt of the accused be clear and beyond any reasonable doubt.

bona fide: Latin meaning "in good faith."

capacity: A legal term referring to the ability or legal power of an individual to perform an act. For example, an insane person lacks the mental capacity to understand the significance of signing a contract.

caveat: Latin meaning "beware."

certiorari: Latin meaning "to be informed of." A writ of certiorari is used by Superior Courts to review the decisions of an inferior body (for example, a lower court or administrative tribunal).

cestui que trust: A reference to the beneficiary in a trust arrangement.

chain of title: A chronological history of the successive owners of a piece of land.

chattel: Belongings other than land (for example, a car) including intangible property (for example, shares in corporations).

circumstantial evidence: A consistent series of facts which will not directly prove the facts in dispute, but by deduction, lead one to come to the conclusion that the alleged crime or act is true.

codicil: A supplementary document to a will, usually offering further details or updating bequests.

collateral contract: A supplementary contract made along with the main contract.

collusion: An arrangement between individuals to commit a fraud or bring harm to another individual.

comity: A term used to describe the courtesy and respect offered by one legal jurisdiction in giving effect to the laws and court decisions of another jurisdiction.

consanguinity: The blood relationship of people descending from the same ancestor.

consideration: In law, something of value (for example, payment of money or property in return for an agreement).

constructive knowledge: Knowledge which is presumed to be known or ought to be known.

constructive trust: A trust created by the courts based on the circumstances of a case such as when a party has no legal right to the benefits of property, yet deserves a share in it because of a valuable contribution (for example, a farmer's wife may receive a share of the farm's assets in a divorce action because she helped support the business).

contribution: The principle of sharing the loss or blame. Contributory negligence by the careless victim of an accident can reduce the court award.

conversion: The unauthorized use or disposition of someone else's property. For example, borrowing someone's car and then selling it without permission.

conveyance: The transfer of ownership in property.

corroboration: Additional evidence backing up a fact or assertion.

costs: In law, usually a reference to the expense of the court action.

count: In criminal cases, a reference to each individual charge.

covenant: A promise.

creditor: The individual who is owed money. The debtor is the individual owing the money.

cross-claim: Claim between co-parties (for example, a claim by one defendant against the other defendant).

culpable: Guilty of or responsible for a criminal act or wrong.

cy-près doctrine: This rule allows the court to alter a will or trust arrangement and to carry out, as best it can, the wishes of the deceased (for example, to give annual donations to a certain charity) when for some reason the original purpose cannot be achieved (for example, the charity may no longer exist).

damage: A loss.

damages: The compensation claimed or awarded in court for damage. There are two common types of damages. Compensatory damages replace the actual loss suffered. Punitive damages punish the wrongdoer and can be awarded in addition to compensatory damages in special circumstances.

debtor: One who owes money. The debtor pays his debt to the creditor.

declaratory judgment: A court decision which settles a disputed fact between parties but orders no remedy.

de facto: Latin meaning "in fact."

de jure: Latin meaning "in law."

delict: A wrong or offence.

de minimis non curat lex: This doctrine stands for the principle that the law does not bother with small matters or trifling offences.

demise: To convey property.

demonstrative evidence: Tangible evidence as opposed to testimony (for example, a photograph or map).

demur: An objection by one party to the facts or law as outlined by the other party.

deposition: Written testimony of a witness under oath, usually in the form of an affidavit. The witness, in this case, is referred to as the "deponent."

desuetude: In reference to laws which have become obsolete.

detinue: An old civil action to recover personal property which has been unlawfully kept by another individual.

devise: The conveyance of land by a will.

dicta: Statements by the court which are not directly related to the issue at hand. Dicta are not vital to the final resolution of the case and are not expressly binding on other courts.

discharge: To excuse or dismiss.

donatio inter vivos: A gift from a living donor.

donatio mortis causa: A gift made in contemplation of death.

due process of law: The course of justice. A reference to fair and equitable procedures.

duress: Unlawful coercion of an individual by threat or actual force to do an act contrary to his will.

duty: A legal or moral responsibility to do or not to do something.

encumbrance: An interest held by an individual, other than the owner, in property.

equity: A body of law which seeks to find the fairest solution to a court action. The rules of equity will be applied where the solution offered by the common law is too harsh or unfair.

escheat: The forfeiting of property to the State. It frequently occurs when there are no heirs to an estate.

estate: In reference to wills, this is the sum total of the real and personal property of the deceased.

et al.: Latin meaning "and others."

executory: Of a contract or obligation which hasn't been fulfilled yet.

ex facie: Latin meaning "from the face."

ex parte: Latin meaning "from one side." A court will sometimes grant an *ex parte* injunction to stop an act where time is of importance, even though only one side has been heard.

expressio unius est exclusio alterius: A principle of statutory interpretation which basically means that anything expressly stated is all-inclusive. For example, a statute which allows only one exception to a rule cannot be interpreted as allowing other unexpressed exceptions.

ex turpi causa non oritur actio: A maxim meaning that a court action cannot be based on an illegal or immoral act (for example, you cannot sue on an illegal contract).

face of the record: A reference to the entire record of a court's proceedings.

factum: A lawyer's brief stating the facts in a case and his or her arguments.

fee simple: A right held in land. The "fee simple absolute" grants an individual and his heirs limitless power to hold and deal with the land.

fee tail: A right held in land. The fee tail limits the rights of heirs to deal with the land.

fiduciary: One who agrees to act for the benefit of another individual (for example, a trustee acts for the good of the beneficiaries of the trust).

fieri facias: A court order requiring a sheriff or other official to sell off a debtor's property.

foreclosure: The legal process brought by a mortgagor which ends the rights of a mortgagee (for example, the person who borrowed the money) to property.

fraud: An intentional misrepresentation.

freehold: A right to own a piece of land for an indefinite time or life.

gaol: A term for "jail".

goods: Merchandise or personal property.

guardian ad litem: A court appointed representative for a handicapped or infant party in an action.

habeas corpus: Latin meaning "you must have the body." This ancient writ is used to demand the delivery of a person in custody to a court in order to review the lawfulness of the detention.

headnote: A summation of the issues, arguments, and points of law before the court in a particular case, and the reasons for the decision. The headnote is usually found at the beginning of a case in a legal reporting series (that is, published cases).

hearsay: Evidence based on the word of a person who is not at the hearing to testify as to its veracity (for example, "X" told me that he saw "Y" commit the crime). It is admitted as evidence on rare occasions.

holograph: A handwritten will which is not witnessed.

immovables: Property which cannot be moved, such as land or things attached to land.

impute: To accuse or suggest.

in camera: Latin meaning "in chambers."

indemnify: To compensate.

indictment: A written charge against a person presented to a criminal court. In Canada, an indictment is presented at superior trial court levels, but an "information" is the first document presented at lower court levels. The indictment is usually the "information" re-written for the higher court.

information: A sworn statement charging a person with the commission of an offence. Anyone may "lay" an information. The information is the first document presented to a justice.

infra: Latin meaning "below."

injunction: A court order which commands someone to do or not do a particular act.

innuendo: An implication or suggestion.

in pari delicto: Latin meaning "in equal fault."

insurable interest: In insurance law, this is the legitimate interest that a person has in insuring something or someone. The person with the insurable interest must derive a benefit of some sort from the continued existence of the thing or person.

inter alia: Latin meaning "among other things."

interlocutory: Temporary.

intestate: To die without a valid will.

intra vires: Latin meaning "within the power."

jurisprudence: The philosophy of law and legal systems.

just cause: Reasonable and fair grounds for an act.

laches: This is the principle that someone who does not assert his rights over a long period of time, loses any chance of special treatment by the courts in reclaiming the rights (for example, neglecting to stop trespassers who have used a path over many years).

legacy: A gift in a will.

lessee: One who rents from another.

lessor: One who rents to another.

lien: A claim against personal or real property (for example, a contractor can have a lien against a project if he is not paid).

lis alibi pendens: Latin term meaning "a suit pending elsewhere."

maintenance: In divorce law, it refers to support payments paid by one ex-spouse to the other.

mala fides: Latin meaning "bad faith."

malfeasance: A wrongful act, as opposed to nonfeasance which is a wrongful omission.

mandamus: A writ, issued by a superior court, which commands an inferior body or person to do something. It is sometimes used against inferior court judges who have misused their powers.

material: That which is important and relevant to a matter (for example, a material witness).

may: In law, this word denotes that discretion may be used. "Shall" is an imperative which commands action.

mens rea: Latin meaning "the guilty mind." An important factor in criminal cases which shows an evil intention to commit the offence. A guilty mind must be accompanied by an "actus reus" or wrongful act.

misfeasance: The improper performance of a lawful act.

mitigation: The reduction of loss (for example, in contract law, the innocent party in a breached contract is under a duty to reasonably try to reduce his losses).

moot: That which is undecided (for example, law students sharpen courtroom skills in moot courts arguing hypothetical cases).

movables: In reference to movable property (for example, a car).

necessaries: The essentials of survival or life.

negligence: The failure to use reasonable care or fulfill a legal duty owed in the circumstances.

nisi decree: A temporary order which will eventually become final. In a divorce, the court will issue such a decree for a short period before making the final decree, in case the couple should have a change of heart.

nolo contendere: Latin meaning "I will not contest (it)."

nonfeasance: The omission of an act one has a duty to perform.

non-suit: A court declaration ending an action before it can be decided on its merits (for example, the plaintiff may have failed to present the bare elements of a case).

noscitur a sociis: A Latin maxim stating that the meaning of a word can be taken from the words which surround it. It is a tool of statutory interpretation.

oath: A promise by an individual.

obiter dictum: An opinion by a judge on an issue which is not important to the resolution of the case and not binding on other courts.

paralegal: An individual with legal skills who is not trained to be a lawyer.

parens patriae: A reference to the role of the State as "parent" to us all (for example, it is sometimes used to make children a ward of the province).

parol evidence rule: A reference to oral evidence which changes the meaning or terms of a written contract. The rule prohibits the use of such oral evidence in most situations.

particulars: The details of an issue or the precise act in dispute.

parties: Those who are directly affected by a court matter (for example, plaintiff and defendant).

pecuniary: In reference to money (for example, pecuniary loss).

penal: That which involves a penalty.

per curiam: Latin meaning "by the court."

peremptory challenge: The right of a party to reject a potential juror during jury selection without giving any reason. Each party has a set number of such challenges in criminal or civil jury trials.

perjury: Lying under sworn oath.

personal property: Property other than land (for example, a car).

pleadings: Allegations, claims and defences of the parties to a court action which are formally filed with the court. The pleadings form the basis for the trial arguments.

prerogative writs: Extraordinary Superior Court orders which can be used against inferior courts or public bodies to prevent them from exceeding their jurisdiction. Commonly used for judicial review of administrative tribunal decisions.

prima facie: Latin meaning "on first appearance."

private law: Law that applies between individuals (for example, a contract) as opposed to public law which involves the State.

probate: Pertaining to wills.

probative evidence: Evidence which establishes a fact is true.

promissory: An obligation or a promise.

proviso: A provision of a contract or statute which expands or explains other terms.

public law: That which involves the State and society (for example, criminal law) as opposed to private law which applies between individual citizens only.

quantum meruit: A principle of equity or fairness which states that a person should be compensated for the value of the work performed.

quare: Latin meaning "wherefore."

quasi: Latin meaning "as if."

quo warranto: A prerogative writ which is issued to prevent the unlawful use of authority by someone.

ratio decidendi: The primary reasons for a court decision.

real property: Land.

reasonable man: A fictitious person who provides the standard for behaviour which the courts expect of people. The reasonable man is fair, rational and can foresee damage which might be caused by his own negligence.

regina: Latin referring to the "Queen" or Crown.

replevin: An old civil action which allows the owner of goods to re-claim them from someone who unlawfully takes them.

res judicata: A reference to that which has already been decided by the courts on its merits.

rescind: To withdraw or revoke.

respondent: The party responding to the claims of a party appealing a lower court decision.

restitution: The principle that someone who suffers a loss should be restored to their original position.

retroactive law: A new law which changes rights or obligations created under previous laws.

retrospective law: A new law which changes the effect of an act or omission which occurred under a previous law.

rex: Latin for the "King" or Crown.

riparian: Pertaining to shore or river bank.

semble: Latin meaning "it appears." The word is used when an opinion is offered.

service: A term used in the court system in relation to the delivery of an official court document to a party or witness (for example, a subpoena).

severable: That which can be divided or "cut out." For example, some contracts are severable (that is, having portions which are unrelated to each other).

shall: In law, this is an imperative word which makes an action or obligation mandatory. "May" denotes a discretion.

specific performance: In contract law, the court will sometimes grant this remedy, which compels the parties to fulfill the contract obligations.

standard of care: The degree of care which the law expects of the reasonable man in similar circumstances.

standard of proof: In criminal cases, the case must be proven beyond a reasonable doubt. In civil cases, the case must be proven on a balance of probabilities based upon a preponderance of the evidence.

standing: In law, a term used to denote an individual's interest in a case which allows him to intervene in court.

stare decisis: Latin meaning "to abide by the decision."

stay: To halt. In criminal law, the Crown may "stay" a charge and the subsequent trial, leaving it in limbo for a set period or forever.

subpoena: A court document requiring an individual or thing to be presented at a certain time and place.

talesman: Someone who is chosen from the by-standers in a courtroom or off the street to act as a juror.

testamentary: Referring to a will or document that takes effect after death.

third party: An individual who is not a party to an agreement or event, but has an interest in it.

tort: A civil wrong (for example, defamation) involving a violation of a duty imposed by law.

trover: An old term used to describe a civil court action against an individual who has wrongfully sold goods he or she found.

trust: A right to property which one person holds for the benefit of another.

unconscionable: In contract law, an unconscionable agreement is one which unfairly takes advantage of another party.

unjust enrichment: A principle of equity which states that no person should benefit unjustly at the expense of another person.

venue: A place for trial. When there has been prejudicial publicity in a criminal case, a defence lawyer may ask for a change of venue.

vested: A right or interest becomes "vested" when it is triggered by an event and comes into force.

viva voce: Latin meaning "with the living voice." Usually a reference to oral testimony.

void: Null or having no legal effect.

voidable: That which may be void.

volenti non fit injuria: A Latin maxim stating that one who voluntarily assumes a risk cannot then seek a remedy for any injury or loss.

waiver: The abandonment of a right.

wanton: Reckless.

warranty: A promise.

writ: A court document authorizing an act or making an order.

Index